Collected Poems / 1937–1971

JOHN BERRYMAN

COLLECTED POEMS

1937–1971

EDITED AND INTRODUCED

BY CHARLES THORNBURY

The Noonday Press

Farrar, Straus and Giroux

New York

Copyright © 1989 by Kate Donahue Berryman
All rights reserved
This edition first published in 1991 by The Noonday Press
Printed in the United States of America
Published in Canada by HarperCollinsCanadaLtd
Designed by Cynthia Krupat

Library of Congress Cataloging in Publication Data
Berryman, John, 1914–1972.
[Poems]
Collected poems, 1937–1971 / John Berryman ; edited and introduced
by Charles Thornbury.
Includes indexes.
I. Thornbury, Charles. II. Title.
PS3503.E744A17   1989   811'.54–dc19   89-30944

29895

Contents

THE DISPOSSESSED [1948]

I

II

SONNETS TO CHRIS [1947, 1966]

HOMAGE TO MISTRESS BRADSTREET
[1953]

from *HIS THOUGHT MADE POCKETS & THE PLANE BUCKT* [1958]

Formal Elegy [1964]

LOVE & FAME [1971]

I

DELUSIONS etc of John Berryman [1972]

I. OPUS DEI

II

III

EARLY POEMS

from "TWENTY POEMS"
in FIVE YOUNG AMERICAN POETS [1940]

from POEMS [1942]

Editor's Note

Collected Poems 1937–1971 brings together for the first time John Berryman's seven collections of short poems. This new edition incorporates only the collections he published and includes as well *Homage to Mistress Bradstreet*, one of his two long poems. The inclusive dates, 1937 to 1971, correspond to the dates of composition of the earliest and latest poems rather than the dates of the publication of his collections. *Henry's Fate and Other Poems* (1976) is not collected here because Berryman himself did not select and arrange the volume; *The Dream Songs* (1969), a self-contained major work, will continue to be published as a separate volume.

As editor of *Collected Poems 1937–1971*, my job was determined by the kind of edition the publisher requested—one that was general rather than exclusively scholarly. The complete history of the changes and transmissions of each collection and poem, for example, was not to be documented. Nevertheless, since my duty was to present an accurate text—believing the general reader is as interested in having an accurate text as the scholarly one—it was agreed that I would document all instances where I chose a reading different from that of the published first or revised edition of each collection.

The Editor's Notes, Guidelines, and Procedures, and the Copy-Texts and Variants trace the historical embodiments of Berryman's published texts and describe the nature of the textual problems his manuscripts, corrected galleys, and page proofs present. The Copy-Texts and Variants notes, less interpretive than factual, show how the texts for *Collected Poems* were established. My Introduction is addressed to both new and experienced readers of Berryman's poetry. It is arranged in nine parts: the first five present an overview of major themes in Berryman's life and work; the last four inquire into his poetics.

Abbreviations

Introduction

Wary readers of John Berryman's poetry, the kind he respected most because they ask hard questions, find themselves in the best company. Elizabeth Bishop wrote to Robert Lowell in 1956 that she "couldn't make up" her mind about the merits of *Homage to Mistress Bradstreet*. Eleven years later, she was no less baffled by *Berryman's Sonnets* when she wrote to Lowell: "I have been struggling with those sonnets—many beautiful lines but I do find him difficult." Her bafflement, nevertheless, did not diminish her sense of the penetrating power of Berryman's poetry: "One has the feeling a 100 years from now," she wrote to Lowell in 1962, "that *he* may be all the rage—or a 'discovery'—hasn't one?" Three months after Berryman's death, in January 1972, Lowell recalled *his* moments of uncertainty in hearing Berryman's voice:

He never stopped fighting and moving all his life; at first, expert and derivative, later full of output, more juice, more strange words on the page, more obscurity. I'm afraid I mistook it for forcing, when he came into his own. No voice now or persona sticks in my ear as his. It is poignant, abrasive, anguished, humorous.

Other readers heard Berryman's voice and reached different conclusions. As early as 1948, Berryman's poetry seemed surcharged to one reviewer of *The Dispossessed*. "[A] fanfare of shipwrecked syntax, textbook inversions and alliterations." But another reviewer, in *The Times Literary Supplement*, admired his style as "a living compromise between the way people speak and the outsize gestures that poetry traditionally demands." While Berryman bristled at unfavorable reviews, he was pleased to stir up controversy—"Long may they rave," he would say—for opposing views attest to what his poetry asks. He prods us to re-examine our fundamental notions about the design and function of poetry, what poetry *does* for, even to, the poet and the reader.

The critical standards by which Berryman measured other poets suggest an insight into his notions about his own poetry. Generally speaking, especially during the period of his most accelerated development in the mid- to late 1940s, he might have been writing about himself in praising other poets' "intensity" and "urgency and power." He admired Stephen Crane's primitive style and the power of his "refusal to guarantee" the reader's expectations. He was attracted to Edmund Waller's violations of the reader's expectations: "Waller . . . so controlled the forms in his best poems as to produce an expectation differing wholly from previous expectations, and then by violating the expectation got his effects." He found a kinsman in Tristan Corbière's "abrupt phrasing," "violent shifts," and "lightning alternations of the sardonic and the profound." Enlarging the tactic of stylistic violations of expectation to the design of a whole poem, Berryman regarded the first two lines in "The Love Song of J. Alfred Prufrock" as being "diminished or destroyed" in the rest of the poem.

Several of Berryman's early poems signaled the unexpected turns of *Homage to Mistress Bradstreet* and *The Dream Songs*. He described his poem "Winter Landscape," written in early 1939, as pivoting "on a missing or misrepresented element in an agreed-on or imposed design." By 1955, after having completed *Homage*, he could articulate his fundamental poetics: "The two great things [in all writing]," he wrote to his mother, "are to be *clear* and *short*; but rhythms matter too, and unexpectedness. You lead the reader briskly in one direction, then you spin him round, or you sing him a lullaby and then hit him on the head." Berryman's twin standards would appear to be at odds with unexpectedness, but to be "short" may mean that the poem will lurch abruptly, accelerate, and leave the reader standing still. Similarly, to be "clear" may mean that the design and language of a poem take into account, perhaps enact, the unexpected turns of human experience. The poem, it follows, is open to the crosscurrents of the drift-of-life, an openness that gives a sense of being simultaneously polished and jagged, appealing and offensive. In the gaps and silences of lightning shifts, readers may feel as though they have been hit on the head.

Berryman also had his eye on the reader in choosing his (outwardly) defiant tactic: "[C]ontrol . . . the reader," Berryman advises a young writer, "to do half the work" ("Purgatory," *L&F*). Readers are controlled to the extent that they are required to stake a claim in the creation of understanding and meaning. If readers are given the language, characters, and meaning they expect or want to hear, their feelings are unarticulated and their minds unexamined. They may follow nervously; indeed, Berryman believed that the most successful poem rattles the reader's expectations. Readers may be made uneasy because "[t]he serious writer," as Berryman says, "is something of an inquisitor [who] not so much asks questions of the reader as he forces the reader to put to himself the same questions about life that the author has had to put to himself."

Berryman's poetry, as he says of T. S. Eliot's, is "grievous and profound beyond a single poet's." As for readers, they "will have to follow, wherever, wherever." Berryman's making, unmaking, and remaking of sound, sense, and self; his ferocity and tenderness; his songs, satires, petitions, lamentations, and blues require adept readers. His world is Cervantine, Shakespearean, and Joycean. Like Walt Whitman, the American poet he most resembles, Berryman delights equally in tragedy and comedy. He is proud and humble, learned and primitive, nervy and nervous, fantastic and realistic. His characters are victims and masters, self-pitying and brave, lecherous and loving, responsible and irresponsible, alienated and connected. He takes quite literally Coleridge's definition of the "secondary Imagination" that "dissolves, diffuses, dissipates, in order to re-create." He is a poet of Keatsian "Negative Capability" in which the poet, as Keats says, "is capable of being in uncertainties, mysteries, doubts, without any irritable reaching after fact and reason." He believes that intensity, in Keats's words, is "capable of making all disagreeables evaporate."

Some may view Berryman's life as mired in shame and loss, but his poetry rises above a black pathology. ("You can rely upon it," Thoreau said, "you have the best of me in my books.") Those who regard him as abrasively "confessional" might very well see only one tactic of his drama of compensation *and* grace, a complex play of multiple tactics of self-deception and self-understanding. Certainly he attempted to compensate for his shame; at times it is as though he hoped to trick his terror so that he might believe he was acceptable to himself and to others. But his poetry is also his gift, a peculiarly tangled and eloquent gift. Neither he nor his poetry wants to stay in place; his life and poetry are like a "great Pierrot's universe," as Robert Lowell said of 77 *Dream Songs*, "[that] is more tearful and funny than we can easily bear."

Berryman investigates the provisional formations and re-formations of the human personality. Believing the personality to be discontinuous and ever-changing, he rebels against the view that the poem must be polished and autonomous. He assumes that the poet and the reader are bound to an uncertain process of something taking shape, of something circling rather than battened down: "If we take our head in our ears and listen," Berryman responds to Beethoven's music, "You force a blurt: Who was I? / Am I these tutti, am I this rallentando? / This entrance of the oboe?" ("Beethoven Triumphant," *De*). The "sane man" replies, "I am all these." To be these voices and instruments at the same time suggests that readers, too, "contain multitudes," as Whitman says of himself, and to contain multitudes is to set in motion questions and contradictions, an unsettling affront to our need for certainty.

Berryman's manner and matter yield up neither one lock nor one key. His poetry makes a bid for readers to become members of both the choir and the orchestra. The music of the masters, "profound solemn & clear," Berryman says in "Canto Amor" (1945), has its own harmony and grace, but Berryman's poetry is "the other music," a dissonance poised in the act of becoming harmony, a jammed voice sounding out its own articulation, a "flowing ceremony of trouble and light" ("Canto Amor," *TD*). The "ceremony" in his poetry is as important as the "trouble and light." He invites readers to recognize that they are not victims of change, but rather communicants in the cycles of life's ebb and flow, its departures and returns. "Strange lives we lead," he wrote to his mother in 1954; "life is, all, transformation. We must not be glad, or sorry, to be part of it; but we can't help being. And *there* there was some unkindness, somewhere, somewhere? And pity, and kindness."

Like other great moderns and contemporaries—Hardy, Yeats, Bishop, and Lowell—Berryman regards the outcome of human experience as frequently the opposite of what we either expect or hope for. And yet, as it was in Yeats's and Lowell's life and poetry, and before them Emerson's and Whitman's, uncertainty is drawn into the larger orbits of death and rebirth. Berryman's dominant image is that of a figure poised to make ready for the transforming moment of a new beginning. The hero undergoes a series of shocks and misfortunes (a "fall") and arrives at a moment of self-discovery and self-knowledge. Like Henry, Berryman's archetypical alter ego, his heroic figure has "ancient fires for eyes"; his fall is fortunate in that he comes to a moment of transforming intensity with "his head full / & his heart full" (Dream Song 77). But the moment of the new beginning is neither the end of his journey nor the last death and rebirth he will experience. While death and rebirth may be certain, the drift-of-life in between is uncertain; he is continuously "making ready to move on" (Dream Song 77). So if Berryman's abrupt shifts and tentative conclusions refuse to guarantee readers' expectations, they should know that he does not expect them to. He asks for a risky contract; readers who inquire further may find rewards other than confirmation.

The formations and re-formations of Berryman's life. There are many John Berrymans. There is the boy—born John Allyn Smith, Jr., on October 25, 1914, in McAlester, Oklahoma—whose family moved every two or three years, because his father, a banker, either resigned or was fired.

There is the nine-year-old Catholic altar boy admiring his first surrogate father, Fr. Boniface Beri, O.S.B., and the "fox-like child I was," he said many years later, "or assume I was" ("At Chinese Checkers," *TD*). There is the bright and lonely ten-year-old who attended a Catholic boarding school for several months in Chickasha, Oklahoma, while his parents were in Tampa, Florida, attempting to establish a new life. There is the bereft eleven-year-old whose father committed suicide in Clearwater, Florida, in June 1926, only ten months after the family's move. There is the boy who felt that his father's abandonment "blew out [his] most bright candle faith" ("Eleven Addresses to the Lord," #6, *L&F*).

Young Smith becomes the dispossessed son whose mother hastily remarries John Angus McAlpin Berryman, nearly twenty years her senior, in New York City two and a half months after her husband's death. The confused and silently angry adopted son is renamed John Allyn McAlpin Berryman—"a trick a mockery my name," he writes at age twenty-five ("A Point of Age," *TD*)—who feels he is denied the birthright of bearing his father's name. He is the schoolboy at P.S. 69 in Jackson Heights, Long Island, a successful and imaginative student placing in a district spelling bee, winning a prize for his essay on the prevention of cruelty to animals, and writing a science-fiction novel.

He is the short and awkward teenager at South Kent School in Connecticut, nicknamed "Blears" because his "eye glasses were so thick you could perform physics experiments with them," a classmate said. He is the dutiful son whose sense of himself is fused with his mother's ambitions, and he is the unsuccessful athlete who regains some self-esteem by reporting sports events for the school newspaper. He is the protector of his younger brother, Bob, and the successful student who takes great pride in his top academic ranking. He is the bullied and frustrated teenager who, in an impulsive moment of vengeance, must be pulled off the railroad tracks of an oncoming train. He is the precocious teenager who is the first in his prep school to skip the sixth form to enter college.

As an undergraduate at Columbia College (1932–36), Berryman is determined to become a new person. In his freshman year he runs for class office and goes out for sports (crew, wrestling, and track). Despite the Depression and his family's modest income, Berryman's friend E. M. Halliday recalls, his mother "saw to it that John was well dressed and well laundered." Indeed, he changes so dramatically from the frustrated prep student with thick glasses that some admire his poise and self-assurance: "John," Halliday says, "with his lean build but broad shoulders, his sharply cut jaw, and his quizzical hazel eyes flickering behind his metal-framed glasses, radiated charisma." The collegiate Berryman is known as a "tireless & inventive dancing man" ("My Special Fate," *L&F*). He falls passionately in and out of love with the changes of the seasons, but most often he is the "haggard unsuccessful lover." He is alternately serious and flippant, a scholastic monk and a slapstick clown.

Mark Van Doren—Berryman's mentor and friend ("it was the force of his example," Berryman said many years later, "that made me a poet")—remembered the young man as "slender, abstracted, courteous," and he recalled that the young Berryman "lived one life alone and walked with verse as in a trance." The eager apprentice also wishes to be a critic like R. P. Blackmur, another of his surrogate father-heroes: "To be a *critic*," he writes thirty-six years later, "ah, / how deeper & more scientific" ("Olympus," *L&F*). Berryman publishes his first poems and reviews in *The Columbia Review* and Robert Giroux names him one of the magazine editors. He graduates as a member of Phi Beta Kappa and is awarded the Kellett Fellowship to study at Cambridge University in England for two years. All the while, he secretly longs to recover his lost father, especially when he visits his friends' homes "with fathers / universal & intact" ("Freshman Blues," *L&F*); and he dreams, too, of his "*name* / blown by adoring winds all over" ("My Special Fate," *L&F*).

Berryman's journey to Cambridge at once promises a new beginning—"I swamp with possibility" ("Away," *L&F*)—and intensifies his fear of inadequacy: "Black hours over an unclean line. / Fear. Of failure, or, worse, *insignificance*" ("Friendless," *L&F*). But he sets about, in long hours of intense work, re-forming himself, for the colleges of Cambridge are the "haunts of old masters where I may improve" ("Away," *L&F*). On the occasion of his twenty-second birthday, less than two months after settling in his rooms at Clare College, he writes in an unpublished poem: "From this day forth I will absolute change." He becomes the tweedy scholar, grows a beard, wins the prestigious Oldham prize for his knowledge of Shakespeare, and learns to prepare tea the proper English way. He avidly reads biographies and the letters of great poets, especially John Keats's letters; he plans to write a biography of his hero W. B. Yeats. Always self-conscious, he changes his handwriting from undergraduate flourishes to a crabbed and mandarin penmanship, and his American accent takes on the sophistication of Oxbridge rhythms.

After completing his studies at Cambridge in 1938, Berryman's public roles are limited to those of poet, critic, scholar, and teacher. He becomes the tightly wired and learned don dressed in a bow tie and a Brooks Brothers sports jacket. He is the itinerant professor-poet who teaches at

Wayne State, Harvard, Princeton, Cincinnati, Iowa, Minnesota, Washington, California (Berkeley), Brown, and Bread Loaf in Vermont. He writes a biography of Stephen Crane (1950) and starts a Shakespeare book (unfinished); he is the elegant, formal, and shrewd critic of poetry, drama, and fiction in literary magazines; the unashamedly learned editor who works with an accountant's attention to detail on a definitive edition of the text of *King Lear* (also unfinished after many years of work). He is ceremonious and decorous and yet he delights in violating ceremony and decorum. He is the bad, wild poet who is awarded the Pulitzer Prize for *77 Dream Songs* and the National Book Award for *His Toy, His Dream, His Rest*; he is the "meteor-bearded" Regents' Professor at the University of Minnesota.

"[P]arts of my surface," Berryman writes in the last year of his life, "are continually slipping past others" ("Matins," *De*). Likewise, parts of Berryman's inner life slip past others. He is the angry son who is at once ashamed of his father's death and longs to avenge his loss; he seeks out surrogate fathers; he devours the works of major and minor writers, theologians, philosophers, archaeologists, and psychologists. He is the bibliophile of seventeenth- and eighteenth-century editions of poetry and drama, a collector of sayings in crisis and of last words at death; he fears death but longs to embrace it. He is the self-wrestler, the scared and searing self-critic, the hard worker who agonizes over periods of calm that seem to him laziness. He is alternately strong and sickly, almost a hypochondriac. He is the lover of Bessie Smith, Bach, Beethoven, and Mozart; the stubborn craftsman; the avid moviegoer; the failed playwright. He continues to be the dutiful son of a possessive mother, but he is also the possessive son of a dutiful mother.

His personality resembles the warring name of his fictional character Alan Severance in *Recovery*: Alan (an allusion to his father, Allyn?) is Celtic for "harmony" and Severance means "tearer-apart of people, disrupter." He becomes the husband married three times, the "sexual athlete," the womanizer, the father of a son in his second marriage, two daughters in his third, and one child, as he said, "off the record." He is as cruel as a Pharaoh in insulting and blaming others for his misfortunes and as admirable as a good Samaritan in his deep empathy with the pains and difficulties of friends and acquaintances. He is unashamedly patriotic, at once jealous of the national honor and chagrined by Americans' shallow knowledge of their country's history. He is the poet who is distressed by an American society that values his success in the media more than his achievement in his poetry. He is the generous and profligate spender, the proud pauper, the mad charmer, the bristling, stagy, and swaggering egotist; he is the fiercely loyal friend, the untrustworthy and betraying friend, the alcoholic, the public clown, the witty conversationalist, the believer in a "God of rescue," and the suicide in Minneapolis at age fifty-seven on January 7, 1972.

Berryman's intensity—his affliction and his means of grace. Like his alter ego Henry in *The Dream Songs*, Berryman believed he was afflicted by "a sense of total L O S S" that created in him "an absolute disappearance of continuity & love" (Dream Song 101). As a result, when someone mentions " 'worthless' . . . he took it in, / degraded Henry, at the ebb of love— / O at the end of love . . ." (Dream Song 109). Perhaps it was the violations in his youth that created in him a radically incomplete sense of identity, but whatever the cause, he frequently and acutely expected to be shamed, betrayed, and abandoned. When the environment of shame and loss seemed to rage, he felt fragmented, insecure, needing, helpless, and terrified. When the turbulence moderated, he gave the impression of an engaging personality negotiating a tightrope of conflicting urgencies. "Berryman the man," Jane Howard wrote in *Life* in 1965, "is as fully complex as Berryman the poet. . . . You never know whether to treat him as an august man of letters or as a prankish little boy, because he is always, simultaneously, both." Berryman often seemed stymied in his hope to "wipe out," as he would say, his unpredictable and undesirable selves. "The law," in Berryman's and Henry's mind, is that "we must, owing to chiefly shame / lacing our pride, down what we did" (Dream Song 58).

Since grace and dignity are hard won for the person who experiences shame and loss so profoundly, Berryman's expectations throughout his life issued in a distrust of stability. "My occasional absolute confidence is what worries me," Berryman wrote to Halliday in 1937; "experience says man never got what he counted on." "[W]hat should be normal life," he wrote to his mother on his thirtieth birthday (October 25, 1944), "comes to have, transient & tolerable, the air of a vacation, unreal interim." Similarly, Berryman said to an interviewer in 1967: "I'm not an enemy of good news at all, mind you. When news is good, it's fine with me— but I usually expect it to be bad."

Believing he was destined to suffer, Berryman's questions often had to do with what form the suffering would take and how he might endure it. At times he believed that suffering should not be, as he wrote to a friend in 1948, "kept going" and that he should "head through" suffering.

Characteristically, he took himself up, for these were his *"provisional"* feelings. And indeed they were: "My idea is this," he said to an interviewer in 1970, "the artist is extremely lucky who is presented with the worst possible ordeal which will not actually kill him. At that point he's in business." "What seems to happen [when one suffers]," Berryman wrote in 1948, "is that one is *dared* to move, and a great boulder is thrown down on one, and then certain men are able to move. We have to be very grateful for the dare." But to take up the dare to endure suffering was not enough. Berryman's view of suffering is what Nietzsche called "joyful wisdom" (that which does not kill me makes me stronger) and what Yeats identified as "tragic gaiety." In the aftermath of shame and loss, one maintains one's dignity by defying adversity with a bitter and compassionate laughter.

But it was not the suffering that Berryman desired; one might even say that he did not desire to suffer at all. His sense of "tragic gaiety" was an effort to turn suffering in on itself, as though the flame might be so intense that it would purify and make him new. He desired most to replace his intensity of loss with an intensity of grace. At some level of self-understanding, Berryman seemed to be aware that intensity, whether destructive or constructive, was the habitual center of his craving and expectation. He sought out intensity in almost every activity—conversation, dancing, drinking, lecturing, writing, even his reading:

How shall I tell you how I am reading it? [he wrote to his mother in 1942 about Dostoevsky's *Crime and Punishment*]. As if I were driving a pack of hounds through a wood, feverishly; only every tree and bush is so unbearably interesting and exciting that I'd like to stop and examine it for a long time, but the hounds are off ahead and won't stop. . . . [M]y faculties are raging out in front of me. I haven't felt so powerfully in a long time. Even my unhappiness is acute, sharp, engaging.

As a young man, Berryman was aware of the paradoxical power of intensity, and he began to investigate how he might use it in the style and composition of his poetry. In an unpublished poem, four days before his twenty-second birthday, he came to the conclusion: "I derive a curious ease from contemplation of the intense, the / Unalterable place which will be mine." Eleven days earlier, he wrote of a similar intensity he desired in his life and poetry:

Idiom and reference are but
Statistics of catastrophe,
Intensity is the lever that
Riots the nerve within the bone. . . .

The next day (October 11, 1936) he wrote to his mother: "I want more and more only intensity or the ineluctable authority of precise poetic statement." Berryman was drawn to the same intensity in the writing of poetry as he wanted in it, one being necessary to accomplish the other. He frequently spoke of the "valuable heat" of composition that he found most present in writing a long poem like "Boston Common" (*TD*) in 1942:

[E]ach stanza appears a kind of mountain. . . . Until yesterday I could work only at night; during the days I read William James and Aristotle and Donne and generally *waited*, in a state best described as frenzy; at midnight I began. . . . Each session brings more mistakes than the last, as the effort needed increases, as my fatigue increases, and as I approach the unsayable centre. Most of them, so far, I have been able to correct—a poor term, "correct," just as "mistakes" is, but you understand: mistakes, I mean, considered as a deviation from the top of intensity and truth [Letter to his mother, June 1942].

John Keats—"the lovely man," Henry says—would have understood Berryman's "unsayable centre": "[T]he excellence of every art," Keats wrote, "is its intensity capable of making all disagreeables evaporate from their being in close relationship with Beauty and Truth." (This quotation was one of the epigraphs Berryman considered using for *Homage*.) Both recognized that, for them, the actual composition of a poem was as important as the completion of it, for both seemed to hope to refire an intensity that evaporates the old self and tempers the new. Each new poem offers the possibility of the exhilarating grace of a new beginning, what Berryman sometimes experienced as "a freeing, with the creation of every real poem." Each new poem comes as a gift and a prayer: "Gift us," Berryman prays to God, "with long cloaks & adrenaline" ("Eleven Addresses to the Lord," #4, *L&F*).

"The sense of change . . . will abide." The supreme expression of Berryman's intensity in his life and poetry was his fear of death and his desire to embrace it. "How impatient [John] had been for death the late Dream Songs make clear," writes Eileen Simpson, Berryman's first wife and the author of *Poets in Their Youth*. Simpson suggests that Berryman's being

a poet did not, as she and others had sometimes believed, contribute to his suicide. On the contrary, "It was the poetry that kept him alive"; because of his "certainty that there were all those poems still to be written," he lived nearly twenty years longer than his father. Berryman's friend Saul Bellow cites the poem "Despair" (*L&F*), written several years after *The Dream Songs*, as an explanation of the suicide: "It seems to be DARK all the time. . . . I certainly don't think I'll last much longer." "At last," Bellow comments, "it must have seemed that he had used up all his resources. . . . The cycle of resolution, reform and relapse had become a bad joke which could not continue."

Whatever one's view, Berryman's suicide, in the context of his life, was also a final rebirth, a freeing. "The only comforting reflexion," Berryman wrote several months before his death, "is not / 'we will all rest in Abraham's bosom' & rot of that purport / but: after my death there will be *no more sin*." Berryman would have delighted in Bellow's idea of the "bad joke" of the cycle of resolution, reform, and relapse. "But, Saul," he might have replied, "the cycle *may* end with a final re-formation." He might have cited another poem written about the same time as "Despair": "Rest may be your ultimate gift. Rest or transfiguration!" ("Eleven Addresses to the Lord," #5, *L&F*).

"The sense of change, suns gone up and come down," he wrote in 1939, "Whirls in my tired head, and it will abide" ("At Chinese Checkers," *TD*). Throughout his poetry and diaries, Berryman alternately lamented and celebrated moments of transition, especially the seasons of Christmas, Easter, spring, and his birthday. He either resolved or hoped, as in a primitive rite, for a necessary rebellion and a fresh beginning, a willed death and a new birth. Every new year, as Eileen Simpson writes, he anticipated "a magical rebirth." His ambitious New Year's resolves a little over two months after his first marriage are a typical example:

To keep my temper, and to preserve an even manner; to feign self-possession if I can't achieve it.

Not to exaggerate unless my irony is perfectly clear. To keep my opinions to myself.

To try to bring my humility and my arrogance together. Is a more regular current of feeling *impossible*?

To be a better husband altogether.

And a better friend: to allow, to have faith, to answer letters, to be kind.

To keep the Journal and to make it continually more useful to me.

To learn to know Christ.

One of the engaging qualities of Berryman's character is his ability to act as his own ironic observer. On January 2, 1955, he wrote to his mother: "I made no resolutions. None was necessary. I am *all* resolution." But, in Flannery O'Connor's phrase, his "habit of being" was a habit of seeking *Verklärung*, the moment of transfiguration and ecstasy. "I have been reading some notes about my dead self," Berryman wrote in his diary in January 1940. "Of course it is not dead I am sad to say. What is needed is suicide each year, the dead one then to phoenix into change." Berryman's very grammar points to his moment: the noun becomes the transitive verb that at once names and enacts his desire—"insisting on the verb," as Henry says, "not the noun" (Dream Song 161).

It is in his poetry that Berryman's self-re-forming idiom takes its most pure and primitive form. In the new year of 1937, for example, Berryman writes in an unpublished poem: "A certain peace for my head / In death, I shall make my pause." In another unpublished poem he perceives the cyclical nature of death: "Man is the ground of many deaths." In early January 1945, he probes deeper:

> [C]an old wounds be
> Anything in the new man, man we await,
> Man I am on tiptoe for for years and cling
> To the mirror at morning?

"This spending, surrendering," Berryman concludes, "I hold becoming":

> Grinding more long that it may live more clear,
> Moving at last invisible and dear
> Into the house that was always familiar here.

The language of the poet is the chant of the intense man becoming—a "flowing ceremony of trouble and light," a history of "the fate of the soul," as Henry says, "what it was all about / during its being" (Dream Song 156).

One cannot of course be certain, but Berryman's suicide seven days into the new year tells his story one last time, the moment in which his metaphor becomes his reality. Perhaps his desire "to phoenix into change" was his rescue from his need to live, as he had written of Stephen Crane's, "in the midst of all but unbearable excitement." "Death," therefore, as Berryman says of Crane's suicide fantasy, "ends the terrible excitement under which he is bound to live, death resolves panic, death is 'a way out,' a rescue." In the last year of his life, Berryman frequently spoke of a "God of rescue," and a draft he wrote six months before he died for a book to be titled *Sacrifices* could very well be his own remarkable epitaph:

An entirely new kind of freedom manifested in several ways, in retirement, in death, but invariably in a special retirement or death that contains as one of its chief meanings a repudiation of the earlier "freedom." There is a *conversion*, in short, if we can employ the term without either religious or psychoanalytic overtones. Someone is changed, simply, into someone else.

The poet and the poetry. Not until 1959—confident in the authority of having written *The Dispossessed, Sonnets to Chris,* and *Homage to Mistress Bradstreet*—was Berryman able to articulate publicly the ritual that was buried in his deepest experience. When he inquired into his motives for making poetry, his experience seemed to confirm that poetry "aims . . . at the reformation of the poet":

Poetry is a terminal activity, taking place out near the end of things, where the poet's soul addresses one other soul only, never mind when. And it aims—never mind *either* communication or expression—at the reformation of the poet, as prayer does. In the grand cases—as in our century, Yeats and Eliot—it enables the poet gradually, again and again, to become almost another man; but something of that sort happens, on a small scale, a freeing, with the creation of every real poem.

Berryman's motives for making poetry were more complex than his aiming at his own re-formation, but our recognizing his primary (I want to say primordial) motive leads to an enlightening way of thinking about the design and function of his poetry. On the one hand, Berryman's re-formations appear to be willed changes; as he said after writing *Homage*: "After having done one thing, you want to do something as different as possible." Near the end of *The Dream Songs* he vowed: "I will not come again / or not come with this style" (Dream Song 379), and he did not. On the other hand, Berryman believed that the will, as expressed in ceremony and ritual, may be instinctual—what he called, at the age of twenty-one, "the power of animal will to alter or renew." Furthermore, poetry may be organic, he said several years before his statement about the aim of the poetry, because it "makes use of and adapts to its ends the *basic rhythms* of human life: the systolic-diastolic rhythm of the blood, of breathing, of the alternation of day and night, of cyclical desire and conception, of the procession of the seasons, the stages of youth and age." Willed and organic changes, however, are not necessarily mutually exclusive notions: the poet's apparently willed re-formations may be instinctive responses that are attuned to the alternating rhythms of human life.

At the risk of oversimplifying Berryman's subjects and themes, I would suggest that, beginning with *The Dispossessed* (1948), the rite of re-formation informs the design of all his major collections. Although he arranged most of the poems in his collections chronologically, in order of composition, he selected those that cluster in cycles, cycles moving simultaneously to the alternations of day and night, desire and conception, the procession of the seasons, and the stages of youth and age. Regarded as a whole, his poetry—like his life—was a series of new departures and new beginnings. Some departures are unexpected, some new beginnings are either willed or worried into being, but all are open to a re-formation, a re-formation aimed equally at the poet and the reader.

The poems in Berryman's first major collection, *The Dispossessed*, suggest that neither a new beginning nor a rebirth is possible in the violent and violated world of the late 1930s and World War II. "Winter Landscape" (1939)—the opening poem that simultaneously alludes to "three men in brown" in Brueghel's painting *Hunters in the Snow* and to Hitler's brownshirts—establishes the image of a weary, frozen world. The three hunters, returning from a hunt, are at once frozen in time, like figures on a Grecian urn, and moving in time, unaware of "the evil waste of history / Outstretched" as they descend "[a]nkle-deep in snow down the winter hill." The next five poems present a similarly immobilized modern world where "[d]isfigurement is general" ("The Statue"). It is a world of "storm and gloom" in which the young poet makes his testament of being "prepared to start" ("A Point of Age"), a world where travelers are uncertain of their destination ("The Traveller"), and a world in which a helpless boy learns "well behind his desperate eyes, / The epistemology of loss" ("The Ball Poem"). "Fare Well," the concluding poem of Part I, returns to the winter landscape of the opening ("I slip into a snowbed with no hurt"), and the final stanza suggests that a new departure will be undertaken in the poems that follow. Berryman's emblematic metaphor of the phoenix reappears ("Fare Well" was written in December 1947), but the image of the phoenix—not a verb this time— is a "weak peep" and seems to exist in memory only.

The poems in Parts II, III, and IV follow, with some variations, the thematic design of Part I. Part IV, for example, begins with "Canto Amor," in which the speaker, like Berryman, is at a point of transition ("the midnight of [his] thirtieth year"); he hopes that his marriage will endure in an uncertain world. "The Lightning," the concluding poem of Part IV, mirrors the terza rima form of "Canto Amor" and addresses Berryman's sister-in-law, Marie Mabry, who fears a terrifying lightning storm. The speaker concludes, almost protesting too much, that although the "lightning dances," he "cannot despair." *The Dispossessed* ends (Part V) with the new beginning of the nuclear age in the title poem, part of which Berryman wrote on the day the first atomic bomb was dropped on Hiroshima on August 6, 1945. The new dawn, however, reveals a lifeless landscape (mirroring the winter landscape of the opening poem), and the child of the nuclear age is deformed and grotesque—"the faceless fellow waving from [a woman's] crotch."

Berryman's most dramatic development as a poet—his change from a rhetorical public voice to a sustained nervous idiom—came about during the writing of *Sonnets to Chris. Sonnets* represents his own second birth, and he became the passionate poet, a role he had been rehearsing for over a decade. The first, written on April 26, 1947, seeks a new beginning in spring ("I wished, all the mild days of middle March . . .") in an adulterous affair. By mid-July, as he waits in vain for the usual tryst, he is reminded of ancient graves: "In Shub-ad's grave the fingers of a girl / Were touching still, when they found her, the strings of her lyre" (Sonnet 65). In the aftermath of bitterness, guilt, and their "simultaneous dying" (Sonnet 71)—in the seventeenth-century sense of orgasm and death—the affair ends. Like his experience of reading Dostoevsky, his unhappiness is "acute, sharp, engaging," and he continues writing sonnets. The last, written in September 1947 (the other concluding sonnets were written in 1966), ends with an image of the flame of intensity that has created a new beginning: "I am free now of the fire of this sin . . ." (Sonnet 111).

Berryman's assurance in his new voice spurred him to begin *Homage to Mistress Bradstreet*. On March 22, 1948, the second day of spring, he wrote the first stanza and the first three lines of the second, "and there," Berryman said later, "for almost five years, I stuck." But it was actually his long "pause," like his New Year's resolve for 1937, before yet another beginning. He made notes periodically for several years, and during the first two months of the new year of 1953, he wrote fifty new stanzas: "I was on fire every second," Berryman said, and the poem was completed on March 22. Like the opening poem of *TD, Homage* begins in winter, but then, abruptly, "[t]he winters close, Springs open." "One proud tug greens Heaven," and Bradstreet gives birth to her first child. Later, one of her children asks, "Mother, how *long* will I be dead?" She replies, "[N]ot we one instant die, only our dark does lighten." The poem ends with the burial of Bradstreet, and the poet speaks of a departure and "a sourcing" in the final lines.

And so one might continue with lengthy analyses of *The Dream Songs* (1969), *Love & Fame* (1971), and *Delusions Etc.* (1972), but a few examples will show further how fundamental the theme of formation and re-formation was throughout his poetry. While the rhythms of *The Dream Songs* ebb and flow, they may be more accurately characterized as a series of Henry's departures and returns, his deaths and rebirths. Part I, for example, begins with Henry's first simultaneous death and birth in being forced out of the secure world of the womb: "Then came a departure. / Thereafter nothing fell out as it might or ought" (Dream Song 1). Part I ends with a view of death as a fortunate event: "I had a most marvellous piece of luck. I died" (Dream Song 26); consequently, Part II begins: "good Spring / returns with a dance and a sigh" (Dream Song 27). *The Dream Songs* likewise ends with a new beginning (when Henry begins his songs he is in his mid- to late forties; now he is in his fifties). Song 380 prepares the way with Henry's recovery in a hospital, a recovery that will be "a fresh version of living." In Song 382 Henry is dead once again, and a strange and terrifying dancer comes to his bier and "dances Henry away." But "all is well" in his dance with death, for his rebirth takes place and 383 begins: "It brightens with power, when dawn begins." *The Dream Songs* appropriately ends with a celebration of death and renewal on Thanksgiving Day.

Berryman's last two collections, in their composition, design, and rendering of the personality, are clearly congruent with his own life. The poems of each collection were written between the beginning of the new year and into spring: *Love & Fame* in February and March 1970—"The Search" was written on the first day of spring—and most of *Delusions Etc.* between January and April 1971. The intensity of composition (Berryman described himself as being "hot as a pistol") is a measure of his sense of immediacy and the degree to which he wished to free himself from alcohol and become another person.

In *Love & Fame*, Berryman engages his past youthful self, this time not in the sliding pronouns of *The Dream Songs* but in his verbs, his confusion (or fusion?) of past and present tenses. Each of the four parts represents Berryman's cyclical new beginnings from early youth to middle age (he was fifty-five at the time). In Part I, he accounts primarily for his freshman year at Columbia (1932–33); in Part II, he is in his first year at Cambridge (1936–37); in Part III, his life spreads out through time and space (significantly the section begins with "The Search"); and Part IV establishes another new beginning, his "initiatory faith" in God (late 1969 to early 1970).

"Her & It," the opening poem of *Love & Fame*, begins in the past tense ("I fell in love with a girl") and then shifts to the present: "It's not now near at all the end of winter." As in the opening of *The Dispossessed* and *Homage*, winter establishes the theme of a seasonal death. The two concluding poems of Part I move swiftly from a "Crisis" to a "Recovery," as the titles suggest. In "Crisis," Berryman says he had been "squarely in the middle of Hell" and "more dead than alive." But, he says in the next poem, "I pulled myself reluctantly together at last / & bowed good-bye . . ." ("Recovery"). As he boards his ship to England, he recalls that his "nervous system . . . sprang back into expectation." Part II opens with his leaving the New World for the Old World of Cambridge University, and on board the ship his expectation of a new beginning continues (in the present tense): "I swamp with possibility" ("Away"). The section ends with a "Tea" with a young woman, a new love and a new beginning. The titles of Part III suggest that his formation and re-formation continue not only throughout his own life but also in the larger cycles of time. Part III begins with "The Search" and ends with a descent to death and an ascent toward new life, as the titles suggest, a sort of Dantesque descent and ascent: "The Hell Poem," "Death Ballad," "Purgatory," "Heaven," and "The Home Ballad." Part IV, "Eleven Addresses to the Lord," abruptly shifts to his present life. In the first address, Berryman establishes the "initiatory faith" as his new beginning. Several addresses later, he speaks of "transfiguration!" The addresses conclude with his identifying with the death of Germanicus, a Christian martyr, and he hopes that he, too, may embrace death with Germanicus' courage: "Make too me acceptable at the end of time / in my degree, which then Thou wilt award."

In his last volume, there is more emphasis on the *et cetera* than on the delusions. Although the collection is not so clearly structured by the alternating rhythms of death and rebirth, each section ends with a celebration and affirmation. Part I, the Hours of the Office recounted in the "Opus Dei" poems, begins in winter and ends with the assurance that "the winter will end." The Hours begin before sunrise and progress through dawn, noon, sunset, and midnight. Berryman further suggests in his headnote to "Opus Dei" that "the offices are not within one day said but thro' their hours at intervals over many weeks—such being the

World." The images of rebirth frequently appear in *De*, as in "Beethoven Triumphant" ("Chary with his loins / womanward, [Beethoven] begot us an enigma"). Part III ends with the celebration of the birth of his daughter, and the volume closes with his article of faith in the person of Israel's King David, who, despite his failures ("the wide hell in the world"), defies his adversities with a tragic gaiety: "yea, / all the black same I dance my blue head off!"

Berryman's adaptation of the rhythms of human life frequently turned to questions about the relationship between poetry and the poet. Is the individual life at the mercy of art? Or is art at the mercy of the individual life? At the time he completed *Sonnets* in 1947, Berryman wrote in his diary that he had believed "dogmatically for years" in "the perfect separateness of Life & Art, the poet's life negligible & to-be-lost," but, he resolved, "no more." In his life thereafter, his poetry became "a terminal activity" ("terminal" suggesting both an ending and a juncture) that "aims . . . at the reformation of the poet." It is true, as some critics have said, that his life was at the mercy of his art, but it is equally true that his art was at the mercy of the re-formations of his life.

The sounds of change, the rhythms of poetry. When Berryman sent Wallace Stevens a copy of *The Dispossessed* in 1948, Stevens was courteously aware of Berryman's most sensitive apprehension and hope: "Your poems seem to be packed full so that the very edges of the syllables matter," Stevens wrote, "but I am going to take them slowly." On the back of the letter Berryman commented: "If only a few readers *would hear* them slowly, I think the poems might hope for something."

"All we know is ears" (Dream Song 97), Henry says, and hearing is one of his—and Berryman's—major themes. In one sense, we "play it by ear / out there until all's straight" (Dream Song 278). In another, Berryman believed that his ear accounted for the craft of his art. When Berryman began writing, he felt that, like Henry, his poetry was "keen & viable," but only in listening to the old masters did his art begin (Dream Song 166). In "Ivory," one of his student poems (1935), the speaker suggests that although a poem may appear to be a Yeatsian sanctuary of peace and certainty—"There is no peace / Outside the song"—the speaker-poet believes so at the risk of ignoring a primitive listening to life:

> There is no peace
> Outside the song.

So wrote the poet: while the drums
Beat without: Remotely to his ears, years
Rolled their long thunder.

And when the young Berryman read a poem that was too polished or rhetorical, he wrote in an unpublished poem in 1937: "My ears by easy melody are made mad / And all my brain rings with this competence." As he wrote or revised his poems in the late 1940s and early 1950s, his notes reflect a similar concern: "[C]an't *hear* style," or "where is my ear?" or, more significantly, "control the ear w[ith] mind & heart." Predictably, Berryman judged other poets by the quality of their ear: "Milton is the supreme master of syntax," Berryman said in his 1949 essay on Ezra Pound's poetry; "behind this mastery lies his ear." And on Pound: "I scarcely know what to say about Pound's ear. Fifteen years of listening have not taught me that it is inferior to the ear of the author of *Twelfth Night*." He heard not only the sounds of poetry; in Waller's style of violating the reader's expectation, he also heard "the sound of the change of a national mind."

Berryman asks readers to listen attentively to life, as he assumes the poet has, so that they may hear (and become part of) the sounds of the poet's listening. The degree to which readers respond to the same, or kindred, rhythms might be one test of the poet's effectiveness, but in the matter of reading poetry, Berryman emphasized that a fundamental part of the contract between readers and the poem is that they hear its sounds and rhythms: "People read with their eyes, not their ears." "Poems should be read aloud," Berryman advised, "until you get so that you can hear [them] with your eyes."

As a young man, Berryman set about hearing poems with his eyes. On how he came to hear Yeats's "A Prayer for Old Age," the twenty-two-year-old Berryman wrote to his mother: "Like most of his poems it should be read aloud a hundred times—sometimes only after weeks have I understood an intonation." He also memorized a number of poems by Shakespeare, Donne, Swift, Blake, Wordsworth, Yeats, and Auden as well as those of his contemporaries Dylan Thomas, Theodore Roethke, Bishop, and Lowell. In his classes and readings throughout his life, he recited them with brilliance and vibrancy.

The singular rhythms Berryman heard in his experience are similar to his uncontrollable animals in "The Animal Trainer" and *The Dream Songs*: "Huddled from their recesses, the goblins spring," Henry says, "while the sound goes roaring" (Dream Song 204). In his first ambitious long poem, "Ritual at Arlington" (unpublished), the speaker hears the terrible sounds of his violated past in the voices of the dead: "[L]isten! can you hear / Their tenuous invective, the bones' compelled / Restraint in the ground?" The sounds of the "tenuous invective" of the dead reverberates throughout Berryman's writing, and the terror the sounds call up never changes. He alternately hears "[p]yromaniacal whispers" (Sonnet 6) and "the little cough somewhere . . . a chime" (Dream Song 29). He is terrified by the "enormous sounds / downward . . . [that] up bring real" (Dream Song 120), and the "notes in the sullen ground" whose "solitude is great & dug to last" (Dream Song 268). These terrifying sounds seemed to confirm Berryman's expectation of abandonment; he hears the sounds of his fears of the dead (especially his father) and his own dying. As a result, he renders a strange music: "My harpsichord weird as a koto drums / *adagio* for twilight . . . and the spidery business of love" ("The Dispossessed," *TD*).

If readers are baffled by Berryman's strange and dissonant music, how may they learn to hear it? One short answer is that they might begin by recalling an assumption so simple that one easily forgets it: to hear (in all senses of "hearing") Berryman's poems, they must be read aloud. Michael Dennis Browne, a poet with a fine ear for the music of poetry, describes vividly how his baffled, English-trained ear first heard Berryman's poetry:

It wasn't until I heard John Berryman himself read . . . that I began to feel the real power and energy of [*The Dream Songs*]. . . . He read them *slowly*—more slowly at times than I would have thought possible—but there were also variations within this slowness, sudden bursts and accelerations, sudden drastic increases in volume. And the poems came over to the audience with an extraordinary combination of authority and intimacy—a kind of lyrical power that I had not heard in spoken poetry before.

Readers may not have Browne's advantage of actually hearing Berryman read (several recordings are available), but his description captures how Berryman's power and energy may work. Baffled by *77 Dream Songs*, a friend asked Kate Donahue (Berryman's third wife) how to begin reading the Songs: "Just read the first one over and over and over," she said, "until you hear it. Then read the others." Berryman added: "Well, that's good advice."

Berryman believed that sounds, in some mysterious way, replenish the deep springs of the soul. Like Balzac's description of Sarrasine ("His

soul passed into his ears. . . . He seemed to hear through every pore"),
the poet's listening—and by implication the reader's—may be an actual,
physical experience that empowers the soul. In his unfinished poem
"*Selbst*," written in August 1948, Berryman seemed certain of the mar-
riage of the ear and the soul:

> Some bones, and old clothes, and remorse, two eyes
> None of the best, and if it has a soul
> The soul has ears.

"[T]he *sound* of things," Berryman wrote to a friend a month later, "is
important to the soul—no reason, but they are; or the reason just in the
movement of the blood, the recurrent flash of the lids that interrupt the
world, the rhythms of destruction and rebuilding in the body minute by
minute." But Berryman was not satisfied with a metaphor of the soul's
mysterious listening, for the rhythms of poetry may be so accurate and
so near the nature of experience that they *are* the reality. "The only
permanent thing is rhythm," he wrote in an unpublished "Manifesto,"
"In a poem we hear rhythm as the *pace* of the soul." What Berryman
means by the soul he does not explain, but he seems to assume the
traditional notion of the inner spiritual life. The life of the soul, he sug-
gests, is sustained by the same alternating rhythms as those of the body.
The poem, if the poet has the talent and the luck, at once portrays and
enacts the pace of both body and soul.

The power and control of form. Berryman began writing poetry at the
age of nineteen in late June or early July 1934 with four Petrarchan sonnets
(the earliest extant poems) for his mother's birthday on July 8. The lim-
itations of the sonnet must have appealed to him, but the counterpoint
of the octave and the sestet tapped a personal energy, an apposition of
opposing elements. He also experimented with violating strict rhyme. In
November 1934, shortly after his twentieth birthday, he wrote with great
excitement to E. M. Halliday that he was "experimenting with rime a
good deal." In two quatrains he had written, he said he intentionally used
"two imperfect rimes" because "in so tight and monotonous a form as the
4–3–4–4 quatrain tends to be, four strong rimes seem to me too 'set.'"
He was also "working in the sonnet again" and searching out new ways
to revitalize its traditional use.

But Berryman's ambition at the time was greater than his experience,
and he continued to experiment with tightening and relaxing stanza forms.

In his most ambitious poems throughout the late 1930s, he favored the Yeatsian, "meditative" stanza (eight lines), but a number of others are in seven-, six-, five-, four-, and three-line stanzas. In a poem like "The Trial" (1937), he experimented with terza rima (*axa, bxb*, etc. rounding to *efe, gfg*); in "World-Telegram" (1939) the number of lines in the successive stanzas diminish, alternate, and expand (6, 5, 4, 5, 4, 6, 7, 7); and in "The Animal Trainer" poems (1939 and 1940), the stanzas diminish from eight lines to a single line, in what he called a "sliding stanza" (8, 7, 6, 5, 4, 3, 2, 1).

Berryman experimented with sudden shifts in thought and feeling in his strict stanza forms. In his introduction to "Twenty Poems" (1940) he explained how the break of the verse line in "On the London Train" (written in 1938) may both enact and correspond with the speaker's thought and feeling, in this instance "the ordeal which above all others is humiliating, of loving without return." In the first two stanzas, the speaker observes a man who appears to be lonely and imagines that an unspecified dozen women "fancy him beside a brook, / Their arms with his laced, / Holding him fast." The man longs for one of the women to "take him into her house and care for his wounds." In the third stanza, the speaker draws several conclusions from the imagined scene:

> So it is and has been . .
> Summon an old lover's ghost,
> He'll swear no man has lied
> Who spoke of the painful and most
> Embarrassing ordeal this side
> Satisfaction,—while the green
> Difficulties later are
> More than Zeus could bear.

Berryman cited this stanza as an example of how irony, wit, "abruptness of juxtaposition," and "violence" may be a consequence of verse form. The "first serious conflict between syntax and verse-form," he wrote, occurs in lines 4 and 5—" 'most / Embarrassing' and 'this side / Satisfaction' [which] are split in successive lines." The result of this split is to create an "impression of strain, torsion . . . useful to the subject." Berryman pointed out that in line 6 " 'Satisfaction' is allowed to stand alone, as no other word in the poem does, because it represents a climax." Conflict and alternation continue, however, in the split between lines 6 and 7—"green / Difficulties," which "recalls, as it should recall for the subject, the ordeal which but seemed to end with 'Satisfaction.' " Berryman cited two instances in this stanza where the pressure of verse form allows him to say more than in prose:

The first line of each of the [two] preceding stanzas runs into the second; but "So it is and has been" [at the beginning of the third stanza abruptly comes to] a full stop. A resource of verse form makes the generalization possible. And after the four weak endings which precede it, the heavy regular final line of the stanza takes up the metrical accumulation and acts, again, as generalization, moving from the earth into mythology.

In the early 1940s, Berryman further experimented with the relationship between style and form in the terza rima ("A Poem for Bhain," "The Lightning," and "Canto Amor"). But in the title poem of *The Dispossessed*, written in early 1948 after *Sonnets*, he experimented with the form itself to accommodate the strain and torsion of his style. In a sense, Berryman dispossessed the terza rima rhyme scheme (*aba, bcb, cdc,* etc.) with his own (*xaa, xbb, xcc,* etc., ending with *jxx j*). His end-rhymes alternate between harmony and disharmony, the second and third lines being couplets, so that each stanza is preceded and followed by unrhymed lines. Several end-rhymes are paired unexpectedly, even ironically, as in "watch" and "crotch," "wood" and "understood," "bloomed" and "fumed." And when harmony is suggested in the end-rhyme "dove / love," each is described in unexpected—and undesirable—ways: The dove is "storm-worn" and love is a "spidery business."

The model of composition Berryman desired, he noted while he was writing *Sonnets to Chris* in 1947, is like "Beethoven's onslaughts on the very materials of music." In *Sonnets*, all Petrarchan, he compounded the structural tension between the octave and sestet by creating an expectation of simple syntax and then violated the expectation with a more tangled syntax—what he described as "[c]rumpling a syntax at a sudden need" (Sonnet 47). On a draft of Sonnet 36, for example, he indicated his plan: "beg [in] & end simple, *centre* v[ery] elaborate, / elevated in *diction* & syntax." The octave illustrates how his plan worked:

> Keep your eyes open when you kiss: do: when
> You kiss. All silly time else, close them to;
> Unsleeping, I implore you (dear) pursue
> In darkness me, as I do you again
> Instantly we part . . only me both then

And when your fingers fall, let there be two
Only, 'in that dream-kingdom': I would have you
Me alone recognize your citizen.

Just as a single word marks a climax in "On the London Train," so the phrase "You kiss" in line 2 marks an abrupt shift to his elaborate syntax in the next five lines. And, as in "On the London Train," the conflict between syntax and verse form occurs in lines 4 and 5, "again / Instantly we part," and in 6 and 7, "two / Only." The split results in the "impression of strain, torsion . . . useful to the subject," significantly the subject of parting.

Berryman's method in Sonnet 36 reveals a new development in his ability to fuse disrupted syntax and strict form, a remarkable achievement since there are only two end-rhymes in the eight lines (*abbaabba*). His style now controls his form rather than the reverse. After the simple opening, he violates the reader's expectation in the middle of the couplet of lines 2 and 3: "All silly time else, close them to; / Unsleeping, I implore you (dear) pursue. . . ." Where he had relied on form alone to signify his abrupt shifts and splits in "On the London Train," his violations are now bolder, out in the open. His syntax at once complements and counterpoints his use of form.

In his early poems (before the invention of his *Homage* stanza in 1948), Berryman seemed to use form to sharpen the sense of chaos he frequently described. But his stanza forms might also be seen as a rebellion against their orderly design, as though something were to be gained rather than lost. What seems to be gained is the sense that order and stability are continuously threatened by chaos. His form allows him to have it both ways: he at once mimes chaos and holds it at bay. For example, the threat of the chaos characteristic of Anne Bradstreet's pioneer environment is reflected in Berryman's nervous form, and Bradstreet herself, as Berryman said, rebels against her environment, her barrenness, her marriage, and her "illness, loss, and age." One might make a similar statement about the rebellious relationship between Henry and the alternating beats (5–5–3–5–5–3) of *The Dream Songs* stanza.

About four years after completing *Sonnets*, Berryman wrote almost the same planning note for *Homage* that he had written for Sonnet 36 ("beg. & end simple . . ." etc.). But now the alternations between simple and elevated styles—to be complemented and counterpointed by form—widen to new complexity in a much longer poem:

> beg. & end simple, *centre* v[ery] elaborate,
>> elevated in *diction* & syntax
>
> strong line, & *strokes*—tenuity—sensuous—bulks
>> of *facts*—wit—rich strangeness
>
> Stately vs. rapid / light
> (subdued) limpid & pathetic————<u>full & superb!</u>

Berryman said he modeled *Homage* on Yeats's eight-line stanza in "In Memory of Major Robert Gregory," but he rebelled against his master with the play of his own form. His stanza, Berryman wrote, "breaks not at midpoint [as Yeats's does] but after the third short line." He described his stanza as though the lines are alternations between harmony and dissonance, as though the form sets up boundaries around chaos and imitates (even sharpens) it. After the three-beat break at midpoint, he wrote, "[A] strange four-beat line leads to the balancing heroic couplet of lines five and six, after which seven is again short (three feet, like line three) and then the stanza widens into an alexandrine rhyming all the way back to [line] one." The accentual pattern of the whole stanza, 5–5–3–4–5–5–3–6, is almost a graph of his abrupt shifts. Similarly, his rhyme schemes fluctuate; most are *abxbccba* and *abxbccxa*, but he frequently varies them, for example, *abcbddca* and *axbcbbca*.

The final stanza of *Homage* illustrates Berryman's interplay of form and rhythm:

> O all your ages at the mercy of my loves
> together lie at once, forever or
> so long as I happen.
> In the rain of pain & departure, still
> Love has no body and presides the sun,
> and elfs from silence melody. I run.
> Hover, utter, still,
> a sourcing   whom my lost candle like the firefly loves.

The three-beat third and seventh lines force a sharp turn in the regular rhythms of the lines that precede them, but each operates quite differently. The unrhymed and hovering "forever or" at the end of the second line at once pauses, runs over, and creates pressure on "so long as I happen," and then a full stop. The balancing seventh three-beat line functions the opposite way. While it, too, because it is short, emphasizes, it also reverses the iambic rhythms of the two preceding lines and stutters in trochees and pauses in counterpoint to the final primarily iambic line. Appropriately, in Berryman's notion of tension and strain that is useful to the subject, to "Hover, utter, still" is to plumb "a sourcing" like that of the relationship between the style and form (and rhyme) of *Sonnets*— "A flash of light, an insight" (Sonnet 66).

Berryman's use of form after *Homage* continued to be scored by abrupt alternations, and *The Dream Songs* are orchestrated with an even grander power: "O formal & elaborate, I choose you," Henry says, "but I love too the spare, the hit-or-miss . . ." (Dream Song 265). And yet, his Dream Song stanza sounds out the simple counterpoint of the Petrarchan sonnet he had reworked since 1934. Although *The Dream Songs* depicts, he said, "the kind of hysterical states that modern artists go in for," they are "temperate and held in control, partly by form." Berryman described the three-stanza form of *The Dream Songs* as an "extended three-part sonnet" (six lines per stanza), and, like Hegel's unending triads of thesis-antithesis-synthesis (see Dream Song 78), the triadic alternations of the Dream Song stanzas continuously flex, shift, empty, and refill. Berryman's stresses alternate in triads, 5–5–3–5–5–3 (similar to the alternating stresses of 5–5–3–4–5–5–3–6 in *Homage*), and each short three-beat line either closes down or pivots outward, as the short line functions in *Homage*. His end-rhymes in *The Dream Songs* are hit-or-miss. The stanzas "use various rime schemes," Berryman said in an interview before departing for Ireland to complete the *Songs*:

More and more I'm inclined not to use rime at all. But the notion is to preserve an impression of rime over the three stanzas but without any actual rime at all, even internal rime. . . . The effect is that of a simulation of rime as . . . an end structure, but you actually don't have any. . . . [I]n my songs the rime business is incidental, and it depends on how things go.

The alternating stresses and rhymes of Berryman's stanzas complement the larger design of *The Dream Songs*, for it is structured "according to Henry's nature" in which "open & closed sings on his mystery / furl & unfurl" (Dream Song 260).

The design of *Love & Fame* "furls & unfurls," as it were, according to Berryman's nature. Each of the four parts sets up an expectation and then diminishes or destroys it: "[E]ach of the four movements," Berryman wrote in the revised edition of *Love & Fame*, "criticiz[es] backward the preceding, until Part IV wipes out altogether all earlier presentations of the 'love' and 'fame' of the ironic title." Similarly, his lines abruptly shift. It is as though Berryman returns to the creation of an irregular quatrain, as he had learned in 1934, in which a single line is abruptly shortened (usually the second or third line, but sometimes the first or fourth). The third line of the final stanza in the last of the "Eleven Addresses to the Lord" is a good example:

> Make too me acceptable at the end of time
> in my degree, which then Thou wilt award.
> Cancer, senility, mania,
> I pray I may be ready with my witness.

Like the concluding lines of *Homage*, the penultimate short line (at least in the number of words) is flanked by longer lines that are primarily iambic. The short line calls attention to itself and counterpoints, primarily in trochees, the regular rhythms of the flanking lines. The effect of the rhythms of the three lines together is to create a music that sounds out and brings into control the speaker's terror of death.

In the end, the primitive rite is nearest Berryman's view of how his forms work. His notes on his copy of his essay on Whitman's *Song of Myself* offer a further gloss on how the stanzas of the sonnet may be remade into a rite. Referring to Whitman's "I Saw in Louisiana a Live Oak Growing," he wrote: "This [stanzaic form] modified the Petrarchan sonnet (5–5–3 instead of 4–4–6) into a more organic & explosive form for a primitive *rite*." Similarly, *The Dream Songs* extends the sonnet form (three sestets) and modifies the lines, rather than the stanzas, to 5–5–3–5–5–3. Odd numbers, because they are unharmonious and dynamic (even numbers being harmonious and static), appealed to Berryman's primitive seriousness. Even when he used the balanced eight-line (the early and middle period) and the four-line stanzas (the late period), the stanzas abruptly break and spin the reader around.

A passionate syntax. Just as Berryman was attracted to unpredictability in his forms, so was he drawn to a style that refuses to guarantee the reader's expectations. He wrote to his mother in January 1937 that he hoped to emulate not only Henry Vaughan's "display of power and controlled articulation in form" but also his "continual marvellous energy from line to line." And the continual energy, he recognized, is a matter of style, as Yeats confirmed during Berryman's first and only meeting with the master in London in the spring of 1937: "I never revise now," Yeats said, "but in the interests of a more passionate syntax."

"Passionate syntax" and "marvellous energy from line to line," however, were the standards Berryman had determined for himself in his first extant poems for his mother's birthday on July 8, 1934. The fourth sonnet (of four) addresses her as though she were the muse of his poems yet to be written, and it foreshadows his later notions about the lightning operations of disparate styles. The octave praises his mother's wit and brilliant speech: "a facile word / Struck by the interplay of minds, admit[s] / A verbal brilliance, casual thought transferred." Her abrupt turns of thought—which "as from a cage / Leaps out"—at once summon and counterpoint "poignant beauty to her page." The sestet likewise summons and counterpoints its themes; it concludes that beauty is synonymous with "explosive power" and therefore the very qualities the poet desires in poetry:

> The quality that strains behind the words
> A poet employs to freeze the soul, nor lose
> From a phrase the explosive power of bawling herds—
> This tumbles through her lines—though mind refuse
> An ordered rhyme—like the undertones of birds:
> Fortunate, to weld prose to verse, nor choose!

The sonnet sets multiple counterpoints in motion: in form, the octave counterpoints the sestet; in expression, prose counterpoints poetry; in theme, the static words that "freeze the soul" counterpoint a syntactic energy that has "the explosive power of bawling herds." The effect of his strain and torsion is not so much to suspend opposites in tension as it is, as Berryman said of Stephen Crane's style some fifteen years later, to give the impression of "everywhere . . . a mind at stretch."

The "interplay of minds," the "casual thought transferred," and the "explosive power of bawling herds" inform practically all Berryman's subsequent descriptions of his style. In his 1940 "A Note on Poetry," he compared the "cumbersome expansion" of a prose version of a poem with the "direct, concrete, compact" power of the poem itself: "In the process of translation [from poetry to prose] the particular irony and wit escaped; the abruptness of juxtaposition and the violence were lost." During the intense six months of writing *Sonnets to Chris*, he discovered that prodding and disrupting syntax in a given form is a means by which he, like his mother's "thought transferred," may arrive at an insight:

[xliv

I prod our English: cough me up a word,
Slip me an epithet will justify
My daring fondle, fumble of far fire
Crackling nearby, unreasonable as a surd,
A flash of light, an insight. . . .

(Sonnet 66)

Of his style in *Homage to Mistress Bradstreet* Berryman said, "I wanted . . . [a style] at once flexible and grave, intense and quiet, able to deal with matter both high and low." And his planning notes for *Homage* recall his mother's "thought, as from a cage / Leaps out": "Stately vs. rapid / light / (subdued) limpid & pathetic————full & superb!" Likewise, the style of *The Dream Songs* "leaps out" with the explosive power of Henry's thought: "The river of his wide mind broke the jam, / somebody called his wild wit riverine . . ." (Dream Song 182). Like Berryman's mother's wit ("the interplay of minds"), Henry's interplay of musics resonates with "the slow movement of Schubert's Sonata in A" (Dream Song 204) and the swift alternations of Scarlatti's music that "spurts his wit across [Henry's] brain" (Dream Song 258). In the last years of his life, Berryman came full circle (his youthful desire not to "lose / From a phrase the explosive power of bawling herds") in his description of the merit of the opening poem of *Love & Fame*—"a certain explosive feeling, a certain administrative rhythm-set."

The explosive feeling Berryman desired is accomplished in part by the counterpoint of repeated rhetorical forms and disrupted syntax. The outcome is a peculiarly serious and comic style that happily embraces "matter both high and low." His Chaplinesque muse calls for "a sense of humour / fatal to bardic pretension" ("Images of Elspeth," *L&F*).

Berryman described his early verse as having "no voice of my own" and written in the " 'period style,' the Anglo-American style [Yeats and W. H. Auden] of the 1930's." Prophetic and rhetorical, his somber, public voice of disfigurement, grief, and despair may be illustrated in the opening stanza of "The Statue," written in 1939:

The statue, tolerant through years of weather,
Spares the untidy Sunday throng its look,
Spares shopgirls knowledge of the fatal pallor
Under their evening colour,
Spares homosexuals, the crippled, the alone,
Extravagant perception of their failure;

> Looks only, cynical, across them all
> To the delightful Avenue and its lights.

Randall Jarrell might have had this poem in mind when he referred to Berryman's early poems as "statues talking like a book." There is a textbookish quality in the rhetorical device of repeating the verb at the beginning of the line—"Spares, Spares, Spares, Looks." While the adjectival phrase ("tolerant through years of weather") and the dislocated adjective ("cynical" in line 7) vary the drumming repetition, the rhetorical style not so much invites readers to listen as it commands them to take heed.

When Berryman experimented with rendering other voices in writing plays (most unfinished and all unpublished), the badgering rhetoric of his 1930s style was gradually modified in the 1940s to nervous and individual voices. This discovery of the dramatic mode freed him to write in his own idiom and to invite readers to observe, perhaps empathize with, the personalities his style creates. One of his earliest experiments in the creation of an individual voice was in writing a play during his Christmas break in Paris in late 1936. He wrote to his mother on December 26: "I'm going to keep it [the play] from being pseudo-Elizabethan; [I] want a nervous, mechanical accent, giving way only infrequently to full passion." His weakness, he implies, was to sprint flat out from the opening line to the last, but, he realized, a play calls for "keeping the tempo down in order to get the power when it's needed."

Not until the late 1930s, in poems like "The Animal Trainer (1)" and "The Animal Trainer (2)," did the dramatic mode take hold in his poetry. Two voices—the Heart and the Animal Trainer (i.e., the Poet)—debate symbolically in public masks about the origins of poetry. But each poem does not come out of "a realizable situation," as he had observed while he was writing his first play, and the dramatic mode had not yet influenced his rhetorical style. "The Nervous Songs," most of which were written in 1942, mark the beginning of his change as his characters speak at moments of personal crisis in the "nervous, mechanical accent" he wanted in his first play. His style now begins to work with the power of both a realizable situation and a personal voice, as in "The Song of the Tortured Girl":

> After a little I could not have told—
> But no one asked me this—why I was there.
> I asked. The ceiling of that place was high
> And there were sudden noises, which I made.

The nervous shifts in the girl's thought and feeling enact her pain, and the final stanza holds the tempo down so that the penultimate line is expressed with greater power:

> Through leafless branches the sweet wind blows
> Making a mild sound, softer than a moan;
> High in a pass once where we put our tent
> Minutes I lay awake to hear my joy.
> —I no longer remember what they want.—
> Minutes I lay awake to hear my joy.

Unlike the rhetorical repetition of "Spares, Spares, Spares, Looks," the repeated line ("Minutes I lay awake to hear my joy") is dramatically functional. The girl's joyful memory of the time she lay awake in her tent is unexpectedly interrupted by her cry of despair and resignation ("I no longer remember what they want"), so that the repeating of "Minutes I lay awake to hear my joy" ironically merges her past joy and present suffering. "The Song of the Tortured Girl" also illustrates one of Berryman's favorite definitions, by R. P. Blackmur, of the "art of poetry" that "not only expresses the matter in hand / but adds to the stock of available reality" ("Olympus," *L&F*). The repeated line not only expresses the matter in hand (her present suffering) but also adds to the stock of her, and our, available reality (her past experience and her present memory of joy).

"The Song of the Tortured Girl" illustrates how Berryman's nervous style enacts a moment of high seriousness, but "A Professor's Song" shows how his idiom—in the context of a realizable situation—may be comic:

> Alive now—no—Blake would have written prose,
> But movement following movement crisply flows,
> So much the better, better the much so,
> As burbleth Mozart. Twelve. The class can go.
> Until I meet you, then, in Upper Hell
> Convulsed, foaming immortal blood: farewell.

Berryman discovered his jagged and jazzy voice when he mastered the dramatist's cunning, how the finely made poem may be *unmade*, in a sense, by the individual voice, how the creation of personality and style may be a single enterprise.

Robert Lowell's description of Berryman's mature style, "disrupted and mended," is a useful way of thinking about how it works. Disrupted suggests that a harmony is temporarily broken, perhaps counterpointed, the premise being that there *is* a harmony to be disrupted. Mended suggests not only that the reader may mend the disruption but also that the syntax may somehow, paradoxically, mend itself. The first three stanzas of "Canto Amor," dedicated to his wife Eileen and written in late 1944 and early 1945, illustrate how the disruption and mending may simultaneously address and enact the theme of the harmony and disharmony of marriage:

> Dream in a dream the heavy soul somewhere
> struck suddenly & dark down to its knees.
> A griffin sighs off in the orphic air.
>
> If (Unknown Majesty) I not confess
> praise for the wrack the rock the live sailor
> under the blue sea,—yet I may You bless
>
> always for hér, in fear & joy for hér
> whose gesture summons ever when I grieve
> me back and is my mage and minister.

The style of the first line, neither surcharged nor weak, is appropriate to a harmonious marriage (not till later in the poem do we understand that marriage is the theme): "Dream in a dream the heavy soul somewhere. . . ." But in the second line, the juice suddenly increases in "struck suddenly & dark down" and then abruptly decreases in the third line, "A griffin sighs off in the orphic air." The first line of the second stanza disrupts the ease of the previous line with the parenthetical "Unknown Majesty," and slows to the heavy accents and consonantal *r*'s of the next, "praise for the wrack the rock the live sailor." The stanza concludes with an unexpected turn in that the live sailor is "under the blue sea" and then turns again, stylistically, with the inversion, "yet I may You bless." The stanza now breaks to emphasize the opening of the next ("always for hér") and the heightening is sustained with heavy accents on "her."

Now these paced alternations of style create both a disruptive and a binding energy in that the speaker expresses uncertainty and inquires into it. For example, the disruptive placement of "You" in line 6 is both functional and revealing. It functions to emphasize "You," and it echoes the speaker's nervous desire to believe there is an "Unknown Majesty," significantly the previous disruption. The mending thus takes place in the fusion of opposing beliefs and feelings: the speaker does and does not believe there is a "You" who protects his wife and makes his marriage harmonious. (The poem concludes that marriage is not harmonious but, rather, the "flowing ceremony of trouble and light, / all Loves becoming.")

A more complex disruption of syntax occurs in the third stanza of "Canto Amor," "whose gesture summons ever when I grieve / me back." Sense is tangled, in part, because the syntax places "me" as the indirect object of both "summons" and "grieve" (the line break "grieve / me" also emphasizes "me"). But the tangle of meaning may be regarded as a "passionate syntax"; once we see that "me" is the indirect object of both "grieve" and "summons," several meanings intertwine: (1) "I myself grieve"; (2) "I cause my grief"; (3) "my wife's gesture summons me not to grieve"; and (4) "whenever I grieve, my wife's gesture comforts me." The inverted phrase "ever when" similarly compounds meaning in that "ever" refers to both his own grieving and his wife's "gesture" (meaning both a movement to express her emotion and something she says to convey her intention): (1) she "summons ever" (i.e., "I can always depend on her") and (2) "ever when I grieve" (i.e., "I grieve always"). If commas were to set off "ever when I grieve" (i.e., "whose gesture summons, ever when I grieve, / me back") "me" would clearly be the indirect object of "summons" and the feeling and meaning would be lost.

Berryman's jammed voice may seem to some readers as either affected or a lair of meaning from which they must free themselves. But to put the matter another way, his disrupted syntax also sets in motion a "marvellous energy from line to line." His syntax provokes "a process," as Berryman said of his ambiguous pronouns, "which is at once a process of life and a process of art." His passionate syntax enacts the emergencies and gaps of the drift-of-life—swift movement, concentration, pauses, simultaneous connections and disconnections, overstatement and understatement, humor, irony. A style that disrupts readers' expectations suggests a process in which they, initially, are mostly aware of Berryman's self-conscious style. However, his self-consciousness—his refusal to guarantee readers' expectations—generates another stage of the readers' relationship with the words on the page: they experience, not simply see with their minds, *only* the thought or feeling or experience the words point to. The reader must "endure . . . the manner for the matter" (Dream

Song 305), as Henry says, for Berryman mangles his manner in order to create an experience, an experience that enacts more completely the uncertainty of experience.

Poetry as a transparent reality. Whether or not readers move from self-consciousness to a sense of transparency, Berryman himself made the leap. The language of poetry, he wrote in some notes for an essay to be titled "Poetry and *Logos*" (*ca.* 1965), came to mean to him "the creation of a situation in which something is *said.*" That is, words simply said and said simply with the view that what is said is so transparent that one has no sense of hearing (or reading) words. In a general way, Berryman's newly simple style of the late 1960s seems a dramatic change from his packed and disrupted syntax. And yet, whether his style is simple or complex (there are moments in his last phase where his syntax is disrupted), he holds to the fundamental principle that style must be "fresh as a bubble breaks / As little false" (Sonnet 23) so that it "not only expresses the matter in hand / but adds to the stock of available reality."

In an interview in 1971, Berryman said that "some of the best kind of writing is really transparent . . . you get no impression of viewing art." The interviewer asked for examples, and he replied:

The Odyssey, the *Paradiso* . . . Beethoven's late quartets, where the appearance of art disappears, everything becomes unbelievably simple. The artist just says what he thinks, or how he feels. For example, instead of making a long speech, he says, "I hurt," or he says to the reader "are you hurting?"

Asked to give an example of transparency in twentieth-century poetry, Berryman remembered a line from T. S. Eliot's *Four Quartets*: "At a certain point it occurs to [Eliot] to say 'Humility is endless.' How's that. In verse." Berryman might very well have in mind Eliot's similar notion of the "auditory imagination"—"poetry so transparent," Eliot said in a 1933 lecture, "that we should not see the poetry, but that which we are meant to see through the poetry, poetry so transparent that in reading it we are intent on what the poem *points at*, and not on the poetry" (Eliot, too, cited Beethoven's later works as an example of going "*beyond* music"). Both Berryman and Eliot owe something to Coleridge's statement that the great poet has the "power of so carrying the eye of the reader as to make him almost lose consciousness of the words—to make him *see* everything."

This is the theory, but one reader's (or writer's) transparency may

[1

be another's dark glass. In the same 1971 interview, Berryman offered a useful example of how he saw transparency at work:

Take a line from *The Tempest*, "turfy mountains, where live nibbling sheep." Now, that is absolutely magnificent, but incredibly simple. The art comes in placing, pure syntax.

Admittedly, "turfy" is good, and "nibbling" is good, and it's nicely held together. That's what happens, turf is what you nibble if you're a sheep. But, it really is so powerful because "live" is so low-keyed. You expect something bigger. The height at the front of the line, and another height at the end of the line, so you want something way low-keyed down in the middle.

Where linguists may see a parallel structure in "turfy mountains" and "nibbling sheep," Berryman hears a heightening and diminishing of movement and sound.

The eighth of his "Eleven Addresses to the Lord" illustrates a similar alternating intensity and delicacy: "Jonquils respond with wit to the teasing breeze." The middle of the line, "with wit," is heightened, almost a spondee; we do not expect jonquils to respond to the breeze with wit. (Another counterpoint might be implied in Wordsworth's well-known daffodils fluttering in the breeze.) This memorable line, however, should be seen—and heard—in the context of the three preceding lines of the opening quatrain of "A Prayer for the Self":

> Who am I worthless that You spent such pains
> and take may pains again?
> I do not understand; but I believe.
> Jonquils respond with wit to the teasing breeze.

The voice of the first three lines speaks simply, and the speaker both makes a statement and poses an inquiry. If the question had ended with the first line—"Who am I worthless that You spent such pains?"—it would emphasize "worthless" and ambiguously refer to Christ's "pains" (i.e., His suffering *and* care because "spent" denotes both expending and care). A more prosaic way of putting it—without the ambiguity of "spent" and "pains"—would be "Why did You suffer for worthless me?" The question continues in the short second line with a qualification and doubt, "and take may pains again?" Stated more directly, the question might be "You may suffer pains for me again?" (The question may also be a statement of hope.) Like "spent," "take" suggests both taking on pains and taking care, that is, "to take pains." "May," placed so that one is tempted to read "take *my* pains again," heightens the apprehension in the question, Christ may or may not "take pains again."

The complex question, so mined with syntactical and rhythmical depth charges, is answered in the low-keyed and direct iambic third line: "I do not understand; but I believe." But then comes another unexpected turn in image, place, thought, and rhythm: "Jonquils respond with wit to the teasing breeze." The juxtaposition of the two final lines plays out the alternating thematic movements of the whole quatrain. On the one hand, Berryman says that his doubt is calmed in faith; on the other hand, the winds of uncertainty—similar to the drums that beat outside the sanctuary of song in his youth and unlike Wordsworth's "correspondent breeze"—are a "teasing breeze."

Berryman's notion of transparency, then, aims, in Keats's phrase, to "tease us out of thought" in a way that corresponds with his notion of "passionate syntax." In his view of both transparency and passionate syntax, he shifts abruptly from one thought or feeling or rhythm to another, and he disrupts accepted conventions of linguistic structures. He provokes thought with the aim of creating intensity; the lightning shift, rather than the apt word, phrase, or image, is his transparent moment. The success of his passionate syntax and transparency very much depends upon the violations of conventions readers are willing to accept. His violations of accepted conventions *provoke* thought so as to *render* reality transparent. Since his style attempts to achieve the opposite of how it actually presents itself, on first reading readers may very well see and hear his abrupt shifts and violations. But if, after thought, incongruity and alternating calm and intensity are standards readers accept, Berryman's passionate syntax creates, as Lowell said of *77 Dream Songs*, a "risk and variety" that is nervously and transparently alive.

The dramatic imagination: a process of life, a process of art. Like Robert Browning and Ezra Pound, Berryman was not so much interested in character in action as in action in character. His early experiments in writing plays raised the question of why and how characters reveal themselves. But his experience in writing poems, beginning as early as 1942 with "The Ball Poem" and "The Nervous Songs," raised the question of his relationship, in the poem, to the characters and the selves he creates. His relationship, he seemed to realize in the mid-1940s, had something to do with his attraction to the primitive origins of poetry in which he expresses and creates his own personality.

All poetry begins, Berryman believed, as a "practical matter," because the poet is compelled to express and dispel his or her fears. Berryman suggested, drawing upon Robert Graves's theory of the origins of poetry, that poems like Stephen Crane's may in fact be "primitively blunt," "like a series of anti-spells":

A savage dreams, is frightened by the dream, and goes to the medicine man to have it explained. The medicine man . . . chants, perhaps he stamps his foot . . . what he says becomes rhythmical . . . and what he says begins to rhyme. Poetry begins—as a practical matter, for *use*. It reassures the savage. . . . And medicine men are shrewd: interpretation enters the chanting, symbols are developed and connected, the gods are invoked, poetry booms.

Berryman must have identified not only with the notion of Crane's "anti-spells" but also with Thomas Beer's observation, quoted by Berryman, that "the mistress of [Crane's] mind was fear"—fear of abandonment, of uncertainty, of death. Whatever Berryman's personal identification with the origin of poetry, this balance of authority and enactment in a primitive ritual applied to the design of a poem is potentially unsettling for the reader, especially as the balance abruptly shifts from line to line or poem to poem. It is a poetry that has, as Berryman observed of Crane's, "the character of a 'dream,' something seen naïvely in a new relation." Berryman came to understand that the alternations may also give the poem the "extraordinary combination of authority and intimacy" that Michael Dennis Browne heard in Berryman's reading of *The Dream Songs*.

Like the frightened primitive, Berryman suggests in his study of Crane, the poet desires most of all to be held in the sway of a ritual that dispels fears of the unexplainable and the uncertain. While his first experience with the power of ritual might very well have been as a Catholic altar boy, the encounter at the age of twenty-one with W. B. Yeats's poetry and plays was probably his first conscious inquiry into how ritual may be at once a personal principle and a poetics. In his undergraduate review of Yeats's *Collected Plays*, he defined ritual as the power to objectify experience—"a code or form of ceremonies, the formal character imposed on any experience as it is given objective existence." In that summer of 1936 he wrote his first long poem, titled "Ritual at Arlington," in which the poet memorializes (and objectifies) the known and unknown soldiers. Personally, he dispels his fear of the dead, particularly the ghost of his father, whose grave he alludes to throughout the poem. What seems to have crystallized in Berryman's poetics in 1936 is his discovery of how the orderly form of ritual (or form) may make, or appear to make, the unknown objective and the uncertain certain. By 1940, in his "A Note on Poetry," he adapted his definition of ritual to an explanation of the function of a poem, which is "to seize an object and make it visible." The use of ritual—this act of making something visible and thus objectifying it—and what it does *for* the poet (and the reader) gradually became his fundamental principle.

One of the cryptic epigraphs to *The Dream Songs*—"But there is another method" (Olive Schreiner, *The Story of an African Farm*)— suggests that Berryman believed there were basically two forms of ritual open to him in the dramatic design of a poem. The first, Schreiner says, "is the stage method" in which we know what will happen to a given character in a given action, a sort of formal ritual with a predictable outcome transferred to the stage:

According to that [method] each character is duly marshalled at first, and ticketed; we know only with immutable certainty that at the right crisis each one will reappear and act his part, and when the curtain falls, all will stand before it bowing. There is a sense of satisfaction in this, and of completeness.

"But there is another method," she continues (this method being Berryman's own), "the method of the life we all lead," in which we observe an unnamed character negotiating an uncertain outcome, similar in kind to the frightened primitive who goes to the medicine man:

Here nothing is prophesied. There is a strange coming and going of feet. Men appear, act and re-act upon each other, and pass away. When the crisis comes, the man who would fit it does not return. When the curtain falls no one is ready. When the footlights are the brightest they are blown out; and what the name of the play is no one knows.

Berryman's view of the music the masters make—"profound solemn & clear" ("Canto Amor," *TD*)—clearly corresponds with Schreiner's "stage method" in which there is satisfaction and completeness. Similarly, Berryman's "other music"—the "flowing ceremony of trouble and light" ("Canto Amor") in poetry, and Schreiner's "other method"—"a strange coming and going of feet" in drama—are not so much complementary notions as they are similarly structured ways of enacting life's refusal to guarantee one's expectations. In his poetry, especially his long poems, Berryman "put people in action [to] see what happens," and what happens is that life takes unexpected turns. "I'm a follower of Pascal," Berryman said to an interviewer in 1970, "in the sense that I don't know what the issue is, or how it is to be resolved." The design and method of the poem, as Berryman saw it, renders the unpredictability of life; the problem was how to incorporate unpredictability without the form of presentation breaking down entirely. Stanzaic form was one way, but he also found another method: creating character in dramatic form.

As Berryman weighed how to use dramatic form in poetry in the 1940s, he also struggled with the problem of how his own personality might be present in the poem. Although style is the surest sign of the poet's presence, it was not enough. In the climate of the 1930s "New Criticism," particularly Eliot's "impersonality of the poet," he did not want to break away entirely, and so he began to experiment with how he might be present in the poem without speaking in the first person. When he was writing his first play in late 1936, he discovered his fundamental dramatic method, a method that resembles Keats's notion of the "chameleon poet." The poet, Keats says in one of his letters, "has no Identity— he is continually in—and filling some other Body." Similarly, Berryman wrote to his mother on December 27, 1936:

I am beginning to see a certain justice in the references to characters' being free agent[s]. To my critical consternation, I see what even cheap novelists and poor actors are getting at when they say "This character I am creating or playing is *real* & makes his own destiny; I but fulfill it." The people literally possess one. . . . [T]hese persons that I have imagined in certain circumstances & actions have a quite uncanny faculty for developing themselves.

Berryman discovered that he had the option of being less concerned about either the Whitman "I" or the Yeatsian mask of his experience. The matter of course is complex; one may persuasively argue, for example, that Berryman's characters are his guises. But the act of creating characters, rather than "poems," freed him from a self-conscious preoccupation with projecting *only* himself. As he pondered how he might be present in the poem as both creator and character, he began to inquire into the question of how his presence might be clearly manifest rather than blatantly overt.

Berryman solved the problem of the poet's presence in the poem with the ambiguous pronoun, through which, he said in 1965, "the poet himself is both left out and put in." "A pronoun," he continued, "may seem a small matter, but she matters, he matters, it matters, they matter. Without this invention . . . I could not have written . . . [*Homage* and

The Dream Songs]." Henry, for instance, Berryman said in another context, "refers to himself as 'I,' 'he,' and 'you,' so that the various parts of his identity are fluid." The reader, too, is forced to participate in the creation of an uncertain identity: "[T]he reader is made to guess who is talking to whom," Berryman says. "Out of this ambiguity arises richness. The reader becomes more aware, is forced to enter into himself."

Berryman identified "The Ball Poem" (1942) as the work in which he learned that "a commitment of [the poet's] identity can be 'reserved,' so to speak, with an ambiguous pronoun." The first line *appears* to be the question "What is the boy now, who has lost his ball[?]" The second line clarifies the question—not "who" or "what" is the boy, but rather how he is to respond to the loss of his ball: "What, what is he to do?" In the next three lines, the "I" of the poem—the poet or the boy or both?—responds to the question by recounting what has happened to the boy: "I saw [the ball] go / Merrily bouncing, down the street, and then / Merrily over—there it is in the water!" The ambiguous "I" creates two points of view: the poet's and the boy's. But the two are one as they witness the moment of something lost. It may be that the two voices speak as a sort of chorus to the sense of loss all readers have experienced; it may also be that the poet desires to become one with the boy; certainly the reader must guess who is speaking.

The pronoun then shifts to "he." While the poet sympathizes with the boy's loss (this particular ball is important to the boy because it cannot be replaced), he identifies a greater loss—and terror—buried deep within them both, their "ultimate shaking grief." On first reading, an "ultimate shaking grief" may seem to be an overstated response to the loss of a ball, but it may be that the speaker has abruptly shifted to a larger inquiry into how one responds to loss. The poet does not intrude upon the boy; he observes what happens (just as the boy has) and identifies with the boy's unarticulated discovery: "He is learning, well behind his desperate eyes, / The epistemology of loss." The poet then speaks in a Whitmanesque "I": "Soon part of me will explore the deep and dark / Floor of the harbour." Although the poet may "suffer and move" ("my mind and my heart move / With all that move me, under the water"), he concludes, "I am not a little boy." The poet does not disallow that he has, momentarily, become *the* little boy; he says, in a way protesting, he is not *a* little boy. So what began as an inquiry into "What is the boy to do now?" ends with the poet's new awareness that he is not a little boy but is this boy at a particular moment. He identifies a loss buried deep within himself that is made particular in the boy's loss. He simultaneously grieves over his own sense of loss and protects not the boy but the little boy in himself.

Berryman said he also discovered in "The Ball Poem" that when "the boy does and does not become [the poet] . . . we are confronted with a process which is at once a process of life and a process of art." He neither defines nor explains the process, but it is similar to a "special pressure," described in his essay "The Development of Anne Frank," of her accelerated maturation: "It took . . . a special pressure forcing [her] child-adult conversion, and exceptional self-awareness and exceptional candour and exceptional powers of expression, to bring that . . . change into view." In light of his view of the twin processes of life and art, we may say that Berryman is and is not writing an autobiography of his own moment of self-awareness in "The Ball Poem." (That the title calls attention to its being a *poem* suggests his distance from his subject.) He is self-aware as he writes the script and empathizes with the boy's feelings, but through the ambiguous pronoun, he simultaneously becomes the boy and plays out a role that is a part of himself (or a role that is not himself, even his opposite self). He simultaneously speaks for and *with* the character he creates—a "special pressure forcing child-adult conversion"—thus dramatizing the creation of himself and respecting the boundaries of a separate self.

In his last volumes, Berryman continued to inquire into his own fluid personality in dramatic terms. Of the opening poem "Her & It" in *Love & Fame*, he wrote: "I notice it makes play with an obsession that ruled 'The Ball Poem' of 1942 as well as, later, *Homage to Mistress Bradstreet* (1948–1953) and *The Dream Songs* (1955–1968): namely, the dissolving of one personality into another without relinquishing the original. . . . In the very long poem, of course, many personalities shift, reify, dissolve, survive, project—remaining one." Berryman's debt to Coleridge is apparent here, and although he limits his principle to the re-formation of the personality, in general terms it resembles Coleridge's definition of the secondary Imagination which "dissolves, diffuses, dissipates in order to re-create."

On the one hand, Berryman believed that the poet speaks in an objective voice (rather than an identifiable personality) for the experiences of human life. In 1948, when a friend suggested that the artist "moves towards himself and God," Berryman disagreed: "I see [the artist] moving towards annihilation—towards becoming a *voice*: first a voice for the *object*, later (very rare, this) a voice for powers and passions and acceptances buried somewhere in men for good—*Tempest*, *Magic Flute*, Schubert C Major Quintet, last works usually." In this view, the poet is like Keats's "chameleon poet": "A Poet is the most unpoetical of any thing in existence; because he has no Identity—he is continually in—for and filling some other Body." On the other hand, Berryman regarded the voice of a poem as individual and subjective, that mysterious and delicate instrument by which we know ourselves as being different from and in relationship with another person. This notion of voice is like Berryman's description of Whitman's "orbic flex": "The poet—one would say, a mere channel, but with its own ferocious difficulties—fills with experiences, a valve opens; he speaks them." Berryman did not regard these two objective and subjective voices as being separate (one speaking as a medium for the human condition, the other expressing personal and "ferocious difficulties"); the two are, he says, "identical." Although each voice speaks for and of different powers and needs, they are identical precisely in the way that the poet simultaneously becomes the boy in "The Ball Poem" and speaks for passions they both feel.

Berryman's dramatic imagination encourages a process of self-inquiry that aims at re-formation and self-definition in which he is willing to be uncertain. It is a drama that allows him to move at will and at need between the predictability of art and the uncertainty of life: form and process, formal speech and individual gesture, will and emotion, consciousness and unconsciousness, objective and subjective realities. In speaking to a character in a poem or in becoming that character, even momentarily, he *plays out*, neither forcing nor merely asserting, subjective and objective realities. The cunning of this dramatic mode allows him (and the reader), in Robert Langbaum's useful phrase, to be *"called into awareness."* As Henry says of himself, "When he dressed up & up, his costumes varied / with the southeast wind, but he remained aware. / Awareness was most of what he had" (Dream Song 370).

No matter how differently readers may respond to any given poem by John Berryman, he invites them to engage simultaneously in a process of life and a process of art. In the end, as Berryman says, they may be "moved, impressed, perhaps changed." Berryman's use of poetry is an effort to reconnect broken connections. His moment is not that of T. S. Eliot's "intersection of the timeless with time"; it is quite a different transfiguration, "a terminal activity taking place out near the end of things." Berryman's timeless moment speaks for, rather than of, "powers and passions and acceptances buried somewhere" in all readers "for good." His terrified and delicate listening, his violations of forms and syntax, his creation of the discontinuous personality, and his rituals of finding the missing element in an uncertain world, all point to one hope and a single prayer: "Unite my various soul, / sole watchman of the wide & single stars."

September 11, 1988
St. John's University
Collegeville, Minnesota

Chronology

1914 Born John Allyn Smith, Jr., October 25, in McAlester, Oklahoma; the first
child of John Allyn ("Allyn"), twenty-seven, a banker in Sasakwa who was
reared in South Stillwater, Minnesota, and Martha ("Peggy") Shaver [Little]
Smith, twenty, formerly an elementary-school teacher in Sasakwa, who was
reared in St. Louis and McAlester. Christened November 29 at St. John
the Evangelist Catholic Church in McAlester; nicknamed "Billy" after his
father's deceased brother, William J. Smith.

1916 Family moves from Sasakwa to Lamar, Oklahoma, because father finds a
new position at a bank (the family moves about every two years in Oklahoma,
first to Lamar, then to Wagoner and Anadarko).

1919 Brother Robert Jefferson—"Bob" as a child, later "Jeff"—born in McAlester
on September 1.

1921 Family moves to Anadarko in January; father is cashier and active vice
president of the First State Bank. Attends West Grade public school.

1923 First communion May 6 at Holy Family Catholic Church, Anadarko.

1924 Serves as an altar boy for Fr. Boniface Beri, O.S.B. Father resigns position
at bank and takes a job as local fish-and-game warden; mother takes a part-
time job.

1925 Confirmed at Holy Family in Anadarko on March 29. Parents and grand-
mother Martha May Little move to Tampa, Florida, where all three buy
and operate the Orange Blossom Restaurant. John and Bob remain in Okla-
homa as boarding students at St. Joseph's Academy, a Catholic convent
school in Chickasha near Anadarko, until mid-December, when they join
their parents in Tampa.

1926 Father speculates in land; crash of Florida land boom; parents sell restaurant
and separate in early April. Mother and sons move to an apartment building
owned by John Angus McAlpin Berryman, fifty-one, in Clearwater, Florida.
Father threatens suicide; mother files for divorce on June 19, charging
John Allyn with adultery. In same month John Allyn found shot dead outside
their apartment and ruled a suicide; father buried in Holdenville, Oklahoma
(near Sasakwa), next to his brother William. Mother marries John Angus
on September 8 in New York City and changes her name to "Jill Angel";
John's name is changed to John Allyn McAlpin Berryman (but not legally
until 1936).

1927 Family moves to Jackson Heights, New York, where John attends Public School 69. Stepfather John Angus is a bond broker in Manhattan.

1928 Wins an essay contest on humane practices in the treatment of animals; places in community-wide spelling bee; writes a science-fiction "novel." Enters South Kent School, a small Episcopal boarding school in South Kent, Connecticut. Family moves to Great Neck, Long Island.

1929 Excels academically; first publications of short articles and reports in the school newspaper. Stock-market crash; mother finds employment as full-time secretary.

1931 Family moves to Manhattan and stepfather works part-time. Young John impulsively attempts suicide at South Kent.

1932 Enters Columbia College, New York City. Meets E. M. ("Milt") Halliday. Family moves to apartment near Columbia. Mark Van Doren becomes mentor. Stepfather mostly unemployed.

1934 Writes first extant poems, four sonnets for his mother's birthday, July 8.

1935 Publishes first poems and reviews (among them, a review of Van Doren's *A Winter Diary and Other Poems*) in *The Columbia Review*, edited by Robert Giroux; wins several poetry prizes (and again in 1936); publishes his first poem in a national magazine, "Note on E. A. Robinson" in *The Nation*; gives first poetry reading. Meets Allen Tate. Stepfather's health declines.

1936 Publishes essay-review "The Ritual of W. B. Yeats," on Yeats's collected plays. Meets R. P. Blackmur. Graduates Phi Beta Kappa, B.A. (English major, philosophy minor); wins a Euretta J. Kellett scholarship to study for two years at Clare College, Cambridge, England. Engaged to Jean Bennett. Sails for England in September. Writes to W. B. Yeats and attends lecture by T. S. Eliot; meets W. H. Auden. Begins writing first play in Paris during Christmas vacation.

1937 Attends lectures by I. A. Richards, F. R. Leavis, and Stephen Spender; completes first play, *Cleopatra*, a one-act dance play; meets Dylan Thomas and W. B. Yeats. Summer vacation with Beryl Eeman in Heidelberg, Paris, and Ghent. Wins Oldham Shakespeare prize. Engaged to Beryl.

1938 Publishes first poems in *The Southern Review*. Returns to New York City; unsuccessfully attempts to find employment. Works on first long play titled *The Architect*. Beryl comes for extended stay with the Berrymans. Meets Bhain Campbell. Mother begins career in advertising.

1939 Beryl returns to England in April. Part-time poetry editor for *The Nation* (and 1940); meets Delmore Schwartz. Mother separated from stepfather. Instructor in English, Wayne University, Ann Arbor, Michigan. By December mentally and physically exhausted, diagnosed *petit mal*, considered to be a form of epilepsy (later, his wife Eileen showed that this was a misdiagnosis).

1940 Briggs-Copeland instructor in English, Harvard University (through spring 1943). Publishes first collection, "Twenty Poems," in *Five Young American Poets* (others include Marion O'Donnell and Randall Jarrell), and "The Loud Hill of Wales," a review of Dylan Thomas's *The World I Breathe*. Bhain Campbell dies of cancer.

1941 Meets Eileen Patricia Mulligan at her New Year's Day party. Classified 4-F for the draft (poor eyesight, or perhaps the official diagnosis of *petit mal*).

1942 Publishes first individual collection, *Poems*, one of a series of poetry pamphlets by New Directions. Breaks engagement to Beryl Eeman; marries Eileen, October 24, the day before his twenty-eighth birthday.

1943 Gives Morris Gray Poetry Reading at Harvard; publishes "Shakespeare's Text," a review of W. W. Greg's *The Editorial Problem in Shakespeare*; Harvard appointment ends; teaches English and Latin at Iona Preparatory School, New Rochelle, New York, for three weeks, but resigns when R. P. Blackmur arranges for a position as instructor in English at Princeton University. Meets Robert Fitzgerald, Erich Kahler, Ralph Ellison, Hermann Broch, Christian Gauss, Edmund Wilson, and Dwight Macdonald.

1944 Rockefeller Foundation Research Fellowship (1944–45, renewed for 1945–46) to work on a critical edition of the text of *King Lear*. Meets Robert Lowell and Jean Stafford.

1945 First recording of his poetry for Library of Congress. Publishes short stories "The Lovers" and "The Imaginary Jew" in *The Kenyon Review*; the latter is awarded the *Kenyon Review*–Doubleday Doran prize; publishes essay-review on Henry James.

1946 Associate in Creative Writing at Princeton (W. S. Merwin is one of his students); publishes essay on F. Scott Fitzgerald.

1947 First infidelity, an account of which is recorded in *Sonnets to Chris* (published as *Berryman's Sonnets* in 1967). Publishes reviews "Lowell, Thomas, & Co." and "Nightingale of the Mire" on a translation of Tristan Corbière's poems. Meets T. S. Eliot. Begins psychoanalysis.

1948 Resident Fellow in Creative Writing (through spring 1949) at Princeton; first major collection of poems, *The Dispossessed*; Shelley Memorial Award (Poetry Society of America) for *The Dispossessed*. Meets Ezra Pound at St. Elizabeths Hospital in Washington, D.C.; meets Saul Bellow. Has several more affairs (and a number of others throughout the 1950s). Publishes "Waiting for the End Boys," a poetry chronicle and omnibus review of poetry in 1947, and "The State of American Writing, 1948: Seven Questions"; writes first stanzas of *Homage to Mistress Bradstreet*; begins sequence of poems, *The Black Book*, which was to be a "Mass for the Dead," about the Nazi murders of the Jews especially in Warsaw (unfinished).

1949 Guarantors Prize (*Poetry*). Involved in publicly defending Pound's being awarded the Bollingen Prize for the *Pisan Cantos*. Publishes essay "The Poetry of Ezra Pound."

1950 Publishes *Stephen Crane*, a biographical and psychological study of Crane's life and poetry. American Academy award for poetry and *Stephen Crane*; National Institute of Arts and Letters Award; Levinson Prize (*Poetry*). Alfred Hodder Fellow at Princeton (1950–51); lecturer for one term at University of Washington, Seattle. Meets Randall Jarrell.

1951 Delivers lectures at Princeton on his critical and textual research on Shakespeare; works on play *Mirabeau* (never completed, nor were *Architect* and *Dictator* in the 1940s); publishes essay "Through Dreiser's Imagination the Tides of Real Life Billowed."

1952 Elliston Lecturer on Poetry, University of Cincinnati (spring term): conducts a poetry workshop, gives ten lectures on modern poetry and seven on Shakespeare's poetry and plays. Publishes introduction to M. G. Lewis's *The Monk*. Awarded a Guggenheim Fellowship for creative writing and research on Shakespeare. Resumes work on *Homage*; writes essay "Marlowe's Damnations" and signs contract with Viking to write a critical study of Shakespeare (not completed).

1953 Completes *Homage to Mistress Bradstreet* in an intense three-month period; first public reading of *Homage* at Princeton. Travels to Europe with Eileen; meets Louis MacNeice and Theodore Roethke; returns to New York City. He and Eileen separate. Publishes *Homage* in *Partisan Review*; publishes essay "Shakespeare at Thirty." Dylan Thomas dies at St. Vincent's Hospital in New York while Berryman stands outside his room. Publishes review of Saul Bellow's *The Adventures of Augie March*.

1954 Lecturer in poetry in Writers' Workshop at State University of Iowa (Iowa City), spring term (his students include W. D. Snodgrass, Donald Justice, Philip Levine, Jane Cooper, and Henri Coulette); studies Hebrew; teaches summer term at Harvard, courses on Shakespeare and fiction; returns to University of Iowa for fall term but is dismissed when he is arrested for intoxication, profanity, and disturbing the peace. Allen Tate assists in move to Minneapolis, Minnesota, about thirty miles from father's birthplace. Intensive period of dream analysis (over 130 of his dreams, which he considers publishing as *St. Pancras Braser*).

1955 Appointed lecturer in Humanities (Ralph Ross chairs the department and becomes a close friend) at the University of Minnesota, Minneapolis, which becomes his home for the rest of his life; his courses include readings from the Gospels, Augustine, Aquinas, Dante, Cervantes, Luther, Freud, and Lenin. Research on *Shakespeare's Friend* (the possible collaboration between Shakespeare and William Haughton). Begins writing Dream Songs at the end of the year.

1956 Divorces Eileen December 19 and marries Elizabeth Ann Levine, twenty-four, a week later. Signs contract with Farrar, Straus for a book on Shakespeare (never completed); publishes *Homage to Mistress Bradstreet*, with drawings by Ben Shahn, as a book—nominated for the Pulitzer Prize; *Partisan Review* Rockefeller Fellowship for poetry (for 1957). Renews friendship with Saul Bellow, who is teaching at the University of Minnesota. Publishes "The Case of Ring Lardner"; translates Paul Claudel's *"Le Chemin de la Croix"* for Antal Dorati's musical composition *Cantata Dramatica* (not used by Dorati but later performed in 1959 as "The Way of the Cross").

1957 Harriet Monroe Poetry Prize (University of Chicago) for *Homage*. Son Paul born March 5. Promoted to Associate Professor of Interdisciplinary Studies (with tenure in Humanities and English) at University of Minnesota. Sent to India in the summer by the United States Information Service (State Department) to give twenty-six lectures on American literature at fourteen universities (also visits Japan). Joins Ann and Paul in Italy; family stays in Spain for several months. Writes essay on Whitman, " 'Song of Myself': Intention and Substance."

1958 Publishes *His Thought Made Pockets & the Plane Buckt*, a chapbook of poems; works on *Shakespeare Handbook*, commissioned by T. Y. Crowell but never completed; writes essays on individual works of Babel, Shakespeare, Stephen Crane, Hemingway, and Eliot for *Arts of Reading*; begins developing plans for *The Dream Songs*. Admitted to Regent Hospital in New York City for exhaustion. Ann leaves with son, Paul.

1959 Publishes first book of poems in England, *Homage to Mistress Bradstreet and Other Poems*. Admitted to Glenwood Hills Hospital, Minneapolis, for exhaustion and alcoholism (from 1959 to the end of his life, Berryman is admitted to hospitals almost annually—sometimes more frequently—for alcoholism and nervous exhaustion). Divorced from Ann on April 28. Publishes "From the Middle to the Senior Generations," a review of poems by Roethke, Shapiro, Cummings, and Williams; teaches at University of Utah in June; publishes first Dream Songs.

1960 Visiting lecturer, University of California (Berkeley), Department of Speech, spring term. Receives Brandeis University Creative Arts Award. Publishes *The Arts of Reading*, an anthology with commentary by Ralph Ross, Allen

Tate, and Berryman, and introduction to Thomas Nashe's *The Unfortunate Traveller*.

1961 Meets Kathleen ("Kate") Donahue, twenty-two, in spring. Teaches in the summer at Indiana School of Letters. Marries Kate on September 1. Writes essay on *Don Quixote*, "The Freedom of the Don" and the first draft of "The Development of Anne Frank."

1962 Teaches in the summer at Bread Loaf School of English, Vermont—courses on the fiction of Henry James and Stephen Crane and "Deep Form in Minor and Major Poetry"—where he renews his friendship with William Meredith and visits Robert Frost; Writer-in-Residence, Brown University, September through spring 1963. Writes essay on *The Tempest*, "Shakespeare's Last Word." First daughter, Martha ("Twissy"), born December 1.

1963 Family vacations in rural Rhode Island and Washington, D.C. Receives award from the Ingram Merrill Foundation.

1964 *77 Dream Songs* (the first three parts of *The Dream Songs*). Russell Loines Award (National Institute of Arts and Letters). He and Kate buy, in Minneapolis, the first and only house he would own.

1965 Pulitzer Prize for *77 Dream Songs*. Publishes afterword to *The Titan* by Theodore Dreiser.

1966 Guggenheim Fellowship for 1966–67 to complete *The Dream Songs*. Lives with his family in Dublin, Ireland, from September to June 1967; drinks heavily; visits England, the Continent, and Greece.

1967 Publishes *Berryman's Sonnets* and *Short Poems*. Receives Academy of American Poets and National Endowment for the Arts award for "distinguished service to American letters." Admitted to Abbott Hospital in Minneapolis for alcohol treatment.

1968 Publishes *His Toy, His Dream, His Rest*, the concluding four parts of *The Dream Songs*.

1969 National Book Award and Bollingen Prize for *His Toy, His Dream, His Rest*. Publishes the complete *The Dream Songs*. Appointed Regents' Professor of Humanities, University of Minnesota. Admitted to Hazelden Center in Minneapolis for alcoholic rehabilitation for five weeks.

1970 Resumes work on his critical biography of Shakespeare (early drafts begun in 1951); begins writing *Love & Fame* in early February and by the end of the month is in the hospital for intoxication; second rehabilitation treatment at St. Mary's Intensive Alcohol Treatment Center in Minneapolis in early May. On May 12 undergoes "a sort of religious conversion" and recovers a sense of a "God of rescue." Holiday trip with family to Mexico. Readmitted to St. Mary's for third alcoholic treatment (October through November).

Considers converting to Judaism but becomes a professed Catholic; joins Alcoholics Anonymous. Publishes *Love & Fame*.

1971 Works on *Recovery*, a thinly disguised autobiographical novel about alcoholic rehabilitation. Receives honorary doctorate from Drake University (Iowa). Mother moves to Minneapolis in May; second daughter, Sarah Rebecca, born June 13; holiday trip to Colorado with daughter Martha and son, Paul. Senior Fellowship, National Endowment for the Humanities to work on a biography of Shakespeare; *Love & Fame* (revised British edition) published; sends manuscript of *Delusions etc of John Berryman* to Farrar, Straus & Giroux.

1972 Leaps to his death on the morning of January 7 from the Washington Avenue Bridge in Minneapolis, landing on the embankment of the west side of the Mississippi River; given a Catholic funeral and buried in Resurrection Cemetery, Mendota Heights, St. Paul, Minnesota.

POSTHUMOUS PUBLICATIONS

1972 *Delusions Etc.*

1973 *Recovery* (unfinished novel), foreword by Saul Bellow.

1976 *The Freedom of the Poet* (essays and short stories), edited and with a preface by Robert Giroux.

1977 *Henry's Fate & Other Poems (1967–1972)*, selected and introduced by John Haffenden.

1988 *We Dream of Honour: John Berryman's Letters to His Mother*, selected and introduced by Richard J. Kelly.

THE
DISPOSSESSED

[1 9 4 8]

Winter Landscape

The three men coming down the winter hill
In brown, with tall poles and a pack of hounds
At heel, through the arrangement of the trees,
Past the five figures at the burning straw,
Returning cold and silent to their town,

Returning to the drifted snow, the rink
Lively with children, to the older men,
The long companions they can never reach,
The blue light, men with ladders, by the church
The sledge and shadow in the twilit street,

Are not aware that in the sandy time
To come, the evil waste of history
Outstretched, they will be seen upon the brow
Of that same hill: when all their company
Will have been irrecoverably lost,

These men, this particular three in brown
Witnessed by birds will keep the scene and say
By their configuration with the trees,
The small bridge, the red houses and the fire,
What place, what time, what morning occasion

Sent them into the wood, a pack of hounds
At heel and the tall poles upon their shoulders,
Thence to return as now we see them and
Ankle-deep in snow down the winter hill
Descend, while three birds watch and the fourth flies.

The Dispossessed

The Statue

The statue, tolerant through years of weather,
Spares the untidy Sunday throng its look,
Spares shopgirls knowledge of the fatal pallor
Under their evening colour,
Spares homosexuals, the crippled, the alone,
Extravagant perception of their failure;
Looks only, cynical, across them all
To the delightful Avenue and its lights.

Where I sit, near the entrance to the Park,
The charming dangerous entrance to their need,
Dozens, a hundred men have lain till morning
And the preservative darkness waning,
Waking to want, to the day before, desire
For the ultimate good, Respect, to hunger waking;
Like the statue ruined but without its eyes;
Turned vaguely out at dawn for a new day.

Fountains I hear behind me on the left,
See green, see natural life springing in May
To spend its summer sheltering our lovers,
Those walks so shortly to be over.
The sound of water cannot startle them
Although their happiness runs out like water,
Of too much sweetness the expected drain.
They trust their Spring; they have not seen the statue.

Disfigurement is general. Nevertheless
Winters have not been able to alter its pride,
If that expression is a pride remaining,
Coriolanus and Rome burning,
An aristocracy that moves no more.
Scholars can stay their pity; from the ceiling
Watch blasted and superb inhabitants,
The wreck and justifying ruined stare.

Since graduating from its years of flesh
The name has faded in the public mind
Or doubled: which is this? the elder? younger?
The statesman or the traveller?
Who first died or who edited his works,
The lonely brother bound to remain longer
By a quarter-century than the first-born
Of that illustrious and lost family?

The lovers pass. Not one of them can know
Or care which Humboldt is immortalized.
If they glance up, they glance in passing,
An idle outcome of that pacing
That never stops, and proves them animal;
These thighs breasts pointed eyes are not their choosing,
But blind insignia by which are known
Season, excitement, loosed upon this city.

Turning: the brilliant Avenue, red, green,
The laws of passage; marvellous hotels;
Beyond, the dark apartment where one summer
Night an insignificant dreamer,
Defeated occupant, will close his eyes
Mercifully on the expensive drama
Wherein he wasted so much skill, such faith,
And salvaged less than the intolerable statue.

The Disciple

Summoned from offices and homes, we came.
By candle-light we heard him sing;
We saw him with a delicate length of string
Hide coins and bring a paper through a flame;
I was amazed by what that man could do.
And later on, in broad daylight,
He made someone sit suddenly upright
Who had lain long dead and whose face was blue.

But most he would astonish us with talk.
The warm sad cadence of his voice,
His compassion, and our terror of his choice,
Brought each of us both glad and mad to walk
Beside him in the hills after sundown.
He spoke of birds, of children, long
And rubbing tribulation without song
For the indigent and crippled of this town.

Ventriloquist and strolling mage, from us,
Respectable citizens, he took
The hearts and swashed them in an upland brook,
Calling them his, all men's, anonymous.
. . He gained a certain notoriety;
The magical outcome of such love
The State saw it could not at all approve
And sought to learn where when that man would be.

The people he had entertained stood by,
I was among them, but one whom
He harboured kissed him for the coppers' doom,
Repenting later most most bitterly.
They ran him down and drove him up the hill.
He who had lifted but hearts stood
With thieves, performing still what tricks he could
For men to come, rapt in compassion still.

Great nonsense has been spoken of that time.
But I can tell you I saw then
A terrible darkness on the face of men,
His last astonishment; and now that I'm
Old I behold it as a young man yet.
None of us now knows what it means,
But to this day our loves and disciplines
Worry themselves there. We do not forget.

A Point of Age

I

At twenty-five a man is on his way.
The desolate childhood smokes on the dead hill,
My adolescent brothels are shut down
For industry has moved out of that town;
Only the time-dishonoured beggars and
The flat policemen, victims, I see still.
Twenty-five is a time to move away.

The travelling hands upon the tower call,
The clock-face telescopes a long desire:
Out of the city as the autos stream
I watch, I whisper, Is it time . . time?
Fog is enveloping the bridges, lodgers
Shoulder and fist each other in the mire
Where later, leaves, untidy lives will fall.

Companions, travellers, by luck, by fault
Whose none can ever decide, friends I had
Have frozen back or slipt ahead or let
Landscape juggle their destinations, slut
Solace and drink drown the degraded eye.
The fog is settling and the night falls, sad,
Across the forward shadows where friends halt.

Images are the mind's life, and they change.
How to arrange it—what can one afford
When ghosts and goods tether the twitching will
Where it has stood content and would stand still
If time's map bore the brat of time intact?
Odysseys I examine, bed on a board,
Heartbreak familiar as the heart is strange.

In the city of the stranger I discovered
Strike and corruption: cars reared on the bench
To horn their justice at the citizen's head

And hallow the citizen deaf, half-dead.
The quiet man from his own window saw
Insane wind take the ash, his favourite branch
Wrench, crack; the hawk came down, the raven hovered.

Slow spent stars wheel and dwindle where I fell.
Physicians are a constellation where
The blown brain sits a fascist to the heart.
Late, it is late, and it is time to start.
Sanction the civic woe, deal with your dear,
Convince the stranger: none of us is well.
We must travel in the direction of our fear.

II

By what weird ways, Mather and Boone, we came.
Ethan Allen, father, in the rebel wood
Teach trust and disobedience to the son
Who neither obeys nor can disobey One
No longer, down the reaches of his longing, known.
Speak from the forest and declare my blood
Dishonour, a trick a mockery my name.

You, Shaver, other shade, rébel again,
Great-grandfather, attest my hopeless need
Amongst the chromium luxury of the age
Uncomfortable, threadbare, apt to rage.
Recall your office, exile; tell me now
To devour the annals of the valuable dead,
Fish for the cortex, candour for my pain.

Horizons perish from a hacking eye! . .
The Hero, haggard on the top of time,
Enacts his inconceivable woe and pride
Plunging his enemies down the mountainside,
Lesson and master. We are come to learn
Compassion from the last and piercing scream
Of who was lifted before he could die.

Animal-and-Hero, where you lounge the air
Is the air of summer, smooth and masculine
As skin over a muscle; but the day
Darkens, and it is time to move away.
Old friends unbolt the night wherein you roam;
Wind rises, lightning, rain beats, you begin
The climb the conflict that are your desire.

In storm and gloom, before it is too late
I make my testament. I bequeath my heart
To the disillusioned few who have wished me well;
My vision I leave to one who has the will
To master it, and the consuming art;
What else—the sorrow, the disease, the hate—
I scatter; and I am prepared to start.

III

What is the age of naked man? His time
Scrawls the engrossing tumult on green mould
In a cellar and disreputable place.
Consternation and Hope war in his face.
Writhing upon his bed who achieves sleep
Who is alone? Man in the cradle, old,
Rocks on the fiery earth, smoke is his fame.

Prophecy is another smoke, and lost.
To say that country, time to come, will be
The island or harbour city of our choice
Argues the sick will raving in the voice.
The pythoness is mute upon her bier,
Cassandra took a thrust she would not see
And dropt for daughter an inarticulate ghost.

The animal within the animal
How shall we satisfy? With toys its fear,
With incantation its adorable trust?
Shall we say 'We were once and we shall be dust'
Or nourish it with confident lies and look

The Dispossessed

Contentment? What can the animal bear?
Whose version brightens that will not appal?

Watch in the valleys for the sign of snow.
Watch the light. Where the riotous leaves lay
Will arise a winter man at the New Year
And speak. No eye will be dry, none shall fear.
—That time is not yet, and our eyes are now:
Twenty-five is a time to move away.
Late on the perilous wood the son flies low.

The projection of the tower on the pine
Wavers. The wind will fan and force the fire
Streaming across our ditches to find wood.
All that someone has wished or understood
Is fuel to the holocaust he lives;
It spreads, it is the famine of his desire,
The tongue teeth eyes of your will and of mine.

What then to praise, what love, what look to have?
The animals who lightless live, alone
And dark die. We await the rising moon.
When the moon lifts, lagging winter moon,
Its white face over time where the sun shone
Gold once, we have a work to do, a grave
At last for the honourable and exhausted man.

Detroit, 1940

The Traveller

They pointed me out on the highway, and they said
'That man has a curious way of holding his head.'

They pointed me out on the beach; they said 'That man
Will never become as we are, try as he can.'

They pointed me out at the station, and the guard
Looked at me twice, thrice, thoughtfully & hard.

I took the same train that the others took,
To the same place. Were it not for that look
And those words, we were all of us the same.
I studied merely maps. I tried to name
The effects of motion on the travellers,
I watched the couple I could see, the curse
And blessings of that couple, their destination,
The deception practised on them at the station,
Their courage. When the train stopped and they knew
The end of their journey, I descended too.

The Ball Poem

What is the boy now, who has lost his ball,
What, what is he to do? I saw it go
Merrily bouncing, down the street, and then
Merrily over—there it is in the water!
No use to say 'O there are other balls':
An ultimate shaking grief fixes the boy
As he stands rigid, trembling, staring down
All his young days into the harbour where
His ball went. I would not intrude on him,
A dime, another ball, is worthless. Now
He senses first responsibility
In a world of possessions. People will take balls,
Balls will be lost always, little boy,
And no one buys a ball back. Money is external.
He is learning, well behind his desperate eyes,
The epistemology of loss, how to stand up
Knowing what every man must one day know
And most know many days, how to stand up
And gradually light returns to the street,
A whistle blows, the ball is out of sight,
Soon part of me will explore the deep and dark
Floor of the harbour . . I am everywhere,
I suffer and move, my mind and my heart move
With all that move me, under the water
Or whistling, I am not a little boy.

The Dispossessed

Fare Well

Motions of waking trouble winter air,
I wonder, and his face as it were forms
Solemn, canorous, under the howled alarms,—
The eyes shadowed and shut.
Certainly for this sort of thing it is very late,
I shudder, while my love longs and I pour
My bright eyes towards the moving shadow . . where?
Out, like a plucked gut.

What has been taken away will not return,
I take it, whether upon the crouch of night
Or for my mountain need to share a morning's light,—
No! I am alone.
What has been taken away should not have been shown,
I complain, torturing, and then withdrawn.
After so long, can I still long so and burn,
Imperishable son?

O easy the phoenix in the tree of the heart,
Each in its time, his twigs and spices fixes
To make a last nest, and marvellously relaxes,—
Out of the fire, weak peep! . .
Father I fought for Mother, sleep where you sleep!
I slip into a snowbed with no hurt
Where warm will warm be warm enough to part
Us. As I sink, I weep.

The Spinning Heart

The fireflies and the stars our only light,
We rock, watching between the roses night
If we could see the roses. We cannot.
Where do the fireflies go by day, what eat?
What categories shall we use tonight?
The day was an exasperating day,
The day in history must hang its head
For the foul letters many women got,
Appointments missed, men dishevelled and sad
Before their mirrors trying to be proud.
But now (we say) the sweetness of the night
Will hide our imperfections from our sight,
For nothing can be angry or astray,
No man unpopular, lonely, or beset,
Where half a yellow moon hangs from a cloud.

Spinning however and balled up in space
All hearts, desires, pewter and honeysuckle,
What can be known of the individual face?
To the continual drum-beat of the blood
Mesh sea and mountain recollection, flame,
Motives in the corridor, touch by night,
Violent touch, and violence in rooms;
How shall we reconcile in any light
This blow and the relations that it wrecked?
Crescent the pressures on the singular act
Freeze it at last into its season, place,
Until the flood and disorder of Spring.
To Easterfield the court's best bore, defining
Space tied into a sailor's reef, our praise:
He too is useful, he is part of this,

Inimitable, tangible, post-human,
And Theo's disappointment has a place,
An item in that metamorphosis
The horrible coquetry of aging women.
Our superstitions barnacle our eyes
To the tide, the coming good; or has it come?—
Insufficient upon the beaches of the world
To drown that complex and that bestial drum.

Triumphant animals,—upon the rest
Bearing down hard, brooding, come to announce
The causes and directions of all this
Biting and breeding,—how will all your sons
Discover what you, assisted or alone,
Staring and sweating for seventy years,
Could never discover, the thing itself?
                                    Your fears,
Fidelity, and dandelions grown
As big as elephants, your morning lust
Can neither name nor control. No time for shame,
Whippoorwill calling, excrement falling, time
Rushes like a madman forward. Nothing can be known.

On the London Train

Despite the lonesome look
The man in the corner has,
Across the compartment,
Doubtless a dozen daze
Daily their eyes on him intent
And fancy him beside a brook,
Their arms with his laced,
Holding him fast.

Whilst he for some virgin
Endures the vacant night
Without rest, and would go
On bare knees, eyes shut tight,
To Tomsk or San Diego

If she'd but let him in,
Bind his hurt knees, or say
'There is a doctor down the way.'

So it is and has been . .
Summon an old lover's ghost,
He'll swear no man has lied
Who spoke of the painful and most
Embarrassing ordeal this side
Satisfaction,—while the green
Difficulties later are
More than Zeus could bear.

Austere in a sheltered place
The sea-shell puzzles Destiny,
Who set us, man and beast
And bird, in extremity
To love and twig a nest.
The frown on the great face
Is recompense too little for
Who suffer on the shore.

Caravan

The lady in her silver-
grey spectacular
Dressing-room prepares,
Twisting at the mirror,
Of son and daughter the careers.

Also in the evening
He who collects dung
Conjures an August moon
Where he may once bring
Her flushed and salt, supine.

The blue vase having final
Wit glitters fragile
Until at the horizon

To sky and sea all
Divides, throwing off season.

Thus kept delicately
In appalling storm the
Buds will begin again
Their white difficulty
To the mature and green.

Waves, guilt, all winter tears
Draw tingling nearer
And hang a glass for apparition . .
As the words here are
At work upon salvation.

The Possessed

This afternoon, discomfortable dead
Drift into doorways, lounge, across the bridge,
Whittling memory at the water's edge,
And watch. This is what you inherited.

Random they are, but hairy, for they chafe
All in their eye, enlarging like a slide;
Spectral as men once met or crucified,
And kind. Until the sun sets you are safe.

A prey to your most awkward reflection,
Loose-limbed before the fire you sit appalled.
And think that by your error you have called
These to you. Look! the light will soon be gone.

Excited see from the window the men fade
In the twilight; reappear two doors down.
Suppose them well acquainted with the town
Who built it. Do you fumble in the shade?

The key was lost, remember, yesterday,
Or stolen,—undergraduates perhaps;

But all men are their colleagues, and eclipse
Very like dusk. It is too late to pray.

There was a time crepuscular was mild,
The hour for tea, acquaintances, and fall
Away of all day's difficulties, all
Discouragement. Weep, you are not a child.

The equine hour rears, no further friend,
Intolerant, foam-lathered, pregnant with
Mysterious grave watchers in their wrath
Let into tired Troy. You are near the end.

Midsummer Common loses its last gold,
And grey is there. The sun slants down behind
A certain cinema, and the world is blind
But more dangerous. It is growing cold.

Light all the lights, heap wood upon the fire
To banish shadow. Draw the curtains tight.
But sightless eyes will lean through, and wide night
Darken this room of yours. As you desire.

Think on your sins with all intensity.
The men are on the stair, they will not wait.
There is a paper-knife to penetrate
Heart & guilt together. Do it quickly.

Parting as Descent

The sun rushed up the sky; the taxi flew;
There was a kind of fever on the clock
That morning. We arrived at Waterloo
With time to spare and couldn't find my track.

The bitter coffee in a small café
Gave us our conversation. When the train
Began to move, I saw you turn away
And vanish, and the vessels in my brain

Burst, the train roared, the other travellers
In flames leapt, burning on the tilted air
Che si cruccia, I heard the devils curse
And shriek with joy in that place beyond prayer.

Cloud and Flame

The summer cloud in summer blue
Capricious from the wind will run,
Laughing into the tender sun,
Knowing the work that it must do.
When One says liberty is vain
The cloud will come to summer rain.

After his college failure, Swift
Eight hours a day against his age
Began to document his rage
Towards the decades of strife and shift.
From claims that pride or party made
He kept in an exacting shade.

Cornford in a retreat was lost;
A stray shot like an aimless joke
His learning, spirit, at one stroke
Dispersed, his generation's cost.
The harvest value of his head
Is less than cloud, is less than bread.

The One recalls the many burn,
Prepared or unprepared: one flame
Within a shade can strike its name,
Another sees the cloud return.
And Thirkill saw the Christ's head shake
At Hastings, by the Bloody Lake.

Letter to His Brother

The night is on these hills, and some can sleep.
Some stare into the dark, some walk.
Only the sound of glasses and of talk,
Of cracking logs, and of a few who weep,
Comes on the night wind to my waking ears.
Your enemies and mine are still,
None works upon us either good or ill:
Mint by the stream, tree-frogs, are travellers.

What shall I say for anniversary?
At Dachau rubber blows forbid
And Becket's brains upon the pavement spread
Forbid my trust, my hopeful prophecy.
Prediction if I make, I violate
The just expectancy of youth,—
Although you know as well as I whose tooth
Sunk in our heels, the western guise of fate.

When Patrick Barton chased the murderer
He heard behind him in the wood
Pursuit, and suddenly he knew hé fled:
He was the murderer, the others were
His vigilance. But when he crouched behind
A tree, the tree moved off and left
Him naked while the cry came on; he laughed
And like a hound he leapt out of his mind.

I wish for you—the moon was full, is gone—
Whatever bargain can be got
From the violent world our fathers bought,
For which we pay with fantasy at dawn,
Dismay at noon, fatigue, horror by night.
May love, or its image in work,
Bring you the brazen luck to sleep with dark
And so to get responsible delight.

1938

Desires of Men and Women

Exasperated, worn, you conjure a mansion,
The absolute butlers in the spacious hall,
Old silver, lace, and privacy, a house
Where nothing has for years been out of place,
Neither shoe-horn nor affection been out of place,
Breakfast in summer on the eastern terrace,
All justice and all grace.

                At the reception
Most beautifully you conduct yourselves—
Expensive and accustomed, bow, speak French,
That Cinquecento miniature recall
The Duke presented to your great-grandmother—

And none of us, my dears, would dream of you
The half-lit and lascivious apartments
That are in fact your goal, for which you'd do
Murder if you had not your cowardice
To prop the law; or dream of you the rooms,
Glaring and inconceivably vulgar,
Where now you are, where now you wish for life,
Whence you project your naked fantasies.

World-Telegram

Man with a tail heads eastward for the Fair.
Can open a pack of cigarettes with it.
Was weaving baskets happily, it seems,
When found, the almost Missing Link, and brought
From Ceylon in the interests of science.
The correspondent doesn't know how old.

Two columns left, a mother saw her child
Crushed with its father by a ten-ton truck

Against a loading platform, while her son,
Small, frightened, in a Sea Scout uniform,
Watched from the Langley. All needed treatment.

Berlin and Rome are having difficulty
With a new military pact. Some think
Russia is not too friendly towards London.
The British note is called inadequate.

An Indian girl in Lima, not yet six,
Has been delivered by Caesarian.
A boy. They let the correspondent in:
Shy, uncommunicative, still quite pale,
A holy picture by her, a blue ribbon.

Right of the centre, and three columns wide,
A rather blurred but rather ominous
Machine-gun being set up by militia
This morning in Harlan County, Kentucky.
Apparently some miners died last night.
'Personal brawls' is the employers' phrase.

All this on the front page. Inside, penguins.
The approaching television of baseball.
The King approaching Quebec. Cotton down.
Skirts up. Four persons shot. Advertisements.
Twenty-six policemen are decorated.
Mother's Day repercussions. A film star
Hopes marriage will preserve him from his fans.

News of one day, one afternoon, one time.
If it were possible to take these things
Quite seriously, I believe they might
Curry disorder in the strongest brain,
Immobilize the most resilient will,
Stop trains, break up the city's food supply,
And perfectly demoralize the nation.

11 May 1939

The Dispossessed

Conversation

Whether the moorings are invisible
Or slipt, we said we could not tell,
But argument held one thing sure
Which none of us that night could well endure:
The ship is locked with fog, no man aboard
Can make out what he's moving toward,
There's little food, few love, less sleep,
The sea is dark and we are told it's deep.

Where is an officer who knows this coast?
If all such men long since have faced
Downward, one summon. Who knows how,
With what fidelity, his voice heard now
Could shout directions from the ocean's floor?
Traditional characters no more
Their learnéd simple parts rehearse
But bed them softly down from the time's curse.

A snapt short log pitched out upon the hearth,
The flaming harbinger come forth
Of holocausts that night and day
Flake from the mind its skinny sovereignty.
We watched the embers cool, embers that brought
To one man there the failing thought
Of cities stripped of knowledge, men,
Our continent a wilderness again.

These are conclusions of the night, we said;
And drank; and were not satisfied.
The fire died down, smoke in the air
Assumed the alarming postures of our fear,—
The overhead horror, in the padded room
The man who will not tell his name,
The guns and subtle friends who face
Into this delicate and dangerous place.

1938

Ancestor

The old men wept when the Old Man in blue
Bulked in the doorway of the train, Time spun
And in that instant's revolution Time
(Who cannot love old men) dealt carelessly
Passions and shames upon his hardihood,
Seeing the wet eyes of his former staff:

. . Crossing from Tennessee, the river at flood,
White River Valley, his original regiment,
The glowflies winking in the gully's dusk,
Three horses shot from under him at Shiloh
Fell, the first ball took Hindman's horse as well
And then the two legs from an orderly

Rain on the lost field, mire and violence,
Corruption; Klan-talk, half-forgotten tongue
Rubbed up for By-Laws and its Constitution,
The Roman syllables
                              he an exile fled,
Both his plantations, great-grandmother's too
Gone, fled south and south into Honduras
Where great-grandmother was never reconciled
To monkeys or the thought of monkeys
                                                  once
Tricked into taking bites of one, she kept
Eight months her bed
                              fire on the colony,
Lifting of charges, and a late return,
The stranger in his land, and silence, silence . .

(Only the great grey riddled cloak spoke out
And sometimes a sudden breath or look spoke out)

Reflecting blue saw in the tears of men,
The tyrant shade, shade of the last of change,
And coughed once, twice, massive and motionless;

Now Federal, now Sheriff, near four-score,
Controlled with difficulty his old eyes
As he stepped down, for the first time, in blue.

World's Fair

The crowd moves forward on the midway, back
And forward, men and women from every State
Insisting on their motion like a clock.
I stand by the roller-coaster, and wait.
An hour I have waited, fireworks on the lake
Tell me it's late, and yet it is not that
Which rattles at the bottom of my mind,
Slight, like a faint sound sleepy on the wind
To the traveller when he has lost his track.

Suddenly in torn images I trace
The inexhaustible ability of a man
Loved once, long lost, still to prevent my peace,
Still to suggest my dreams and starve horizon.
Childhood speaks to me in an austere face.
The Chast Mayd only to the thriving Swan
Looks back and back with lecherous intent,
Being the one nail known, an excrement;
Middleton's grave in a forgotten place.

That recognition fades now, and I stand
Exhausted, angry, beside the wooden rail
Where tireless couples mount still, hand in hand,
For the complex drug of catapult and fall
To blot out the life they cannot understand
And never will forgive. The wind is stale,
The crowd thins, and my friend has not yet come.
It is long past midnight, time to track for home
And my work and the instructor down my mind.

Travelling South

A red moon hung above the pines that night
Travelling, as we travelled, south. First one,
Then two, streamers of cloud across the moon
Crept and trivided the cold brooding light
Like blood. The captive hum under the hood
Pacing, the pebbles plunging, throbbing mind
Raced through the night, afraid of what we'd find
For brother at the end, sightless or dead.

The same womb bore us. What is the time of man?
At what time does he rise and go to bed?
When shall a young man bend his hopeful head
Upon the block, under a red red moon,
And lose that dear head? I was dull with fear,
The car devoured the darkness, the moon hung,
Blood over the pines, and the cold wind sang
Welcome, welcome the executioner.

O then the lighted house, the nurse, at last
Painfully but his real face, his hand
Moving, his voice to melt the frozen wind;
Trouble but trouble that would soon be past;
Injury, but salvation. The headsman stood
Once at the block, looked on the young man stark,
And let that young man rise. In the flowing dark
The pines consumed the moon and the moon of blood.

At Chinese Checkers

I

Again—but other faces bend with mine
Upon the board—I settle to this game
And drive my marbles leaping or in line
Towards the goal, the triangular blue aim
Of all my red ones, as it was before.

Sitting with strangers by a Northern lake
I watch the opening and the shutting door,
The paradigms of marble shift and break.

II

The table moves before my restless eyes,
Part of an oak, an occupation once,
This town humming with men and lumber, cries,
Will, passionate activity that since
Dwindled, died when the woods cut without plan
Were thirty years ago exhausted. Now
The jackpine where the locomotive ran
Springs up wild; the docks are rotten with snow.

III

Last night for the first time I saw the Lights,
The folding of the Lights like upright cloud
Swinging as, in a childhood summer, kites
Swung, and the boys who owned the kites were proud.
What pride was active in that gorgeous sky?
What dreadful leniency compelled the men
Southward, the crumpled men? Questions went by,
Swung in the dark back and were gone again.

IV

Far on the dunes the wind is rising, sand
Drifts with it, drops; under the rounding moon
Deer, hesitating from the wood, will stand
Until their promise is a lonely dune
And they come forward, masters for the time
Of all that mountainous dead world, cold light.
The glittering rocks are naked as a tomb
Where the sea was; alteration is the night.

V

Insistent voices recall me to the play.
I triple over blue and yellow, sit
Erect and smile; but what it is they say
My ears will not accept, I mangle it,
I see their faces change, I hear the wind
Begin to whistle under the shut door,
The door shudders, I cannot hold my mind,
Backward, east, south it goes in the wind's roar.

VI

I am again in the low and country room
Where all that is was heart-wrung, had by hard
Continual labour. We are at the game:
Excited childish cries over the board,
The old man grumbling in the darkness there
Beside the stove, Baynard is still, intent,
And to my left his sister has her chair,
Her great eyes to the flashing marbles bent.

VII

The shy head and the delicate throat conceal
A voice that even undisciplined can stir
The country blood over a Southern hill.
Will Ingreet's voice bring her renown, bring her
That spontaneous acclaim an artist needs
Unless he works in the solitary dark?
What prophecy, what hope can older heads
Proclaim, beyond the exhaustion of the work?

VIII

How shall we counsel the unhappy young
Or young excited in their thoughtlessness
By game or deviltry or popular song?
Too many, blazing like disease, confess

The Dispossessed

In their extinction the consuming fear
No man has quite escaped: the good, the wise,
The masters of their generation, share
This pressure of inaction on their eyes.

IX

I move the white, jumping the red and green,
Blue if I can, to finish where the blue
Marbles before they issued forth began,
And fill the circles, as I ought to do.
Can I before the children win that place?
Their energies are here at work, not mine:
The beautiful absorption on Sue's face
My crowded travelling face cannot design.

X

The fox-like child I was or assume I was
I lose, the abstract remember only; all
The lightness and the passion for running lose
Together with all my terror, the blind call
At midnight for the mother. How shall we know
The noon we are to be in night we are?
The altering winds are dark and the winds blow
Agitation and rest, unclear, unclear.

XI

Deep in the unfriendly city Delmore lies
And cannot sleep, and cannot bring his mind
And cannot bring those marvellous faculties
To bear upon the day sunk down behind,
The unsteady night, or the time to come.
Slack the large frame, he sprawls upon his bed
Useless, the eloquent mouth relaxed and dumb,
Trouble and mist in the apathetic head.

XII

What prophecies, what travel? Strangers call
Across the miles of table, and I return,
Bewildered, see burnt faces rise and fall
In the recapitulation of their urn.
I speak; all of us laugh; the game goes on.
The Northern wind is moaning still outside.
The sense of change, suns gone up and come down,
Whirls in my tired head, and it will abide.

XIII

Against my will once in another game
I spat a piece of tooth out—this was love
Or the innocence of love, long past its time
Virgin with trust, which time makes nothing of.
The wind is loud. I wonder, Will it grow,
That trust, again? Can it again be strong?
What rehabilitations can the heart know
When the heart is split, when the faithful heart is wrong?

XIV

Venus on the half-shell was found a dish
To madden a fanatic: from the nave
Rolled obloquy and lust. Sea without fish,
Flat sea, and Simonetta had a grave
Deeper than the dark cliff of any tooth,
Deeper than memory. Obstinate, malicious,
The man across the table shouts an oath,
The sea recedes, strangers possess the house.

XV

Marbles are not the marbles that they were,
The accurate bright knuckle-breakers boys
In alleys, where there is no one to care,
Use, in the schoolyard use at noon, and poise
As Pheidias his incomparable gold.

The Dispossessed

The gold is lost. But issued from the tomb,
Delmore's magical tongue. What the sea told
Will keep these violent strangers from our room.

XVI

The marbles of the blood drive to their place,
Foam in the heart's level. The heart will mend,
Body will break and mend, the foam replace
For even the unconsolable his taken friend.
Wind is the emblem of the marbles' rest,
The sorrowful, the courageous marble's hurt
And strange recovery. Stubborn in the breast
The break and ache, the plunging powerful heart.

1939

The Animal Trainer (1)

I told him: The time has come, I must be gone.
It is time to leave the circus and circus days,
The admissions, the menagerie, the drums,
Excitements of disappointment and praise.
In a suburb of the spirit I shall seize
The steady and exalted light of the sun,
And live there, out of the tension that decays,
Until I become a man alone of noon.

Heart said: Can you do without your animals?
The looking, licking, smelling animals?
The friendly fumbling beast? The listening one?
That standing up and worst of animals?
What will become of you in the pure light
When all your enemies are gone, and gone
The inexhaustible prospect of the night?

—But the night is now the body of my fear,
These animals are my distraction. Once
Let me escape the smells and cages here,

Once let me stand naked in the sun,
All these performances will be forgotten.
I shall concentrate in the sunlight there.

Said the conservative Heart: Your animals
Are occupation, food for you, your love
And your immense responsibility;
They are the travellers by which you live.
(Without you they will pace and pine, or die.)

—I reared them, tended them (I said) and still
They plague me, they will not perform, they run
Into forbidden corners, they fight, they steal.
Better to live like an artist in the sun.

—You are an animal trainer, Heart replied.
Without your animals leaping at your side
No sun will save you, nor this bloodless pride.

—What must I do then? Must I stay and work
With animals, and confront the night, in the circus?

—You léarn from animals. You léarn in the dark.

The Animal Trainer (2)

I told him: The time has come, I must be gone.
It is time to leave the circus and circus days,
The admissions, the menagerie, the drums,
Excitements of disappointment and praise.
In a suburb of the spirit I shall seize
The steady and exalted light of the sun
And live there, out of the tension that decays,
Until I become a man alone of noon.

Heart said: Can you do without these animals?
The looking, licking, smelling animals?
The friendly fumbling beast? The listening one?
The standing up and worst of animals?

The Dispossessed

What will become of you in the pure light
When all your enemies are gone, and gone
The inexhaustible prospect of the night?

—But the night is now the body of my fear,
These animals are my distraction! Once
Let me escape the smells and cages here,
Once let me stand naked in the sun,
All their performances will be forgotten.
I shall concentrate in the sunlight there.

Said the conservative Heart: These animals
Are occupation, food for you, your love
And your despair, responsibility:
They are the travellers by which you live.
Without you they will pace and pine, or die.

—What soul-delighting tasks do they perform?
They quarrel, snort, leap, lie down, their delight
Merely a punctual meal and to be warm.
Justify their existence in the night!

—The animals are coupling, and they cry
'The circus *is*, it is our mystery,
It is a world of dark where animals die.'

—Animals little and large, be still, be still:
I'll stay with you. Suburb and sun are pale.

—Animals are your destruction, and your will.

☙ III ❧

1 September 1939

The first, scattering rain on the Polish cities.
That afternoon a man squat' on the shore
Tearing a square of shining cellophane.
Some easily, some in evident torment tore,
Some for a time resisted, and then burst.
All this depended on fidelity . .
One was blown out and borne off by the waters,
The man was tortured by the sound of rain.

Children were sent from London in the morning
But not the sound of children reached his ear.
He found a mangled feather by the lake,
Lost in the destructive sand this year
Like feathery independence, hope. His shadow
Lay on the sand before him, under the lake
As under the ruined library our learning.
The children play in the waves until they break.

The Bear crept under the Eagle's wing and lay
Snarling; the other animals showed fear,
Europe darkened its cities. The man wept,
Considering the light which had been there,
The feathered gull against the twilight flying.
As the little waves ate away the shore
The cellophane, dismembered, blew away.
The animals ran, the Eagle soared and dropt.

The Dispossessed

Desire Is a World by Night

The history of strangers in their dreams
Being irresponsible, is fun for men,
Whose sons are neither at the Front nor frame
Humiliating weakness to keep at home
Nor wince on principle, wearing mother grey,
Honoured by radicals. When the mind is free
The catechetical mind can mince and tear
Contemptible vermin from a stranger's hair
And then sleep.

                In our parents' dreams we see
Vigour abutting on senility,
Stiff blood, and weathered with the years, poor vane;
Unfortunate but inescapable.
Although this wind bullies the windowpane
Are the children to be kept responsible
For the world's decay? Carefully we choose
Our fathers, carefully we cut out those
On whom to exert the politics of praise.

Heard after dinner, in defenceless ease,
The dreams of friends can puzzle, dazzle us
With endless journeys through unfriendly snow,
Malevolent faces that appear and frown
Where nothing was expected, the sudden stain
On spotless window-ledges; these we take
Chuckling, but take them with us when we go,
To study in secret, late, brooding, looking
For trails and parallels. We have a stake
In this particular region, and we look
Excitedly for situations that we know.
—The disinterested man has gone abroad;
Winter is on the by-way where he rode
Erect and alone, summery years ago.

When we dream, paraphrase, analysis
Exhaust the crannies of the night. We stare,

Fresh sweat upon our foreheads, as they fade:
The melancholy and terror of avenues
Where long no single man has moved, but play
Under the arc-lights gangs of the grey dead
Running directionless. That bright blank place
Advances with us into fearful day,
Heady and insuppressible. Call in friends,
They grin and carry it carefully away,—
The fathers can't be trusted,—strangers wear
Their strengths, and visor. Last, authority,
The Listener borrow from an English grave
To solve our hatred and our bitterness . .
The foul and absurd to solace or dismay.
All this will never appear; we will not say;
Let the evidence be buried in a cave
Off the main road. If anyone could see
The white scalp of that passionate will and those
Sullen desires, he would stumble, dumb,
Retreat into the time from which he came
Counting upon his fingers and his toes.

Farewell to Miles

We are to tell one man tonight good-bye.
Therefore in little glasses Scotch, therefore
Inane talk on the chaise longue by the door,
Therefore the loud man, the man small and shy
Who squats, the hostess as she has a nut
Laughing like ancestor. Hard, hard to find
In thirteen bodies one appropriate mind,
It is hard to find a knife that we can cut.

The dog is wandering among the men
And wander may: who knows where who will be,
Under what master, in what company,
When what we hope for has not come again
For the last time? Schedules, nerves will crack
In the distortion of that ultimate loss;

The Dispossessed

Sad eyes at frenzied eyes will look across,
Blink, be resigned. The men then will come back.

How many of these are destined there? Not one
But may be there, staring; but some may trick
By attack or by some prodigy of luck
The sly dog. McPherson in the Chinese sun
May achieve the annihilation of his will;
The urbane and bitter Miles at Harvard may
Discover in time an acid holiday
And let the long wound of his birth lie still.

Possibilities, dreams, in a crowded room.
Fantasy for the academic man,
Release, distinction. Let the man who can,
Does any peace know, now arise and come
Out of the highballs, past the dog, forward.
(I hope you will be happier where you go
Than you or we were here, and learn to know
What satisfactions there are.) No one heard.

Wayne, 1940

The Moon and the Night and the Men

On the night of the Belgian surrender the moon rose
Late, a delayed moon, and a violent moon
For the English or the American beholder;
The French beholder. It was a cold night,
People put on their wraps, the troops were cold
No doubt, despite the calendar, no doubt
Numbers of refugees coughed, and the sight
Or sound of some killed others. A cold night.

On Outer Drive there was an accident:
A stupid well-intentioned man turned sharp
Right and abruptly he became an angel
Fingering an unfamiliar harp,
Or screamed in hell, or was nothing at all.

Do not imagine this is unimportant.
He was a part of the night, part of the land,
Part of the bitter and exhausted ground
Out of which memory grows.

                          Michael and I
Stared at each other over chess, and spoke
As little as possible, and drank and played.
The chessmen caught in the European eye,
Neither of us I think had a free look
Although the game was fair. The move one made
It was difficult at last to keep one's mind on.
'Hurt and unhappy' said the man in London.
We said to each other, The time is coming near
When none shall have books or music, none his dear,
And only a fool will speak aloud his mind.
History is approaching a speechless end,
As Henry Adams said. Adams was right.

All this occurred on the night when Leopold
Fulfilled the treachery four years before
Begun—or was he well-intentioned, more
Roadmaker to hell than king? At any rate,
The moon came up late and the night was cold,
Many men died—although we know the fate
Of none, nor of anyone, and the war
Goes on, and the moon in the breast of man is cold.

White Feather

   (after a news item)

Imagine a crowded war-time street
Down Under. See as little as I:
The woman gives him as they meet
Passing, something . . a feather. Try
To make out this man who was going by.
The eye stared at the feather.

He could remember sand and sand,
The punishing sun on their guns; he chose
As the men approached the western end
To move to the left. Who would suppose
A Lieutenant in civilian clothes?
The feather stared back.

He dropt his glass eye in her hand.
. . Humiliation or fantasy,
He thought; I have seen too much sand
For judgment or anger; it may be I,
All men, deserve the feather's lie.
The eye stared at the feather.

The Enemies of the Angels

I

The Irish and the Italians own the place.
Anyone owns it, if you like, who has
A dollar minimum; but it is theirs by noise.
Let them possess it until one o'clock,
The balconies' tiers, huddled tables, shroud-
ed baleful music, and the widening crack
Across the far wall watching a doomed crowd,
The fat girl simpering carnations to the boys.

This is a paradise the people seek,
To hide, if they but knew, being awake,
Losses and crisis. This is where they come
For love, for fun, to forget, dance, to conceal
Their slow perplexity by the river. Who
But pities the kissing couple? Who would feel
Disdain, as she does, being put on show
By whom she loves? And pity . . our images of home.

The arrival of the angels is delayed
An even minute, and I am afraid
We clapped because they fail to, not because

[38

They come. Their wings are sorry. The platform
A little shudders as they back and frisk,
We'd maul the angels, the whole room is warm,—
A waste, and a creation without risk;
Jostling, pale as they vanish, the horse-faced chorine paws.

The impersonator is our special joy
And puzzle: did the nurse announce a boy
Or not? But now the guy is all things, all
Women and most men howl when he takes off
Our President, the Shadow, Garbo or Bing
And other marvellous persons. 'Sister Rough'
The sailors at their table, gesturing,
Soprano, whistling. Still, recall him, and recall

Mimics we wish we all were, and we are.
We lack a subject just, we lack a car,
We would see two Mayors bowing as we pass,
We wish we had another suit, we wish
Another chance, we would have Western life
Where the hero reins and fans, horseflesh ís flesh.
But the heckling man and his embarrassed wife
Play us across the mirrored room. Where is my glass?

II

My tall and singular friend two feet away,
Where do you go at the end of another day?
What is your lot, your wife's lot, under the Lord?
If you between two certain ages, more
Nor less, are, and if you revere the Flag
Or whether, Friend, you find a flag a bore
And whether Democracy blooms or you see it sag,
What is your order number at your Local Board?

Where do you all go? Not with whom you would;
But where you went as little boys, when good,
To the plains' heaven of the silver screen.
This comic in a greatcoat is your will,
The faery presence walking among men

The Dispossessed

Who mock him: sly, baffled, and powerful
For imagination is his, and imagination
Ruins, compels; consider the comedian again.

The orchestra returns and tunes before
A spot, a flash, the M.C. through the door
Glides like a breakfast to your vision—gay
Indelicate intimate, 'Jerk, what do you know?'
An aging, brimstone acrobat in pink
Monkeys her way across the blue boards. Who
Resists her? Who would be unkind to think
A human wheel, a frozen smile, is human woe?

Consider, students, at the convalescent hour
The fantasy which last week you saw fair,
Which loses now its eye; its eye is gone.
Where shall the ten be found to safe us? For
The enemies of the angels, hard on sleep,
Weary themselves to find the Gentlemen's door.
It is not a little one. Perhaps you weep,
Three eyes weep in the world you inhabit alone.

All this resist. Who wish their stays away
Or wish them tighter tighter—the mourners pray
In narrowing circles—these are women lost,
Are men lost in the drag of women's eyes,
Salt mouths. Go with the tide, at midnight dream
Hecklers will vanish like a radical's lies,
And all Life slides from drink to drink, the stream
Slides, and under the stream we join a happy ghost.

A Poem for Bhain

Although the relatives in the summer house
Gossip and grumble, do what relatives do,
Demand, demand our eyes and ears, demand us,

You and I are not precisely there
As they require: heretics, we converse
Alert and alone, as over a lake of fire

Two white birds following their profession
Of flight, together fly, loom, fall and rise,
Certain of the nature and station of their mission.

So by the superficial and summer lake
We talk, and nothing that we say is heard,
Neither by the relatives who twitter and ache

Nor by any traveller nor by any bird.

Boston Common

A Meditation upon The Hero

I

Slumped under the impressive genitals
Of the bronze charger, protected by bronze,
By darkness from patrols, by sleep from what
Assailed him earlier and left him here,
The man lies. Clothing and organs. These were once
Shoes. Faint in the orange light
Flooding the portico above: the whole
Front of the State House. On a February night.

II

Dramatic bivouac for the casual man!
Beyond the exedra the Common falls,
Famous and dark, away; a lashing wind;
Immortal heroes in a marble frame
Who broke their bodies on Fort Wagner's walls,
Robert Gould Shaw astride, and his
Negroes without name, who followed, who fell
Screaming or calm, wet cold, sick or oblivious.

The Dispossessed

III

Who now cares how? here they are in their prime,—
Paradigm, pitching imagination where
The crucible night all singularity,
Idiosyncrasy and creed, burnt out
And brought them, here, a common character.
Imperishable march below
The mounted man below the Angel, and
Under, the casual man, the possible hero.

IV

Hero for whom under a sky of bronze,
Saint-Gaudens' sky? Passive he seems to lie,
The last straw of contemporary thought,
In shapeless failure; but may be this man
Before he came here, or he comes to die,
Blazing with force or fortitude
Superb of civil soul may stand or may
After young Shaw within that crucible have stood.

V

For past her assignation when night fell
And the men forward,—poise and shock of dusk
As daylight rocking passes the horizon,—
The Angel spread her wings still. War is the
Congress of adolescents, love in a mask,
Bestial and easy, issueless,
Or gets a man of bronze. No beating heart
Until the casual man can see the Angel's face.

VI

Where shall they meet? what ceremony find,
Loose in the brothel of another war
This winter night? Can citizen enact
His timid will and expectation where,

Exact a wedding or her face O where
Tanks and guns, tanks and guns,
Move and must move to their conclusions, where
The will is mounted and gregarious and bronze?

VII

For ceremony, in the West, in the East,
The pierced sky, iced air, and the rent of cloud
As, moving to his task at dawn, who'd been
Hobbledehoy of the cafeteria life
Swung like a hobby in the blue and rode
The shining body of his choice
To the eye and time of his bombardier;—
Stiffened in the racket, and relaxed beyond noise.

VIII

'Who now cares how?'—the quick, the index! Question
Your official heroes in a magazine,
Wry voices past the river. Dereliction,
Lust and bloodlust, error and goodwill, this one
Died howling, craven, this one was a swine
From childhood. Man and animal
Sit for their photographs to Fame, and dream
Barbershop hours . . vain, compassionate parable.

IX

'Accidents of history, memorials'—
A considering and quiet voice. 'I see
Photograph and bronze upon another shore
Do not arrive; the light is where it is,
Indifferent to honour. Let honour be
Consolation to those who give,
None to the Hero, and no sign of him:
All unrecorded, flame-like, perish and live.'

The Dispossessed

X

Diminishing beyond the elms. Rise now
The chivalry and defenders of our time,
From Spain and China, the tortured continents,
Leningrad, Syria, Corregidor,—
Upon a primitive theme high variations
Like soaring Beethoven's.—Lost, lost
Whose eyes flung faultless to one horizon
Their fan look. Fiery night consumes a summoned ghost.

XI

Images of the Possible, the top,
Their time they taxed,—after the tanks came through,
When orderless and by their burning homes'
Indelible light, with knee and nail they struck
(The improvised the real) man's common foe,
Misled blood-red statistical men.
Images of conduct in a crucible,
Their eyes, and nameless eyes, which will not come again.

XII

We hope will not again. Therefore those eyes
Fix me again upon the terrible shape,
Defeated and marvellous, of the man I know,
Jack under the stallion. We have passed him by,
Wandering, prone, and he is our whole hope,
Our fork's one tine and our despair,
The heart of the Future beating. How far far
We sent our subtle messengers! when he is here.

XIII

Who chides our clamour and who would forget
The death of heroes: never know the shore
Where, hair to the West, Starkatterus was burnt;
And undergo no more that spectacle—

Perpetually verdant the last pyre,
Fir, cypress, yew, the phoenix bay
And voluntary music—which to him
Threw never meat or truth. He looks another way,

XIV

Watching who labour O that all may see
And savour the blooming world, flower and sound,
Tending and tending to peace,—be what their blood,
Prayer, occupation may,—so tend for all:
A common garden in a private ground.
Who labour in the private dark
And silent dark for birthday music and light,
Fishermen, gardeners, about their violent work.

XV

Lincoln, the lanky lonely and sad man
Who suffered in Washington his own, his soul;
Mao Tse-tung, Teng Fa, fabulous men,
Laughing and serious men; or Tracy Doll
Tracing the future on the wall of a cell—
There, there, on the wall of a cell
The face towards which we hope all history,
Institutions, tears move, there the Individual.

XVI

Ah, it may not be so. Still the crucial night
Fastens you all upon this frame of hope:
Each in his limited sick world with them,
The figures of his reverence, his awe,
His shivering devotion,—that they shape
Shelter, action, salvation.
 . . Legends and lies. Kneel if you will, but rise
Homeless, alone, and be the kicking working one.

The Dispossessed

XVII

None anywhere alone! The turning world
Brings unaware us to our enemies,
Artist to assassin, Saint-Gaudens' bronze
To a free shelter, images to end.
The cold and hard wind has tears in my eyes,
Long since, long since, I heard the last
Traffic unmeshing upon Boylston Street,
I halted here in the orange light of the Past,

XVIII

Helpless under the great crotch lay this man
Huddled against woe, I had heard defeat
All day, I saw upon the sands assault,
I heard the voice of William James, the wind,
And poured in darkness or in my heartbeat
Across my hearing and my sight
Worship and love irreconcilable
Here to be reconciled. On a February night.

1942

IV

Canto Amor

Dream in a dream the heavy soul somewhere
struck suddenly & dark down to its knees.
A griffin sighs off in the orphic air.

If (Unknown Majesty) I not confess
praise for the wrack the rock the live sailor
under the blue sea,—yet I may You bless

always for hér, in fear & joy for hér
whose gesture summons ever when I grieve
me back and is my mage and minister.

—Muses: whose worship I may never leave
but for this pensive woman, now I dare,
teach me her praise! with her my praise receive.—

Three years already of the round world's war
had rolled by stoned & disappointed eyes
when she and I came where we were made for.

Pale as a star lost in returning skies,
more beautiful than midnight stars more frail
she moved towards me like chords, a sacrifice;

entombed in body trembling through the veil
arm upon arm, learning our ancient wound,
we see our one soul heal, recovering pale.

Then priestly sanction, then the drop of sound.
Quickly part to the cavern ever warm
deep from the march, body to body bound,

descend (my soul) out of dismantling storm
into the darkness where the world is made.
. . Come back to the bright air. Love is multiform.

Heartmating hesitating unafraid
although incredulous, she seemed to fill
the lilac shadow with light wherein she played,

whom sorry childhood had made sit quite still,
an orphan silence, unregarded sheen,
listening for any small soft note, not hopeful:

The Dispossessed

caricature: as once a maiden Queen,
flowering power comeliness kindness grace,
shattered her mirror, wept, would not be seen.

These pities moved. Also above her face
serious or flushed, swayed her fire-gold
not earthly hair, now moonless to unlace,

resistless flame, now in a sun more cold
great shells to whorl about each secret ear,
mysterious histories, white shores, unfold.

New musics! One the music that we hear,
this is the music which the masters make
out of their minds, profound solemn & clear.

And then the other music, in whose sake
all men perceive a gladness but we are drawn
less for that joy than utterly to take

our trial, naked in the music's vision,
the flowing ceremony of trouble and light,
all Loves becoming, none to flag upon.

Such Mozart made,—an ear so delicate
he fainted at a trumpet-call, a child
so delicate. So merciful that sight,

so stern, we follow rapt who ran a-wild.
Marriage is the second music, and thereof
we hear what we can bear, faithful & mild.

Therefore the streaming torches in the grove
through dark or bright, swiftly & now more near
cherish a festival of anxious love.

Dance for this music, Mistress to music dear,
more, that storm worries the disordered wood
grieving the midnight of my thirtieth year

and only the trial of our music should
still this irresolute air, only your voice
spelling the tempest may compel our good:

Sigh then beyond my song: whirl & rejoice!

THE NERVOUS SONGS

Young Woman's Song

The round and smooth, my body in my bath,
If someone else would like it too.—I did,
I wanted T. to think 'How interesting'
Although I hate his voice and face, hate both.
I hate this something like a bobbing cork
Not going. I want something to hang to.—

A fierce wind roaring high up in the bare
Branches of trees,—I suppose it was lust
But it was holy and awful. All day I thought
I am a bobbing cork, irresponsible child
Loose on the waters.—What have you done at last?
A little work, a little vague chat.

I want that £3.10 hat terribly.—
What I am looking for (*I am*) may be
Happening in the gaps of what I know.
The full moon does go with you as yóu go.
Where am I going? I am not afraid . .
Only I would be lifted lost in the flood.

The Song of the Demented Priest

I put those things there.—See them burn.
The emerald the azure and the gold
Hiss and crack, the blues & greens of the world
As if I were tired. Someone interferes

The Dispossessed

Everywhere with me. The clouds, the clouds are torn
In ways I do not understand or love.

Licking my long lips, I looked upon God
And he flamed and he was friendlier
Than you were, and he was small. Showing me
Serpents and thin flowers; these were cold.
Dominion waved & glittered like the flare
From ice under a small sun. I wonder.

Afterward the violent and formal dancers
Came out, shaking their pithless heads.
I would instruct them but I cannot now,—
Because of the elements. They rise and move,
I nod a dance and they dance in the rain
In my red coat. I am the king of the dead.

The Song of the Young Hawaiian

Ai, they all pass in front of me those girls!
Blazing and lazy colours. The swaying sun
Brushes the brown tips of them stiffly softly
And whispers me: Never take only one
As the yellow men the white the foreigners do.—
No no, I dance them all.

The old men come to me at dusk and say
'Hang from their perches now the ruined birds;
They will fall. We hear strange languages.
Rarely a child sings now.' They cough and say
'We are a dying race.' Ai! if we are!
You will not marry me.

Strengthless the tame will of the elders' eyes.—
The green palms, the midnight sand, the creaming surf!
The sand at streaming noon is black. I swim
Farther than others, for I swim alone.
. . (Whom Nangganangga smashed to pieces on
The road to Paradise.)

A Professor's Song

(. . rabid or dog-dull.) Let me tell you how
The Eighteenth Century couplet ended. Now
Tell me. Troll me the sources of that Song—
Assigned last week—by Blake. Come, come along,
Gentlemen. (Fidget and huddle, do. Squint soon.)
I want to end these fellows all by noon.

'That deep romantic chasm'—an early use;
The word is from the French, by our abuse
Fished out a bit. (Red all your eyes. O when?)
'A poet is a man speaking to men':
But I am then a poet, am I not?—
Ha ha. The radiator, please. Well, what?

Alive now—no—Blake would have written prose,
But movement following movement crisply flows,
So much the better, better the much so,
As burbleth Mozart. Twelve. The class can go.
Until I meet you, then, in Upper Hell
Convulsed, foaming immortal blood: farewell.

The Captain's Song

The tree before my eyes bloomed into flame,
I rode the flame. This was the element,
Forsaking wife and child, I came to find,—
The flight through arrowy air dark as a dream
Brightening and falling, the loose tongues blue
Like blood above me, until I forgot.

. . Later, forgetting, I became a child
And fell down without reason and played games
Running, being the fastest, before dark
And often cried. Certain things I hid
That I had never liked, I leapt the stream
No one else could and darted off alone . .

The Dispossessed

You crippled Powers, cluster to me now:
Baffle this memory from my return,
That in the coldest nights, murmuring her name
I sought her two feet with my feet, my feet
Were warm and hers were ice and I warmed her
With both of mine. Will I warm her with one?

The Song of the Tortured Girl

After a little I could not have told—
But no one asked me this—why I was there.
I asked. The ceiling of that place was high
And there were sudden noises, which I made.
I must have stayed there a long time today:
My cup of soup was gone when they brought me back.

Often 'Nothing worse now can come to us'
I thought, the winter the young men stayed away,
My uncle died, and mother broke her crutch.
And then the strange room where the brightest light
Does not shine on the strange men: shines on me.
I feel them stretch my youth and throw a switch.

Through leafless branches the sweet wind blows
Making a mild sound, softer than a moan;
High in a pass once where we put our tent,
Minutes I lay awake to hear my joy.
—I no longer remember what they want.—
Minutes I lay awake to hear my joy.

The Song of the Bridegroom

A sort of anxiousness crystal in crystal has . .
Fragile and open like these pairs of eyes.
All over all things move to stare at it.
One's single wish now: to be laid away
Felted in depths of caves, dark cupboards that
No one would open for a long time.—

Do not approach me! If I am on show
Compassion waves you past, you hoverers,
Forms brutal, beating eyes upon my window.
Because if I am desolate I have—
Have emanations, and it is not safe.
Rising and falling fire, ceremonial fire.

Not long . . not long but like a journey home
Frightening after so distant years
And such despairs . . And then fatigue sets in.
Lead me up blindly now where I began,
I will not wince away into my one.
I extend my hand and place it in the womb.

Song of the Man Forsaken and Obsessed

Viridian and gamboge and vermilion
Are and are not.—The hut is quiet,
Indistinct as letters. When I wake I wait.
Nothing comes.—The brown girl brings me rice
And one day months ago I might have stood—
So far were firm my feet—had that ship come—
And painted, softening my brush with blood.

Hardly, whatever happens from today.
—Certainly the little old woman
With a white eye, who takes all things away,
Comes and stares from the corner of my bed
If I could turn. My nails and my hair loosen,
The stiff flesh lurches and flows off like blood.

Grateful the surf of death drawing back under
(Offshore to fan out, vague and dark again)
My legs, my decayed feet, cock and heart.
If I were rid of them, somehow propped up . .
My vivid brain alone with a little vermilion!

[53

The Pacifist's Song

I am the same yes as you others, only—
(Also for mé the plain where I was born,
Bore Her look, bear love, makes its mindless pull
And matters in my throat, also for me
The many-murdered sway my dreams unshorn,
Bearded with woe, their eyes blasted and dull)

Only I wake out of the vision of death
And hear One whisper whether man or god
'Kill not . . . Your ill from evil comes . . . Bear all';—
Only I must forsake my country's wrath
Who am earth's citizen, must human blood
Anywhere shed mourn, turning from it pale

Back to the old and serious labour, to
My restless labour under the vigilant stars,
From whom no broad storm ever long me hides.
What I try, doomed, is hard enough to do.
We breed up in our own breast our worse wars
Who long since sealed ourselves Hers Who abides.

Surviving Love

The clapper hovers, but why run so hard?
What he wants, has,—more than will make him ease;
No god calls down,—he's not been on his knees
This man, for years, and he is off his guard.
What then does he dream of
Sweating through day?—Surviving love.

Cold he knows he comes, once to the dark,
All that waste of cold, leaving all cold
Behind him hearts, forgotten when he's tolled,
His books are split and sold, the pencil mark
He made erased, his wife
Gone brave & quick to her new life.

And so he spins to find out something warm
To think on when the glaze fastens his eyes
And he begins to freeze. He slows and tries
To hear a promise: 'After, after your storm
I will grieve and remember,
Miss you and be warm and remember.'

But really nothing replies to the poor man,
He never hears this, or the voice he hears
(He thinks) he loses ah when next appears
The hood of the bell, seeing which he began.
His skull rings with his end,
He runs on, love for love.

The Lightning

Sick with the lightning lay my sister-in-law,
Concealing it from her children, when I came.
What I could, did, helpless with what I saw.

Analysands all, and the rest ought to be,
The friends my innocence cherished, and you and I,
Darling,—the friends I qualm and cherish and see.

. . The fattest nation!—wé do not thrive fat
But facile in the scale with all we rise
And shift a breakfast, and there is shame in that.

And labour sweats with vice at the top, and two
Bullies are bristling. What he thought who thinks?
It is difficult to say what one will do.

Obstinate, gleams from the black world the gay and fair,
My love loves chocolate, she loves also me,
And the lightning dances, but I cannot despair.

The Dispossessed

Rock-Study with Wanderer

'Cold cold cold of a special night'
Summer and winter sings under the beast
The ravished doll   Hear in the middle waste
The blue doll of the west cracking with fright

The music & the lights did not go out
Alas   Our foreign officers are gay
Singers in the faery cities shiver & play
Their exile dances through unrationed thought

Waiting for the beginning of the end
The wedding of the arms   Whose charnel arms
Will plough the emerald mathematical farms
In spring, spring-flowers to the U.N. send?

          *   *   *

Waiting I stroll within a summer wood
Avoiding broken glass in the slant sun
Our promises we may at last make good
The stained glass shies when the cathedral's won

Certainly in a few years call it peace
The arms & wings of peace patrol us all
The planes & arms that planes & arms may cease
Pathos (theanthropos) fills evenfall

When shall the body of the State come near
The body's state stable & labile? When
Irriding & resisting rage & fear
Shall men in unison yet resemble men?

[56

Detroit our heart   When terribly we move
The sea is ours   We walk upon the sea
The air is ours   Hegemony, my love,
The good life's founded upon LST

The twilight birds wake   A paralysis
Is busy with societies and souls
Whose gnarled & pain-wild bodies beg abyss
Paraplegia dolorosa   The world rolls

A tired and old man resting on the grass
His forehead loose as if he had put away
Among the sun & the green & the young who pass
The whole long fever of his passionate day

. . To the dark watcher then an hour comes
Neither past nor future, when the chuffing sea
Far off like the rough of beast nearby succumbs
And a kind of sleep spreads over rock & tree

Nightshade not far from the abandoned tomb
Hangs its still bells & fatal berries down
The flowers dream   Crags shadows loom
The caresses of the animals are done

Under faint moon they lie absorbed and fair
Stricken their limbs flow in false attitudes
Of love   Dovetailed into a broken mirror
Stained famous glass are, where the watcher broods

All wars are civil   So the thing will die
Your civilization a glitter of great glass
The lusts have shivered you are shaken by
And step aside from in the moonlit grass

Stare on, cold riot of the western mind
Rockwalking man, what can a wanderer know?

The Dispossessed

Rattle departing of his friend and kind
And then (the widow sang) sphincter let go

*   *   *

Draw draw the curtain on a little life
A filth a fairing   Wood is darkening
Where birdcall hovered now I hear no thing
I hours since came from my love my wife

Although a strange voice sometimes patiently
Near in the air when I lie vague and weak
As if it had a body tries to speak . .
I must go back, she will be missing me

Whether There Is Sorrow in the Demons

Near the top a bad turn some dare. Well,
The horse swerves and screams, his eyes pop,
Feet feel air, the firm winds prop
Jaws wide wider until
Through great teeth rider greets the smiles of Hell.

Thick night, where the host's thews crack like thongs
A welcome, curving abrupt on cheek & neck.
No wing swings over once to check
Lick of their fire's tongues,
Whip & chuckle, hoarse insulting songs.

Powers immortal, fixed, intractable.
Only the lost soul jerks whom they joy hang:
Clap of remorse, and tang and fang
More frightful than the drill
An outsize dentist scatters down a skull;

Nostalgia rips him swinging. Fast in malice
How may his masters mourn, how ever yearn
The frore pride wherein they burn?
God's fire. To what *qui tollis*
Stone-tufted ears prick back towards the bright Palace?

Whence Lucifer shone Lucifer's friends hail
The scourge of choice made at the point of light
Destined into eternal night;
Motionless to fulfil
Their least, their envy looks up dense and pale.

. . Repine blackmarket felons; murderers
Sit still their time, till yellow feet go first,
Dies soon in them, and can die, thirst;
Not lives in these, nor years
On years scar their despair—which yet rehearse . .

Their belvedere is black. They believe, and quail.
One shudder racks them only, lonely, and
No mirror breaks at their command.
Unsocketed, their will
Grinds on their fate. So was, so shall be still.

The Long Home

bulks where the barley blew, time out of mind
Of the sleepless Master. The barbered lawn
Far to a grey wall lounges, the birds are still,
Rising wind rucks from the sill
The slack brocade beside   the old throne he dreams on.
The portraits' hands are blind.

Below these frames they strain on stones. He mumbles . .
Fathers who listen, what loves hear
Surfacing from the lightless past? He foams.
Stillness locks a hundred rooms.
Louts in a bar aloud, The People, sucking beer.
A barefoot kiss. Who trembles?

Peach-bloom, sorb-apple sucked in what fine year!
I am a wine, he wonders; when?
Am I what I can do? My large white hands.
Boater & ascot, in grandstands

Coups. Concentrations of frightful cold, and then
Warm limbs below a pier.

The Master is sipping his identity.
Ardours & stars! Trash humped on trash.
The incorporated yacht, the campaign cheque
Signed one fall on the foredeck
Hard on a quarrel, to   amaze the fool. Who brash
Hectored out some false plea?

Brownpaper-blind, his morning passions trailed
Home in the clumsy dusk,—how now
Care which from which, trapped on a racing star
Where we know not who we are! . .
The whipcord frenzy curls, he slouches where his brow
Works like the rivals' failed.

Of six young men he flew to breakfast as,
Only the magpie, rapist, stayed
For dinner, and the rapist died, so that
Not the magpie but the cat
Vigil upon the magpie stalks, sulky parade,
Great tail switching like jazz.

Frightened, dying to fly, pied and obscene,
He blinks his own fantastic watch
For the indolent Spring of what he was before;
A stipple of sunlight, clouded o'er,
Remorse a scribble on   the magic tablet which
A schoolboy thumb jerks clean.

Heat lightning straddles the horizon dusk
Above the yews: the fresh wind blows:
He flicks a station on by the throne-side . .
Out in the wide world, Kitty—wide
Night—far across the sea . . Some guardian accent grows
Below the soft voice, brusque:

'You are: not what you wished but what you were,
The decades' vise your gavel brands,

You glare the god who gobbled his own fruit,
He who stood mute, lucid and mute,
Under peine forte et dure to will his bloody lands,
Then whirled down without heir.'

The end of which he will not know. Undried,
A prune-skin helpless on his roof.
His skin gleams in the lamplight dull as gold
And old gold clusters like mould
Stifling about his blood, time's helm to build him proof.
Thump the oak, and preside!

An ingrown terrible smile unflowers, a sigh
Blurs, the axle turns, unmanned.
Habited now forever with his weight
Well-housed, he rolls in the twilight
Unrecognizable   against the world's rim, and
A bird whistles nearby.

Whisked off, a voice, fainter, faint, a guise,
A gleam, pin of a, a. Nothing.
—One look round last, like rats, before we leave.
A famous house. Now the men arrive:
Horror, they swing their cold   bright mallets, they're breaking
Him up before my eyes!

Wicked vistas! The wolves mourn for our crime
Out past the grey wall. On to our home,
Whereby the barley may seed and resume.
Mutter of thrust stones palls this room,
The crash of mallets. He   is going where I come.
Barefoot soul fringed with rime.

A Winter-Piece to a Friend Away

Your letter came.—Glutted the earth & cold
With rains long heavy, follows intense frost;
        Snow howls and hides the world
We workt awhile to build; all the roads are lost;

Icy spiculae float, filling strange air;
No voice goes far; one is alone whirling since where,
    And when was it one crossed?
    You have been there.

I too the breaking blizzard's eddies bore
One year, another year: tempted to drop
    At my own feet forlorn
Under the warm fall, frantic more to chop
Wide with the gale until my thought ran numb
Clenching the blue skin tight against what white spikes come,
    And the sick brain estop.
    Your pendulum

Mine, not stilled wholly, has been sorry for,
Weeps from, and would instruct . .   Unless I lied
    What word steadies that cord?
Glade grove & ghyll of antique childhood glide
Off; from our grown grief, weathers that appal,
The massive sorrow of the mental hospital,
    Friends & our good friends hide.
    They came to call.

Hardly theirs, moment when the tempest gains,
Loose heart convulses. Their hearts bend off dry,
    Their fruit dangles and fades.
—Solicitudes of the orchard heart, comply
A little with my longing, a little sing
Our sorrow among steel & glass, our stiffening,
    That hers may modify:
    O trembling Spring.—

Immortal risks our sort run, to a house
Reported in a wood . . mould upon bread
    And brain, breath giving out,
From farms we go by, barking, and shaken head,
The shrunk pears hang, Hölderlin's weathercock
Rattles to tireless wind, the fireless landscape rock,
    Artists insane and dead
    Strike like a clock:

If the fruit is dead, fast. Wait. Chafe your left wrist.
All these too lie, whither a true form strays.
Sweet when the lost arrive.
Foul sleet ices the twigs, the vision frays,
Festoons all signs; still as I come to name
My joy to you my joy springs up again the same,—
The thaw alone delays,—
Your letter came!

New Year's Eve

The grey girl who had not been singing stopped,
And a brave new no-sound blew through acrid air.
I set my drink down, hard. Somebody slapped
Somebody's second wife somewhere,
Wheeling away to long to be alone.
I see the dragon of years is almost done,
Its claws loosen, its eyes
Crust now with tears & lust and a scale of lies.

A whisky-listless and excessive saint
Was expounding his position, whom I hung
Boy-glad in glowing heaven: he grows faint:
Hearing what song the sirens sung,
Sidelong he web-slid and some rich prose spun.
The tissue golden of the gifts undone
Surpassed the gifts. Miss Weirs
Whispers to me her international fears.

Intelligentsia milling. In a semi-German
(Our loss of Latin fractured how far our fate,—
Disinterested once, linkage once like a sermon)
I struggle to articulate
Why it is our promise breaks in pieces early.
The Muses' visitants come soon, go surly
With liquor & mirrors away
In this land wealthy & casual as a holiday.

The Dispossessed

Whom the Bitch winks at. Most of us are linsey-
woolsey workmen, grandiose, and slack.
On m'analyse, the key to secrets. Kinsey
Shortly will tell us sharply back
Habits we stuttered. How revive to join
(Great evils grieve beneath : eye Caesar's coin)
And lure a while more home
The vivid wanderers, uneasy with our shame?

Priests of the infinite! ah, not for long.
The dove whispers, and diminishes
Up the blue leagues. And no doubt we heard wrong—
Wax of our lives collects & dulls; but was
What we heard hurried as we memorized,
Or brightened, or adjusted? Undisguised
We pray our tongues & fingers
Record the strange word that blows suddenly and lingers.

Imagine a patience in the works of love
Luck sometimes visits. Ages we have sighed,
And cleave more sternly to a music of
Even this sore word 'genocide'.
Each to his own! Clockless & thankless dream
And labour Makers, being what we seem.
Soon soon enough we turn
Our tools in; brownshirt Time chiefly our works will burn.

I remember: white fine flour everywhere whirled
Ceaselessly, wheels rolled, a slow thunder boomed,
And there were snowy men in the mill-world
With sparkling eyes, light hair uncombed,
And one of them was humming an old song,
Sack upon sack grew portly, until strong
Arms moved them on, by pairs,
And then the bell clanged and they ran like hares.

Scotch in his oxter, my Retarded One
Blows in before the midnight; freezing slush
Stamps off, off. Worst of years! . . no matter, begone;
Your slash and spells (in the sudden hush)

We see now we had to suffer some day, so
I cross the dragon with a blessing, low,
While the black blood slows. Clock-wise,
We clasp upon the stroke, kissing with happy cries.

Of 1947

Narcissus Moving

Noise of the vans woke us before we would
At the second landing a fine mirror cracked
Scratches appeared on all the valued wood
And this was the Fairway's last official act

Unfit to form attachment he is flying
The weather favours jokers of this kind
News of the hairy cousins was supplying
Barkers with gossip not to speak his mind

Blond to the dawn comes down himself in green
Verging on joy   I see his knuckles white
With joy and yet he stood all night unseen
In reverie upstairs under the skylight

The neglected corners said what they were for
'Limpid the lapse & sweet relapse of water
Upon my trembling image, ah, no more'
He whispered and stole downstairs to the slaughter

With a bannister he laid a blue bone bare
A tongue tore hard but one boot in a groin
Sank like a drift   A double fist of hair
Like feathers members that will not rejoin

Flat slams below there but I blew my drag
Against my ash and strained, ash on the tile
Spoilt the good washroom, weary with a jag
I chinned the sill to watch a wicked mile

The walls of stone bury to some pavane
The garden   A bloody rubbish a dancing shoe
'Two-Eyes could bear no more' like the dusty swan
Shut of its cage and doubtful what to do

A vile tune from the shattered radio
Incredibly arises & dies at once . .
A deeper silence, then we slowly know
Somewhere in the empty mansion one tap runs

'A Negress gnawed my lip up a terrible place
Why not? the rising sun will light me poor'
Only upon a young man's most blond face
Un silence de la mort de l'amour

The Dispossessed

'and something that . . . that is theirs—no longer ours'
stammered to me the Italian page. A wood
seeded & towered suddenly. I understood.—

The Leading Man's especially, and the Juvenile Lead's,
and the Leading Lady's thigh that switches & warms,
and their grimaces, and their flying arms:

our arms, our story. Every seat was sold.
A crone met in a clearing sprouts a beard
and has a tirade. Not a word we heard.

Movement of stone within a woman's heart,
abrupt & dominant. They gesture how
fings really are. Rarely a child sings now.

My harpsichord weird as a koto drums
adagio for twilight, for the storm-worn dove
no more de-iced, and the spidery business of love.

The Juvenile Lead's the Leader's arm, one arm
running the whole bole, branches, roots, (O watch)
and the faceless fellow waving from her crotch,

Stalin-unanimous! who procured a vote
and care not use it, who have kept an eye
and care not use it, percussive vote, clear eye.

That which a captain and a weaponeer
one day and one more day did, we did, *ach*
we did not, *They* did . . cam slid, the great lock

lodged, and no soul of us all was near was near,—
an evil sky (where the umbrella bloomed)
twirled its mustaches, hissed, the ingenue fumed,

poor virgin, and no hero rides. The race
is done. Drifts through, between the cold black trunks,
the peachblow glory of the perishing sun

in empty houses where old things take place.

The Dispossessed

SONNETS TO
CHRIS

[1 9 4 7 , 1 9 6 6]

He made, a thousand years ago, a-many songs
for an Excellent lady, wif whom he was in wuv,
shall now he publish them?
Has he the right, upon that old young man,
to bare his nervous system
& display all the clouds again as they were above?

As a friend of the Court I would say, Let them die.
What does anything matter? Burn them up,
put them in a bank vault.
I thought of that and when I returned to this country
I took them out again. The original fault
will not be undone by fire.

The original fault was whether wickedness
was soluble in art. History says it is,
Jacques Maritain says it is,
barely. So free them to the winds that play,
let boys & girls with these old songs have holiday
if they feel like it.

[1]

I wished, all the mild days of middle March
This special year, your blond good-nature might
(Lady) admit—kicking abruptly tight
With will and affection down your breast like starch—
Me to your story, in Spring, and stretch, and arch.
But who not flanks the wells of uncanny light
Sudden in bright sand towering? A bone sunned white.
Considering travellers bypass these and parch.

This came to less yes than an ice cream cone
Let stand . . though still my sense of it is brisk:
Blond silky cream, sweet cold, aches: a door shut.
Errors of order! Luck lies with the bone,
Who rushed (and rests) to meet your small mouth, risk
Your teeth irregular and passionate.

[2]

Your shining—where?—rays my wide room with gold;
Grey rooms all day, green streets I visited,
Blazed with you possible; other voices bred
Yours in my quick ear; when the rain was cold
Shiver it might make shoulders I behold
Sloping through kite-slipt hours, tingling. I said
A month since, 'I will see that cloud-gold head,
Those eyes lighten, and go by': then your thunder rolled.

Drowned all sound else, I come driven to learn
Fearful and happy, deafening rumours of
The complete conversations of the angels, now
As nude upon some warm lawn softly turn
Toward me the silences of your breasts . .   My vow! . .
One knee unnerves the voyeur sky enough.

[3]

Who for those ages ever without some blood
Plumped for a rose and plucked it through its fence? . .
Till the canny florist, amorist of cents,
Unpawned the peppery apple, making it good
With boredom, back to its branch, as it seems he could,—
Vending the thornless rose. We think our rents
Paid, and we nod. O but ghosts crown, dense,
Down in the dark shop bare stems with their Should

Not! Should Not sleepwalks where no clocks agree!
So I was not surprised, though I trembled, when
This morning groping your hand moaning your name
I heard distinctly drip . . somewhere . . and see
Coiled in our joys flicker a tongue again,
The fall of your hair a cascade of white flame.

[4]

Ah when you drift hover before you kiss
More my mouth yours now, lips grow more to mine
Teeth click, suddenly your tongue like a mulled wine
Slides fire,—I wonder what the point of life is.
Do, down this night where I adore you, Chris,
So I forsake the blest assistant shine
Of deep-laid maps I made for summits, swine-
enchanted lover, loafing in the abyss?

Loaf hardly, while my nerves dánce, while the gale
Moans like your hair down here. But I lie still,
Strengthless and smiling under a maenad rule.
Whose limbs worked once, whose imagination's grail
Many or some would nourish, must now I fill
My strength with desire, my cup with your tongue,
    no more Melpomene's, but Erato's fool? . .

[5]

The poet hunched, so, whom the worlds admire,
Rising as I came in; greeted me mildly,
Folded again, and our discourse was easy,
While he hid in his skin taut as a wire,
Considerate as grace, a candid pyre
Flaring some midday shore; he took more tea,
I lit his cigarette . . once I lit Yeats' as he
Muttered before an Athenaeum fire
The day Dylan had tried to slow me drunk
Down to the great man's club. But you laught just now
Letting me out, you bubbled 'Liar' and
Laught . .   Well, but thén my breast was empty, monk
Of Yeatsian order: yesterday (truth now)
Flooding blurred Eliot's words sometimes,
        face not your face, hair not you blonde but iron.

[6]

Rackman and victim twist: sounds all these weeks
Of seconds and hours and days not once are dumb,
And has your footfall really not come
Still? O interminable strength that leaks
All day away alert . . I am who seeks
As tautly now, whom the vague creakings strum
Jangled this instant, as when the monstrous hum
Your note began!—since when old silence spéaks.

Deep down this building do I sometimes hear
Below the sighs and flex of the travelling world
Pyromaniacal whispers? . .   *Not to be*
They say *would do us good* . . easy . . the mere
Lick and a promise of a sweet flame curled
Fast on its wooden love: *silence our plea*.

Sonnets to Chris

[7]

I've found out why, that day, that suicide
From the Empire State falling on someone's car
Troubled you so; and why we quarrelled. War,
Illness, an accident, I can see (you cried)
But not this: what a bastard, not spring wide! . .
I said a man, life in his teeth, could care
Not much just whom he spat it on . . and far
Beyond my laugh we argued either side.

'One has a right not to be fallen on! . . . .'
(Our second meeting . . yellow you were wearing.)
Voices of our resistance and desire!
Did I divine then I must shortly run
Crazy with need to fall on you, despairing?
Did you bolt so, before it caught, our fire?

[8]

College of cocktails, a few gentlemen,
Of whippersnappers and certain serious boys,
Who better discriminates than I your noise
From the lemon song and black light assertion
Of the academies of eternity? . .   Your fen—
Yet it's your fen yields this perfume I poise
Full against Helen, and Isotta: toys
To time's late action in this girl. Again
As first when I sat down amongst your trees
I respect you and am moved by you! Hér you
Taught not, nor could, but comrades of hers you have,
She sleeps, she rouses, near you, near she frees
Each morning her strange eyes, eyes that grey blue
Not blue . . for your incurable sins some salve.

[9]

Great citadels whereon the gold sun falls
Miss you O Chris sequestered to the West
Which wears you Mayday lily at its breast,
Part and not part, proper to balls and brawls,
Plains, cities, or the yellow shore, not false
Anywhere, free, native and Danishest
Profane and elegant flower,—whom suggest
Frail and not frail, blond rocks and madrigals.

Once in the car (cave of our radical love)
Your darker hair I saw than golden hair
Above your thighs whiter than white-gold hair,
And where the dashboard lit faintly your least
Enlarged scene, O the midnight bloomed . . the East
Less gorgeous, wearing you like a long white glove!

[10]

You in your stone home where the sycamore
More than I see you sees you, where luck's grass
Smoothes your bare feet more often, even your glass
Touches your palm and tips to your lips to pour
Whatever is in it into you, through which door
O moving softness do you just now pass—
Your slippers' prows curled, red and old—alas
With what soft thought for me, at sea, and sore?

Stone of our situation! iron and stone,
Younger as days to years than the house, yet might
Wé stare as little haggard with time's roil . .
Who in each other's arms have lain—lie—one
Bite like an animal, both do, pause, and bite,
Shudder with joy, kiss . . the broad waters boil!

Sonnets to Chris

[11]

I expect you from the North. The path winds in
Between the honeysuckle and the pines, among
Poison ivy and small flowerless shrubs,
Across the red-brown needle-bed. I sit
Or smoking pace. A moment since, at six,
Mist wrapped the knoll, but now birds like a gong
Beat, greet the white-gold level shine. Wide-flung
On a thousand greens the late slight rain is gleaming.

A rabbit jumps a shrub. O my quick darling,
Lie torpid so? Cars from the highway whine,
Dawn's trunks against the sun are black. I shiver.
Your hair this fresh wind would—but I am starting.
To what end does this easy and crystal light
Dream on the flat leaves, emerald, and shimmer? . .

[12]

Mutinous in the half-light, & malignant, grind
Fears on desires, a clutter humps a track,
The body of expectation hangs down slack
Untidy black; my love sweats like a rind;
Parrots are yattering up the cagy mind,
Jerking their circles . . you stood, a week back,
By, I saw your foot with half my eye, I lack
You . . the damned female's yellow head swings blind.

Cageless they'd grapple. O where, whose Martini
Grows sweeter with my torment, wrung on toward
The insomnia of eternity, loud graves!
Hölderlin on his tower sang like the sea
More you adored that day than your harpsichord,
Troubled and drumming, tempting and empty waves.

[13]

I lift—lift you five States away your glass,
Wide of this bar you never graced, where none
Ever I know came, where what work is done
Even by these men I know not, where a brass
Police-car sign peers in, wet strange cars pass,
Soiled hangs the rag of day out over this town,
A juke-box brains air where I drink alone,
The spruce barkeep sports a toupee alas—

My glass I lift at six o'clock, my darling,
As you plotted . . Chinese couples shift in bed,
We shared today not even filthy weather,
Beasts in the hills their tigerish love are snarling,
Suddenly they clash, I blow my short ash red,
Grey eyes light! and we have our drink together.

[14]

Moths white as ghosts among these hundreds cling
Small in the porchlight . .   I am one of yours,
Doomed to a German song's stale metaphors,
The breasty thimble-rigger hums my wring.

I am your ghost, this pale ridiculous thing
Walks while you slump asleep; ouija than morse
Reaches me better; wide on Denmark's moors
I loiter, and when you slide your eyes I swing.

The billiard ball slammed in the kibitzer's mouth
Doctor nor dentist could relieve him of,
Injecting, chipping . . too he clampt it harder . .

Squalor and leech of curiosity's truth
Fork me this diamond meal to gag on Love,
Grinning with passion, your astonished martyr.

Sonnets to Chris

[15]

What was Ashore, then? . .   Cargoed with Forget,
My ship runs down a midnight winter storm
Between whirlpool and rock, and my white love's form
Gleams at the wheel, her hair streams. When we met
Seaward, Thought frank & guilty to each oar set
Hands careless of port as of the waters' harm.
Endless a wet wind wears my sail, dark swarm
Endless of sighs and veering hopes, love's fret.

Rain of tears, real, mist of imagined scorn,
No rest accords the fraying shrouds, all thwart
Already with mistakes, foresight so short.
Muffled in capes of waves my clear signs, torn,
Hitherto most clear,—Loyalty and Art.
And I begin now to despair of port.

(After Petrarch & Wyatt)

[16]

Thrice, or I moved to sack, I saw you: how
Without siege laid I can as simply tell
As whether below the dreams of Astrophel
Lurks the wild fact some scholars would allow
And others will deny in ours! O now
The punishing girl met after Toynbee's bell
Tolled for us all I see too bloody well
To say why then I cheapened a blind bow.

Paid at the shore eyes, ears, a shaking hand,
A pull of blood; behind you coming back,
Already holding, began to be borne away . .
Held. After Mozart, saw you bend and stand
Beside my seat . . held. I recovered . .   Rack
The consumer! I rushed out Stockton street one day.

[17]

The Old Boys' blazers like a Mardi-Gras
Burn orange, border black, their dominoes
Stagger the green day down the tulip rows
Of the holiday town. Ever I passioned, ah
Ten years, to go where by her golden bra
Some sultry girl is caught, to dip my nose
Or dance where jorums clash and King Rex' hose
Slip as he rules the tantrum's orchestra,
Liriodendron, and the Mystick Krewe!
Those images of Mardi-Gras' sweet weather
Beckoned—but how has their invitation ceased?
. . The bells brawl, calling (I cannot find you
With me there) back us who were not together.
Our forward Lent set in before our feast.

[18]

You, Chris, *contrite* I never thought to see,
Whom nothing fazes, no *crise* can disconcert,
Who calm cross crises all year, flouting, alert,
A reckless lady, in whom alone agree
Of bristling states your war and peace; only
Your knuckle broke with smashing objects, curt
Classic dislike, your flowing love, expert
Flat stillness on hot sand, display you wholly.

. . And can you do what you are sorry for? . .
'I'll pin you down and put a biscuit on you'
Your childhood hissed: you didn't: just this side
Idolatry, I cannot see you sor-
ry, darling, no! what other women do
And lie or weep for, flash in your white stride.

[19]

You sailed in sky-high, with your speech askew
But marvellous, and talked like mad for hours,
Slamming and blessing; you transported us,
I'd never heard you talk so, and I knew—
Humbler and more proud—you each time undo
My kitcat but to cram it with these powers
You bare and bury; suddenly, late then, as
Your best 'burnt offering' took me back with you.

No jest but jostles truth! . . I burn . . am led
Burning to slaughter, passion like a sieve
Disbands my circling blood the priestess slights.
—'Remorse does not suit you at all' he said,
Rightly; but what he ragged, and might forgive,
I shook for, lawless, empty, without rights.

[20]

Presidential flags! and the General is here,
Shops have let out, two bands are raising hell
O hell is empty and Nassau street is well,
The little devils shriek, an angel's tear
Falls somewhere, so (but I laugh) would mine, I fear
The Secret Service rang the rising bell
And poor Mr Eliot and the Admiral
Have come, and a damned word nobody can hear.

Two centuries have here misabused our youth:
(Your grey eyes pierce the miles to meet my eyes)
The bicentennial of an affair with truth
(In the southern noon whom do you tyrannize?)
Not turned out well: the cast girl sucks her tooth.
(Secret, let us be true time crucifies.)

[21]

Whom undone David upto the dire van sent
I'd see as far. I can't dislike that man,
Grievously and intensely like him even,
Envy nor jealousy admit, consent
Neither to the night of rustlers I frequent
Nor to this illness dreams them; but I can,
Only, that which we must: bright as a pan
Our love gleams, empty almost empty—lent.

. . Did he, or not, see? I stood close to you
But our lips had broken and you could reply . .
And *is* he clement? does he give us rope?
It is the owner drives one crazy, who
Came, or luck brought him, first; a police spy;
A kind and good man; with a gun; hunts hope.

[22]

If not white shorts—then in a princess gown
Where gaslights pierce the mist I'd have your age,
Young in a grey gown, blonde and royal, rage
Of handlebars at Reisenweber's, frown
Or smile to quell or rally half the town,
To polka partners mad, to flout the stage,
To pale The Lily to an average
Woman, looking up from your champagne, or down.

Myself, ascotted groom, dumb as a mome
Drinking your eyes . .   No Bill comes by to cadge
A Scotch in Rector's, waving his loose tongue;
I tip my skimmer to your friend who clung
Too long, blue-stocking cracked on the *Red Badge*
Stevie's becoming known for . .   We drive home.

They may, because I would not cloy your ear—
If ever these songs by other ears are heard—
With 'love'; suppose I loved you not, but blurred
Lust with strange images, warm, not quite sincere,
To switch a bedroom black. O mutineer
With me against these empty captains! gird
Your scorn again above all at *this* word
Pompous and vague on the stump of his career.

Also I fox 'heart', striking a modern breast
Hollow as a drum, and 'beauty' I taboo;
I want a verse fresh as a bubble breaks,
As little false . .   Blood of my sweet unrest
Runs all the same—I am in love with you—
Trapped in my rib-cage something throes and aches!

[24]

Still it pleads and rankles: 'Why do you love *me*?'
Replies then jammed me dumb; but now I speak,
Singing why each should *not* the other seek—
The octet will be weaker—in the fishful sea.
Your friends I don't like all, and poetry
You less than music stir to, the blue streak
Troubles me you drink: if all these are weak
Objections, they are all, and all I foresee.

Your choice, though! . .   Who no Goliath has slung low.
When one day rushing about your lawn you saw
Him whom I might not name without some awe
If curious Johnson should enquire below,
'Who lifts this voice harsh, fresh, and beautiful?'
—'As thy soul liveth, O king, I cannot tell.'

[25]

Sometimes the night echoes to prideless wailing
Low as I hunch home late and fever-tired,
Near you not, nearing the sharer I desired,
Toward whom till now I sailed back . . but that sailing
Yaws, from the cabin orders like a failing
Dribble, the stores disordered and then fired
Skid wild, the men are glaring, the mate has wired
Hopeless: Locked in, and humming, the Captain's nailing
A false log to the lurching table. Lies
And passion sing in the cabin on the voyage home,
The burgee should fly Jolly Roger: wind
Madness like the tackle of a crane (outcries
Ascend) around to heave him from the foam
Irresponsible, since all the stars rain blind.

[26]

Crouched on a ridge sloping to where you pour
No doubt a new drink late this easy night,
The tooth-drawn town dreams . . censorless, can bite
Rebellion, bodies mauled . . but breaks a snore.
Hessians maraud no more, coaches no more
Crash off north, south; only a smooth car's flight
Hums where the brains rest, an old parasite
Sniff then for breakfast while from Bach you soar

Easy and live in the summer dawn, my striker!
Nothing the borough lets be made here, lest
The professors and the millionaires from bed
Be startled, the Negroes drop trays, build. The tiger
Sprang off heraldic colours into the West,
Where he snoozes . . glossy, and substantially dead.

[27]

In a poem made by Cummings, long since, his
Girl was the rain, but darling you are sunlight
Volleying down blue air, waking a flight
Of sighs to follow like the mourning iris
Your shining-out-of-shadow hair I miss
A fortnight and to-noon. What you excite
You are, you are me: as light's parasite
For vision on . . us. O if my synchrisis
Teases you, briefer than Propertius' in
This paraphrase by Pound—to whom I owe
Three letters—why, run through me like a comb:
I lie down flat! under your discipline
I die. No doubt of visored others, though . .
The broad sky dumb with stars shadows me home.

[28]

A wasp skims nearby up the bright warm air,
Immobile me, my poem of you lost
Into your image burning, a burning ghost
Between the bricks and fixed eyes, blue despair
To spell you lively in this summerfare
Back from your death of distance, my lute tossed
Down, while my ears reel to your marriage, crossed
Brass endless, burning on my helpless glare.

After eighteen years to the Rue Fortunée
Balzac brought Hanska, the Count dead and the lover
Not well to live, home, where the black lock stuck
Stuck! stuck! lights blazed, the crazy valet smashed away,
Idlers assembled, a smith ran to discover—
Ten weeks, and then turned in (like mine) his luck.

[29]

The cold rewards trail in, when the man is blind
They glitter round his tomb (no bivouac):
The Rue Fortunée is the Rue de Balzac,
The Bach-Gesellschaft girdles the world; unsigned,
The treaty rages freeing him to wind
Mankind about an icy finger. Pack
His laurel in, startle him with gimcrack
Recognition.—But O do not remind
Of the hours of morning this indifferent man
When alone in a summery cloud he sweat and knew
She, she would not come, she would not come, now
Or all the lime-slow day . .   Your artisan
And men's, I tarry alike for fame and you,
Not hoping, tame, tapping my warm blank brow.

[30]

Of all that weeks-long day, though call it back
If I will I can—rain thrice, sheets, a torrent
Spaced by the dry sun, Sunday thirst that went
Sharp-set from town to town, down cul-de-sac
To smoke a blind pig for a liquid snack,
Did ever beer taste better, when opulent
Over the State line with the State's consent
We cleared our four throats, climbing off the rack;
Lost our way then: our thirst again: then tea
With a velvet jacket over the flowered choker
Almost a man, who copied tulips *queerer*:
Dinner a triumph—of that day I have wholly
One moment (weeks I played the friendly joker)
Your eyes married to mine in the car mirror.

Sonnets to Chris

[31]

Troubling are masks . . the faces of friends, my face
Met unaware, and your face: where I mum
Your doubleganger writhes, wraiths are we come
To keep a festival, none but wraiths embrace;
Our loyal rite only we interlace,
Laertes' winding-sheet done and undone
In Ithaca by day and night . . we thrum
Hopeful our shuffles, trusting to our disgrace.

Impostors . . O but our truth our fortunes cup
To flash this lying blood. Sore and austere
The crown we cry for, merely to lie ill
In grand evasion, questions not-come-up.—
I am dreaming on the hour when I can hear
My last lie rattle, and then lie truly still.

[32]

How shall I sing, western & dry & thin,
You who for celebration should cause flow
The sensual fanfare of D'Annunzio,
Mozart's mischievous joy, the amaranthine
Mild quirks of Marvell, Villon sharp as tin
Solid as sword-death when the man blinks slow
And accordions into the form he'll know
Forever—voices can nearly make me sin
With envy, so they sound. You they saw not,
Natheless, alas, unto this epigone
Descends the dread labour, the Olympic hour—
When for the garden and the tape of what
We trust, one runs until lung into bone
Hardens, runs harder then . . lucky, a flower.

[33]

Audacities and fêtes of the drunken weeks!
One step false pitches all down . . come and pour
Another . .   Strange, so warningless we four
Locked, crocked together, two of us made sneaks—
Who can't get at each other—midnights of freaks
On crepitant surfaces, a kiss blind from the door . .
One head suspects, drooping and vaguely sore,
Something entirely sad, skew, she not seeks . .

'You'll give me ulcers if all this keeps up'
You moaned . .   One only, ignorant and kind,
Saves his own life useful and usual,
Blind to the witch-antinomy I sup
Spinning between the laws on the black edge, blind
Head—O do I?—I dance to disannul.

[34]

'I *couldn't leave* you' you confessed next day.
Oúr law too binds. Grossly however bound
And jacketed apart, ensample-wound,
We come so little and can so little stay
Together, what can we know? Anything may
Amaze me: this did. Ah, to work underground
Slowly and wholly in your vein profound . .
Or like some outcast ancient Jew to say:

'There *is* Judaea: in it Jerusalem:
In that the Temple: in the Temple's inmost
Holy of holies hides the invisible Ark—
There nothing—there all—vast wing beating dark—
Voiceless, the terrible I AM—the lost
Tables of stone with the Law graved on them!'

Sonnets to Chris

[35]

Nothing there? nothing up the sky alive,
Invisibly considering? . . I wonder.
Sometimes I heard Him in traditional thunder;
Sometimes in sweet rain, or in a great 'plane, I've
Concluded that I heard Him not. You thrive
So, where I pine. See no *adjustment* blunder?
Job was alone with Satan? Job? O under
Hell-ladled morning, some of my hopes revive:

. . Less nakedly malign—loblolly—dull
Eyes on our end . . a table crumples, things
Jump and fuse, a fat voice calls down the sky,
'Too excitable! too sensitive! thin-skull,
I am for you: I shrive your wanderings:
Stand closer, evil, till I pluck your sigh.'

[36]

Keep your eyes open when you kiss: do: when
You kiss. All silly time else, close them to;
Unsleeping, I implore you (dear) pursue
In darkness me, as I do you again
Instantly we part . . only me both then
And when your fingers fall, let there be two
Only, 'in that dream-kingdom': I would have you
Me alone recognize your citizen.

Before who wanted eyes, making love, so?
I do now. However we are driven and hide,
What state we keep all other states condemn,
We see ourselves, we watch the solemn glow
Of empty courts we kiss in . .   Open wide!
You do, you do, and I look into them.

[37]

Sigh as it ends . . I keep an eye on your
Amour with Scotch,—too *cher* to consummate;
Faster your disappearing beer than late-
ly mine; your naked passion for the floor;
Your hollow leg; your hanker for one more
Dark as the Sundam Trench; how you dilate
Upon psychotics of this class, collate
Stages, and . . how long since you, well, *forbore*.

Ah, but the high fire sings on to be fed
Whipping our darkness by the lifting sea
A while, O darling drinking like a clock.
The tide comes on: spare, Time, from what you spread
Her story,—tilting a frozen Daiquiri,
Blonde, barefoot, beautiful,
⠀⠀⠀⠀flat on the bare floor rivetted to Bach.

[38]

Musculatures and skulls. Later some throng
Before a colonnade, eagle on goose
Clampt in an empty sky, time's mild abuse
In cracks clear down the fresco print; among
The exaggeration of poses and the long
Dogged perspective, difficult to choose
The half-forgotten painter's lost excuse:
A vanished poet crowned by the Duke for song.

Yours crownless, though he keep four hundred years
To be mocked so, will not be sorry if
Some of you keeps, grey eyes, your dulcet lust . .
So the old fiction fools us on, Hope steers
Rather us lickerish towards some hieroglyph
Than whelms us home, loinless and sleepy dust.

[39]

And does the old wound shudder open? Shall
I nurse again my days to a girl's sight,
Feeling the bandaged and unquiet night
Slide? Writhe in silly ecstasy? Banal
Greetings rehearse till a quotidian drawl
Carols a promise? Stoop an acolyte
Who stood my master? Must my blood flow bright,
Childish, I chilled and darkened? Strong pulse crawl?

I see I do, it must, trembling I see
Grace of her switching walk away from me
Fastens me where I stop now, smiling pain;
And neither pride don nor the fever shed
More, till the *furor* when we slide to bed,
Enter calenture for the boiling brain.

[40]

Marble nor monuments whereof then we spoke
We speak of more; spasmodic as the wasp
About my windowpane, our short songs rasp—
Not those alone before their singers choke—
Our sweetest; none hopes now with one smart stroke
Or whittling years to crack away the hasp
Across the ticking future; all our grasp
Cannot beyond the butt secure its smoke.

A Renaissance fashion, not to be recalled.
We dinch 'eternal numbers' and go out.
We understand exactly what we are.
. . Do we? Argent I craft you as the star
Of flower-shut evening: who stays on to doubt
I sang true? ganger with trobador and scald!

[41]

And Plough-month peters out . . its thermal power
Squandered in sighs and poems and hopeless thought,
Which corn and honey, wine, soap, wax, oil ought
Upon my farmling to have chivvied into flower.
I burn, not silly with remorse, in sour
Flat heat of the dying month I stretch out taut:
Twenty-four dawns the topaz woman wrought
To smile to me is gone. These days devour
Memory: what were you elbowed on your side?
Supine, your knee flexed? do I hear your words
Faint as a nixe, in our grove, saying farewells? . .
At five I get up sleepless to decide
What I will not today do; ride out: hear birds
Antiphonal at the dayspring, and nothing else.

[42]

The clots of age, grovel and palsy, crave
Mádmen: to gasp, unreasonably weep,
Gravid with ice, staving invincible sleep . .
Still as I watch this two tonight I waive
Half of my fear, envy sues even: grave,
Easy and light with juniors, he, and steep
In his honours she, belov'd, wholly they keep
Together, accustomed; hircine excitement gave
No joy so deep, and died . .   Fill my eyes with tears,
I stare down the intolerable years
To the mild survival—where, you are where, where?
'I *want* to take you for my lover' just
You vowed when on the way I met you: must
Then that be all (*Do*) the shorn time we share?

[43]

You should be gone in winter, that Nature mourn
With me your anarch separation, call-
ing warmth all with you: as more poetical
Than to be left biting the dog-days, lorn
Alone when all else burgeons, brides are born,
Children yet (some) begotten, every wall
Clasped by its vine here . . crony alcohol
Comfort as random as the unicorn.

Listen, for poets are feigned to lie, and I
For you a liar am a thousand times,
Scars of these months blazon like a decree:
I would have you—a liner pulls the sky—
Trust when I mumble me, Than gin-&-limes
You are cooler, darling, O come back to me.

[44]

Bell to sore knees vestigial crowds, let crush
One another nations sottish and a-prowl,
Talon the Norway rat to a barn owl
At wind-soft midnight; split the sleepy hush
With sirens; card-hells create; from a tower push
The frantic hesitator; strike a rowel
To a sad nag; probe, while they whiten & howl,
With rubber gloves the prisoners' genial slush;

Enact our hammer time; only from time
Twitch while the wind works my beloved and me
Once with indulgent tongs for a little free,—
Days, deer-fleet years, to be a paradigm
For runaways and the régime's exiles.
. . The wind lifts, soon, the cold wind reconciles.

[45]

Boy twenty-one, in Donne, shied like a blow,—
His prose, from poems' seductive dynamite,—
I read 'The adulterer waits for the twilight. . .
The twilight comes, and serves his turn.' (Not so:
Midnight or dawn.) I stuttered frightened 'No,
Nóne could decline, crookt, ghastly, from the sight
Of elected love and love's delicious rite
Upon the livid stranger Loves forego.'

. . I am this strange thing I despised; you are.
To become ourselves we are these wayward things.
And the lies at noon, months' tremblings, who foresaw?
And I did not foresee fraud of the Law
The scarecrow restraining like a man, its rings
Blank . . my love's eyes familiar as a scar!

[46]

Are we? You murmur 'not'. What of the night-
bulge on the North Way we could not contain,
Twice I slid to You sudden as the stain
Flushes the wanderer at the water's sight,
And back, but You writhed on Me . . as I write
I tremble . . trust me not to keep on sane
Until you whisper 'Come to me again'
Unless you whisper soon. O come we soon
Together dark and sack each other outright,
Doomed cities loose and thirsty as a dune . .
Lovers we are, whom now the on-tide licks.
Our fast of famed sleep stirs, darling, diurnal,—
Hurry! we (ah), beginning our eternal
Junket on the winds, wake like a ton of Styx.

Sonnets to Chris

[47]

How far upon these songs with my strict wrist
Hard to bear down, who knows? None is to read
But you: so gently . . but then truth's to heed,
The sole word, near or far, shot in the mist.

Double I sing, I must, your utraquist,
Crumpling a syntax at a sudden need,
Stridor of English softening to plead
O to you plainly lest you more resist.

'Arthur lay then at Caerlon upon Usk. . . .'
I see, and all that story swims back . . red
Satin over rushes . . Mother's voice at dusk.

So I comb times and men to cram you rare:
'Faire looketh *Ceres* with her yellow Haire'—
Fairer you far O here lie filteréd.

[48]

I've met your friend at last, your violent friend,
Laughter out of a hard life; and she cut,
Treating in talk one door really as shut
That should be shut, gashes will hardly mend.
'Here is Natasha' at the other end
Of telephones . . 'Heck, I feel wonderful! . . .'
And so do I when I am with her, but
I would she knew she lashed me where I bend.

And so do I when I am with her, only
Her 'they' and 'harmony' harry me lone and wild.
. . How she loves you! and then to disarrange,
Powerful chemist, all the years she's filed
With stubborn work, for the law! . . she means to change.
So do I mean,—less (when I rise up) lonely.

[49]

One note, a daisy, and a photograph,
To slake this siege of weeks without you, all.
Your dawn-eyed envoy, welcome as Seconal,
To call you faithful . . now this cenotaph,
A shabby mummy flower. Note I keep safe,
Nothing, on a ration slip a social scrawl—
Not that it didn't forth some pages call
Of my analysis, one grim paragraph.

The snapshot then—your eyes down, your hair bound:
Your power leashed, but too your blaze is dim . .
By the sea, thinking, long before we met;
Akimbo from your nape, what petrels round
(Out of the print) your unsuspicious slim
Dear figure, warning 'Dream of him
      now you not know whom you will not forget.'

[50]

They come too thick, hail-hard, and all beside
Smother, necessities of my nights and days,
My proper labour that my storm betrays
Weekly lamented, weakly flung aside;
What in the musical wind to work but glide
Among the wind, willing my eyes should daze
Fast on her image, for an exhaustless phrase,
While themes throng, the rapt world one & hers & wide.

They crowd on, crowning what I perforce complain
Remorseful in my journal of, and lest
Thick they fall thin, I beg the calm belongs,—
Traditional meditation. But when my rein
Fails most, still I race feeble to protest
These two months . . decades of excited songs.

Sonnets to Chris

[51]

A tongue there is wags, down in the dark wood O:
Trust it not. It trills malice among friends,
Irrelevant squibs, and lies, to its own ends
Or to no ends, simply because it would O.
To us, us most I hear, it prinks no good O;
Has its idea, Jamesian; apprehends
Truth non-aviarian; meddles, and 'defends'
Honour free . . that such a bill so wily should O!

Who to my hand all year flew to be fed
Makes up his doubts to dart at us . .   —Ah well,
Did you see the *green* of that catalpa tree?—
A certain puisne will lose half its head
For cheek, our keek, our hairy philomel.—
How can you tell?—A little bird told me.

[52]

A sullen brook hardly would satisfy
The Winter-traveller slumps near, Stony Brook;
Prattle of brooks it scorns, only in some crook
Fetches again and now a muddy sigh
Reaches me here.—A liner rocks the sky,
I shudder beneath the trees. I brought a book,
Shut on my brown knee. Once I rise and look
Under the bridge-arch. The third day of July.

Close, going back, I pass (still as a mouse)
The fatuous stranger in the stone strong home
Now you and my friend your husband are away.
And I must gnaw there somewhy. Double day:
In the end I race by cocky as a comb,
Adust . . *Da ist meiner Liebstens Haus.*

[53]

Some sketch sweat' out, unwilling swift & crude,
A hundred more like bats in swelter-day
A-lunge about my office, I'm away
Downstairs for coffee, and to rest, and brood.
. . The *mots* fly, and the flies mope on the food
Where all-age adolescents swig and bray,
An ice-cream-soda jag, the booths are gay . .
The ass-eyes after me unlid, protrude.

And I have fled an-crazy to my task
In the hotbox at the top of Upper Pyne
To work their children music! as ice cubes
Pleasing, colder keeping, more than they ask,
As worthy of them—not of you . .   No sign . .
Ermite-amateur in the midst of the boobs.

[54]

It was the sky all day I grew to and saw.
I cycled southeast through the empty towns,
Flags hanging out, between the summer grains,
Meeting mainly the azure minions of our law.

Near our fake lake an artificial pool
Was full of men and women; all the rest,
Shore for the Fourth. I crookt two roses. Most
I studied the sky's involuntary rule.

I followed a cloud and finally I caught it,
Sprinting my ribbon down the world of green . .
Shadow to shadow, under tropical day . .

Flat country, slow, alone. So in my pocket
Your snapshot nightmares where (cloth, flesh between)
My heart was, before I gave it away.

Sonnets to Chris

[55]

When I recall I could believe you'd go
I start. I can't believe you will come back.
Months on to Monday, and then Monday's rack
Uncertain up the sky unseen winds blow
Bringing what weather I cannot foreknow.
Still I see better in my almanac
Your coming, than in the columns white and black
My going later. All our plans outgrow
My local eyes, locked where somehow we draw
Somewhat together, wince to a single goad,
Each other steady . . steadily closer . . keep.
Closer: against the departures of our law
Let's Dido-like 'forge causes of abode' . .
Whom the sliding stars wheedle as one to sleep.

[56]

Sunderings and luxations, *luxe*, and grief-
unending exile from the original spouse,
Dog-fights! one bites intimate as a louse
The lousy other, Love the twitching leaf
Wide to the weather, hangover-long, jag-brief,
Nulliparous intensities, or as mouse
To cats the child to broken parents, house
Sold, books divided . . divorce as a relief . .

We discussed, drinking, one sad afternoon
In a Connecticut house in cloudy June,
Thinking, whoever was mentioned, still of others.
I thought of you,—come we too to this vile
Loose fagend? earlier *still* loves so defile? . .
Could *our* incredible marriage . . like all others' . . ?

[57]

Our love conducted as in tropic rain
Develops hair and lowers its head: the lash
And weight of rain breed, like the soundless slosh
Divers make round a wrack, régime, domain
Invisible, to us-inured invisible stain
Of all our process; also lightning flash
Limns us audacious, furtive, whom slow crash
On crash jolt like the mud- and storm-blind Wain.

If the rain ceased and the incredible sun
Shone out! . . whom our stars shake, could we emerge
Trustful and clear into the common rank,—
So long deceiving?—Days when Dathan sank
Quick to the pit not past, darling, we verge
Daily O there: have strange changes begun?

[58]

Sensible, coarse, and moral; in decent brown;
Its money doling to an orphanage;
Sober . . well-spirited but sober; sage
Plain nourishing life nor you nor I could down
I doubt, our blinkers lost, blood like a clown
Dancing upon a one-night hot-foot stage,
Brains in a high wind, high brains, the next page
Trembling,—the water's fine, come in and drown.

Since the corruption of the working classes
I am speaking of the Eighteenth Century: kisses
Opening on betrothals, love like a vise.
Where shawm and flute flutter the twilight, where
Conjugal, toothless, has a booth at the Fair,
The Reno brothels boom, suddenly we writhe.

Sonnets to Chris

[59]

Loves are the summer's. Summer like a bee
Sucks out our best, thigh-brushes, and is gone.
The yellow pollen upon the white winds blown
Settles. I feel the summer draining me,
I lean back breathless in an agony
Of charming loss I suffer without moan,
Without my love, or with my love alone.
She left me in the Spring, or I say we

Left, before there we bloomed, our secret garden!
The ghosts of breezes widowy small paths wander,
A fruitless bird pipes its surprising sorrow.
When will she, she come back? . . against whom I harden
My effortless ghost in vain, who moved asunder
Flowers at the come of summer beautiful and narrow.

[60]

Today is it? Is it today? I shudder
For nothing in my chair, and suddenly yawn.
Today I suddenly believe. Since dawn
When I creaked up, my muscles like a rudder
Strain crosswise from this work. I rise and mutter
Something, and hum, pace, and sit down again
Hard. A butterfly in my shoulder then
Stops and aches. My stomach swings like a shutter.

As the undergrounds piston a force of air
Before their crash into the station, you
Are felt before your coming, in the platform's shake.
So light, so small, so far still, to impair
So action and peace . . risks we take make true
Maybe our safeties . . *come*! for our risk's sake.

[61]

Languid the songs I wish I willed . . I try . .
Smooth songs untroubled like a silver spoon
To pour your creamy beauty back, warm croon
Blind, soft . . but I have something in my eye,
I see by fits, see what there, rapid and sly,
Difficult, so that it will be off soon,
I'd better *fix* it! frantic as a loon,
Smarting, world-churned, some convulsed song I cry.

Well . . (also I plead, I have something in mind,
My bobsled need, the need for me you'll find
If you look deeper: study our winter-scene) . .
Thinking is well, but worse still to be caught
The wholly beautiful just beyond thought,—
Small trees in mist far down an endless green!

[62]

Tyranny of your car—so far resembles
Beachwagons all, all with officious hope
Conscript my silly eyes—offers a trope
For your grand sway upon these months my shambles:
Your cleaver now to other women's brambles
I'll not contrast—no, all of you have scope,
Teeth breasts tongues thighs eyes hair: as rope to rope
You point to point compare, and the subject trembles.

What makes yóu then this ominous wide blade
I'd run from O unless I bleat to die?
Nothing: you are not: woman blonde, called Chris.
It is I lope to be your sheep, to wade
Thick in my cordial blood, to howl and sigh
As I decide . . if I could credit this.

Sonnets to Chris

[63]

Here too you came and sat a time once, drinking.
I could have cut their throats to be alone.
Yet all the hour I slumped here like a stone
My heart smiled, I smiled while my heart was sinking.
Happier than I seemed for their hoodwinking,
My smile was under . . over . . so was the moan
Arcane I kept out of the 'master' tone
Native to me I adopted . . my rabid thinking.

Juggler and cull! and places, words, call up
Inscrutable disturbance bound to you
Partout! partout some crowning or some crime;
As Julian spending a nickel, Win a dime,
Mazes of instant silence must pursue,—
Obsession's hypocrites, time's, their own dupe.

[64]

The dew is drying fast, a last drop glistens
White on a damaged leaf askew from me.
A pine-cone calmed here in a red-brown sea
Collects its straying forces now and listens:
A veery calls; south, a slow whistle loosens
My lone control. The flat sun finally
Flaws through the evergreen grove, and can be he—
If Chris comes—our renewed love lights and christens.

Tarry today? . . weeks the abandoned knoll
And I have waited. The needles are soft . . feel.
The village bell, or the college, tells me seven.
Much longer not sustains—will it again?—
Castaway time I scrabble tooth and nail,
I crush a cigarette black, and go down.

[65]

Once when they found me, some refrain *'Quoi faire?'*
Striking my hands, they say repeatedly
I muttered; although I could hear and see
I knew no one.—I am silent in my chair,
And stronger and more cold is my despair
At last, for I have come into a country
Whose vivid Queen upon no melody
Admits me. *Manchmal glaub ich, ich kann nicht mehr.*

Song follows song, the chatterer to the fire
Would follow soon . .   Deep in Ur's royal pits
Sit still the courtly bodies, a little bowl
By each, attired to voluntary blitz . .
In Shub-ad's grave the fingers of a girl
Were touching still, when they found her, the strings of her lyre.

[66]

Astronomies and slangs to find you, dear,
Star, art-breath, crowner, conscience! and to chart
For kids unborn your distal beauty, part
On part that startles, till you blaze more clear
And witching than your sister Venus here
To a late age can, though her senior start
Is my new insomnia,—swift sleepless art
To draw you even . . and to draw you near.

I prod our English: cough me up a word,
Slip me an epithet will justify
My daring fondle, fumble of far fire
Crackling nearby, unreasonable as a surd,
A flash of light, an insight: I am the shy
Vehicle of your cadmium shine . . your choir.

Sonnets to Chris

[67]

Faith like the warrior ant swarming, enslaving
Or griding others, you gave me soft as dew,
My darling, drawing me suddenly into you,
Your arms' strong kindness at my back, your weaving
Thighs agile to me, white teeth in your heaving
Hard, your face bright and dark, back, as we screw
Our lives together—twin convulsion—blue
Crests curl, to rest . . again the ivy waving.

Faiths other fall. Afterwards I kissed you
So (Chris) long, and your eyes so waxed, marine,
Wider I drowned . . light to their surface drawn
Down met the wild light (derelict weeks I missed you
Leave me forever) upstreaming; never-seen,
Your radiant glad soul surfaced in the dawn.

[68]

Where the lane from the highway swerves the first drops fell
Like lead, I bowed my head and drifted up.
Now in the grove they pat like footsteps, but
Not hers, Despair's. In slant lines sentinel
Silver and thin, it rains so into Hell,
Unvisited these thousand years. I grope
A little in the wind after a hope
For sun before she wakes . . all might be well.

All might yet be well . .   I wandered just
Down to the upper lane now, the sky was clearing,
And as I scrawl, the sun breaks. Ah, what use?
She said if rain, no,—in vain self-abuse
I lie a fairy will! cloud disappearing
Not lonelier, leaving like me: we must.

[69]

For you am I collared to quit my dear
My redhaired mild good and most beautiful
Most helpless and devoted wife? I pull
Crazy away from this; but too from her
Resistlessly I draw off, months have, far
And quarrelling—irrelation—numb and dull
Dead Sea with tiny aits . . Love at the full
Had wavered, seeing, foresuffering us here.

Unhappy all her lone strange life until
Somehow I friended it. And the Master catches
Me strongly from behind, and clucks, and tugs.
He has, has he? my heart-relucting will.
She spins on silent the great needle scratches.
—This all, Chris? and stark kisses, stealthy hugs?

[70]

October's both, back in the Sooner State
Where the thin winds worry the soul, we both were born;
And we have cast our origin, and the Horn
Neither (frankly) has scanted, others imitate
Us; and we have come a long way, late
For depth enough, betimes enough for torn
Hangnails of nerves and innocent love, we turn
Together in this vize lips, eyes, our Fate.

When the cam slid, the prodigious fingers tightened
And we began to fuse, weird afternoon
Early in May (the Third), we both were frightened,
A month we writhed, in sudden love like a scrimmage;
June's wide loss worse; the fortnight after June
Worst. Vize and woe worked us this perfect image!

Sonnets to Chris

[71]

Our Sunday morning when dawn-priests were applying
Wafer and wine to the human wound, we laid
Ourselves to cure ourselves down: I'm afraid
Our vestments wanted, but Francis' friends were crying
In the nave of pines, sun-satisfied, and flying
Subtle as angels about the barricade
Boughs made over us, deep in a bed half made
Needle-soft, half the sea of our simultaneous dying.

'Death is the mother of beauty.' Awry no leaf
Shivering with delight, we die to be well . .
Careless with sleepy love, so long unloving.
What if our convalescence must be brief
As we are, the matin meet the passing bell? . .
About our pines our sister, wind, is moving.

[72]

A Cambridge friend put in,—one whom I used
To pay small rope at chess to, who in vain
Luffed up to free a rook,—and through the strain
Of ten-year old talk cocktails partly loosed
I you forgot forgot forgot for the first
Hour in months of watches . . Mozart's pain
I heard then, in the cranny of the hurricane,
As since the chrisom caught me up immersed

I have heard nothing but the sough of the sea
And wide upon the open sea my friend
The sea-wind crying, out of its cave to roam
No more, no more . . until my memory
Swung you back like a lock: I sing the end,
Tolerant Aeolus to call me home.

[73]

Demand me again what Kafka's riddles mean,
For I am the penal colony's prime scribe:
From solitary, firing against the tribe
Uncanny judgments ancient and unclean.
I am the officer flat on my own machine,
Priest of the one Law no despair can bribe,
On whom the mort-prongs hover to inscribe
'I FELL IN LOVE' . .   O none of this foreseen,
Adulteries and divorces cold I judged
And strapped the tramps flat. Now the harrow trembles
Down, a strap snaps, I wave—out of control—
To you to change the legend has not budged
These years: make the machine grave on me (stumbles
Someone to latch the strap) 'I MET MY SOUL.'

[74]

All I did wrong, all the Grand Guignol years,
Tossed me here still able to touch you still.
I took the false turn on the fantastic hill
Continually, until the top appears.
Even my blind (last night) disordered tears
Muster me into morning. When I grew ill
In the South, I only taxed my doctors' skill
To pass me to you fixed . .   The damned sky clears
Into a decent sun (this week's the worst
Ever I see-saw) half an hour: this town
My tomb becomes a kind of paradise . .
How then complain? Rain came with a burst,
Ridding the sky. Was it this evil clown
Or surviving lover you called to you? . . *twice.*

18 July

Sonnets to Chris

[75]

Swarthy when young; who took the tonsure; sign,
His coronation, wangled, his name re-said
For euphony; off to courts fluttered, and fled;
Professorships refused; upon one line
Worked years; and then that genial concubine.
Seventy springs he read, and wrote, and read.
On the day of the year his people found him dead
I read his story. Anew I studied mine.

Also there was Laura and three-seventeen
Sonnets to something like her . . twenty-one years . .
He never touched her. Swirl our crimes and crimes.
Gold-haired (too), dark-eyed, ignorant of rimes
Was she? Virtuous? The old brume seldom clears.
—Two guilty and crepe-yellow months
    Chris! be our surviving actual scene.

[76]

The two plantations Greatgrandmother brought
My bearded General, back in a world would burn,
I thresh excited as I see return
Odd in this symbol you me last night taught . .
Your Two-fields rapt into the family ought
To save us: sensitivity, elegant, fern-
subtle, knit upon vigour enough to turn
A nation's strong decline. I grind my thought
A bit more, and I bare the quick of the have
And have not, half have, less than half, O this
Fantasy of your gates ajar, gates barred.
Poaching and rack-rent do you hope will save
True to ourselves *us*, darling? owners, Chris!—
Heiress whose lovely holdings lie
    too forkt for truth; called also Koblegaard.

[77]

Fall and rise of her midriff bells. I watch.
Blue knee-long shorts, striped light shirt. Bright between
Copt hills of the cushion a lazy green
Her sun-incomparable face I watch.
A darkness dreams adown her softest crotch,
A hand dreams on her breast, two fingers lean,
The ring shows like a wound. Her hair swirls clean
Alone in the vague room's morning-after botch.

Endymion's Glaucus through a thousand years
Collected the bodies of lovers lost, until
His own beloved's body rustled and sighed . .
So I would, O to spring—blotting her fears,
The others in this house, the house, road, hill—
As once she up the stair sprang to me, lips wide!

[78]

On the wheat-sacks sullen with the ceaseless damp,
Sidney and I sat hours and talked of you,
I talked of you. Potting porter. Just a few
Fireflies were out, no stars, no moon; no lamp.
The Great Dane licked my forearm like a stamp,
Surprisingly, in total darkness. Who
Responds with peaceful gestures, calm and new
This while, your home-strong love's ferocious tramp?

Insonorous and easy night! I lusk,
Until we rise and strike rake-handles in
The nervous sacks to prod and mix with air;
Lest a flame sing out invisible and brusk
About the black barn . .   Princeton (and my chin
Sank on the rake-end) suddenly
    I longed for sick, your toxic music there.

[79]

I dreamt he drove me back to the asylum
Straight after lunch; we stood then at one end,
A sort of cafeteria behind, my friend
Behind me, nuts in groups about the room;
A dumbwaiter with five shelves was waiting (some-
thing's missing here) to take me up—I bend
And lift a quart of milk to hide and tend,
Take with me. Everybody is watching, dumb.

I try to put it first among some worm-
shot volumes of the N. E. D. I had
On the top shelf—then somewhere else . . slowly
Chris comes up in a matron's uniform
And with a look (I saw once) infinitely sad
In her grey eyes takes it away from me.

[80]

Infallible symbolist!—Tanker driven ashore,
An oil-ship by a tropical hurricane
Wrecked on a Delaware beach, the postcard's scene;
On the reverse, words without signature:
Je m'en fiche du monde sans toi—in your
Hand for years busy in the liquid main
To tank you on—your Tulsa father's vein,
Oil. All the worked and wind-slapt waters roar.

O my dear I am sorry, sorry, and glad! and glad
To trope you helpless, there, and needing me,
Where the dangerous land meets the disordered sea . .
Rich on the edge we wait our salvage, sad
And joyous, nervous, that the hired men come
Whom we require, to scrap us single, strap us home.

[81]

Four oval shadows, paired, ringed each by sun,
The closer smaller pair behind, third pair
Beating symmetrical to the sides in air
Apparently—the water-spiders' dun
Bodies above unlike their shadows run,
Skim with six wires about a black-backed, fair-
bellied and long tube which does not appear
In the atomic drawings on the shallow mud.

My shadow on the vines and brook-sheet should—
If so it were as Gath in Babylon—
Show a lover's neurons waiting for a letter,
The complex patient, or man's fission's crack
Of comfortable doom. Wé do this better: . .
A four-square hypocrite squats there in black.

[82]

Why can't, Chris, why shouldn't *they* fall in love?
Mild both, both still in mix of studies, still
Unsteadied into life, novices of the will,
Formed upon others (us), disciples of
The Master and the revisionists: enough
Apart from their attraction, to unstill
The old calm loves (cyclonic loves) until
The electric air shocks them together, rough,
But better in love than grief, who can afford
No storms (ours). Fantasy! . . Forget.
—This pencil's leaving Pennsylvania's farms,
Seats 37, 12 Standees, I'm tired
Unspeakably of standing: Kiss me, and let—
Let me sit down and take you in my arms.

[83]

Impossible to speak to her, and worse
To keep on silent, silent hypocrite
Bound for my kindness or my lack of it
Solely to strength you crumple or you nurse
By not being or being with me. Curse
This kindness tricks her to think bit by bit
We *will* be more together . . better . . sit
The poor time out, and then the good rehearse—

When neither my fondness nor my pity can
O no more bend me to Eileen with love,
Gladden the sad eyes my lost eyes have seen
With such and so long ache, ah to unman.
When she calls, small, and grieving I must move,
The horror and beauty of your eyes burn between.

[84]

How shall I do, to pass the weary time
Of fading entertainments while you're gone?
Early I'll rise still, then from dawn to dawn
To meet you in our grove not once will climb.
Your fingers to my shoulder in some rime
I'll manage only, and your instep drawn
In the morning light remember only; on
Any dropt cue follow you off, and mime

My senseless presence in your presence not,
My comments rather skew—They'll say 'I wonder
What is ín Berryman lately? I find him stranger
Than usual'—working their nickel in the slot
They'll try again, dreamless they drag from yonder
Vexed to my leather chair this lathered ranger.

[85]

Spendthrift Urethra—Sphincter, frugal one—
Masters from darkness in your double sway
Whom favouring either all chaotic stray—
Adjust us to our love! . . *Unlust* undone,
Wave us together out of the running sun
Suddenly, and rapt from our shore-play,
My loss your consolation and protégé,
Down at a stroke whelmed, while the waters run.

O serious as our play, my nervous plea!
. . Hallucinatory return to the warm and real
Dark, still, happy apartment after the riot . .
Wounded, be well, and sleep sound as the sea
Vexed in wide night by no wind, but the wheel
Roils down to zero . . steady . . archaic quiet.

[86]

Our lives before hopelessly our mistake!—
We should have been together seething years,
We should have been the tomb-bat hangs and hears
Sounds inconceivable, been a new snowflake,
We should have been the senile world's one sake,
Vestigial lovers, tropical and fierce
Among fatigues and snows, the gangs and queers,
We should have been the bloom of a cockcrow lake.

. . A child's moon, child's fire!—What I love of you
Inter alia tingles like a whole good day,
A hard wind, or a Strad's consummate pluck,
Proficient, full and strong, shrewd as the blue
Profound sky, pale as a winter sky you lay
And with these breasts whiter than stars gave suck.

[87]

Is it possible, poor kids, you must not come out?
Care for you none but Chris, to whom you cry?
Here in my small book must you dance, then die?
Rain nor sun greet you first, no friendly shout?
If the army stands, moves not ahead one scout?
Sits all your army ever still, small fry?
And never to all your letters one reply?
No echo back, your games go on without?
Dignity under these conditions few
I feel might muster steadily, and you
Jitterbug more than you pavane, poor dears . .
Only you seem to want to hunt the whole
House through, scrutators of the difficult soul
Native here—and pomp's not for pioneers.

[88]

Anomalous I linger, and ignore
My blue conviction she will now not come
Whose grey eyes blur before me like some sum
A shifting riddle to fatigue . . I pore . .
Faster they flicker, and flag, moving on slower,
And I move with them—who am I? a scum
Thickens on a victim, a delirium
Begins to mutter, which I must explore.

O rapt as Monteverdi's '. . . *note . . . note . . .*'
I glide aroused—a rumour? or a dream?
An actual lover? Elmo's light? erlking?
—'I know very well who I am' said Don Quixote.
The sourceless lightning laps my stare, the stream
Backs through the wood, the cosy spiders cling.

[89]

'If long enough I sit here, she, she'll pass.'
This fatuous, and suffering-inversion,
And Donne-mimetic, O and true assertion
Tolls through my hypnagogic mind; alas
I hang upon this threshold of plate-glass,
Dry and dull eyes, in the same weird excursion
As from myself our love-months are, some Persian
Or Aztec supersession—the land mass
Extruded first from the archaic sea,
Whereon a desiccation, and species died
Except the one somehow learnt to breathe air:
Unless my lungs adapt me to despair,
I'll nod off into the increasing, wide,
Marvellous sleep my hopelets herald me.

[90]

For you an idyl, was it not, so far,
Flowing and inconvulsive pastoral,
I suddenly made out tonight as, all
The pallor of your face fled like a star,
It clenched and darkened in your avatar,
The goddess grounded. Lovers' griefs appal
Women, who with their honey brook their gall
And succor, as they can, the men they mar.

Down-soft my joy in the beginning, O
Dawn-disenchanted since, I hardly remember
The useful, urine-retentive years I sped.
—I said as little as I could, sick; know
Your strange heart works; wish us into September
Only alive, and lovers, and abed.

Sonnets to Chris

[91]

Itself a lightning-flash ripping the 'dark
Backward' of you-before, you harrowed me
How you and the wild boy (larcener-to-be)
Took horses out one night, full in the stark
Pre-storm midnight blackness, for a lark,
At seventeen, drunk, and you whipt them madly
About the gulph's rim, lightning-split, with glee
About, about. A decade: . . I embark.

How can we know with whom we ride, or soon
Or later, ever? You . . what are yóu like?
A topic's occupied me months, month's mind.
But I more startled may, than who shrank down
And wiped his sharp eyes with a helpless look,
The great tears falling, when Odysseus struck him, find.

[92]

What can to you this music wakes my years
(I whistle you a wistful specimen)
Become, to you affable and supple, when
The music they call music fills your ears?
How far? Alive to my animals' tears?
Haunted by cagy sighs? Or the cries of men
Versed are you in? . .   Your Tetragrammaton—
J.B., M·o, B·e, and F.S.—hears.

No quarrel here once! Pindar sang both sides,—
Two thousand years their easy marriage lasted,
Until some coldness grew . . deaf pride of art . .
Only one now to rile the other rides
Across sometimes: neither admits he's fasted,
They stare with desire, and spar . . and crib . . and part.

[93]

The man who made her let me climb the derrick
At nine (not far from—four—another child)
Produced this steady daring keeps us wild . .
I remember the wind wound on me like a lyric.
One resignation on to more, some cleric
Has told us, helms, would make the Devil mild
At last; one boldness so in the spirit filed
Brings boldness on—collective—atmospheric—

Character in the end, contented on a slope
Brakeless, a nervy ledge . . we overgrow
My derrick into midnights and high dawn,
The riot where I'm happy—still I hope
Sometime to dine with you, sometime to go
Sober to bed, a proper citizen.

[94]

Most strange, my change, this nervous interim.—
The utter courtship ended, tokens won,
Assurance salted down . . all this to stun
More than excite: I blink about me grim
And dull and anxious, rather than I skim
Light bright & confident: like a weak pun
I stumble neither way: Hope weighs a ton:
Tired certainly, but much less tired than dim.

—I wére absence' adept, a glaring eye;
Or I were agile to this joy, this letter,
You say from Spring Hill: 'I am not the same.'—
No more am I: I'm neither: without you I
Am not myself. My sight is dying. Better
The searchlights' torture which we overcame!

[95]

'Old Smoky' when you sing with Robin, Chris,
Sometimes at night, and your small voices hover
Mother-and-son but sourceless, O yours over
The hesitating treble must be his,
I glide about my metamorphosis
Gently, a tryst of troubled joy—discover
Our pine-grove grown a mountain—the *true* lover
Soft as a flower, hummingbird-piercing, is.

I saw him stretch out farther than a wish
And I have seen him gutted like a fish
At hipshot midnight for you, by your side.—
Last night there in your love-seat, you away,
I sang low to my niece your song, and stray
Still from myself into you singing slide.

[96]

It will seem strange, no more this range on range
Of opening hopes and happenings. Strange to be
One's *name* no longer. Not caught up, not free.
Strange, not to wish one's wishes onward. Strange,
The looseness, slopping, time and space estrange.
Strangest, and sad as a blind child, not to see
Ever you, never to hear you, endlessly
Neither you there, nor coming . .   Heavy change!—

An instant there is, Sophoclean, true,
When Oedipus must understand: his head—
When Oedipus *believes*!—tilts like a wave,
And will not break, only ἰοὺ ἰού
Wells from his dreadful mouth, the love he led:
Prolong to Procyon this. This begins my grave.

[97]

I say *I laid siege—you enchanted me* . .
Magic and warfare, faithful metaphors
As when their paleolithic woods and tors
The hunter and the witchwife roamed, half free,
Half to the Provider and the Mystery-
riddler bound: the kill, the spell: your languors
I wag my wolf's tail to—without remorse?—
You shudder as I'd pierce you where I knee

l . .   Only we little wished, or you to charm
Or I to make you shudder, you to wreck
Or I to hum you daring on my arm.
Abrupt as a dogfight, the air full of
Tails and teeth—the meshing of a trek—
All this began: knock-down-and-drag-out love.

[98]

Mallarmé siren upside down,—rootedly!
Dare the top crotch, the utmost two limbs plume
Cloudward, the bole swells just below . .   See, from
Her all these leaves and branches! . . world-green . . free
To be herself: firm-subtle-grey-brown barky,
A skin upon her gravest thought: to roam,
Sea-disinclined . . through the round stair I come,
A hollow. Board loose down near your rooftree.

. . I biked out leisurely one day because
My heart was breaking, and swung up with the casual
Passion of May again your sycamore . .
Hand trembling on the top, everything was
Beautiful, inhuman, green and real as usual.—
Your hypocrite hangs on the truth, sea-sore.

[99]

A murmuration of the shallow, Crane
Sees us, or so, twittering at nightfall
About the eaves, coloured and houseless soul,
Before the mucksweat rising of the Wain.
No black or white here; and our given brain
Troubles us incompletely; if we call
Sometimes to one another, if we fall
Sorry, we soon forget; wing'd, but in vain.

He fell in love once, when upon her *arms*
He concentrated what I call his faith . .
He died, and dropt into a German hole,
A generation or our culture's swarms
Accumulated honey for your wraith—
Does his wraith watch?—ash-blond and candid soul!

[100]

I am interested alone in making ready,
Pointed, more splendid, O the Action which
Attends your whim; bridge interim; enrich
That unimaginable-still, with study
So sharp at time the probe shivers back bloody;
Test the strange circuit but to trust the switch.
The Muse is real, the random shades I stitch—
Devoted vicarage—somewhere real, and steady.

Burnt cork, my leer, my Groucho crouch and rush,
No more my nature than Cyrano's: we
Are 'hindered characters' and mock the time,
The curving and incomprehensible hush
Einstein requires before that colloquy
Altared of joy concludes our pantomime!

[101]

Because I'd seen you not believe your lover,
Because you scouted cries come from no cliff,
Because to supplications you were stiff
As Ciro, O as Nero to discover
Slow how your subject loved you, I would hover
Between the slave and rebel—till this life
Arrives: '. . . was astonished as I would be if
I leaned against a house and the house fell over . . .'

Well, it fell over, over: trust him now:
A stronger house than looked—*you leaned*, and crash,
My walls and ceiling were to be walked on.—
The same thing happened once in Chaplin, how
He solved it now I lose.—Walk on the trash . .
Walk softly, triste,—little is really gone.

[102]

A penny, pity, for the runaway ass!
A nickel for the killer's twenty-six-mile ride!
Ice for the root rut-smouldering inside!
—Eight hundred weeks I have not run to Mass.—
Toss Jack a jawful of good August grass!
'Soul awful', pray for a soul sometimes has cried!
Wire reasons he seasons should still abide!
—Hide all your arms where he is bound to pass.—

Who drew me first aside? her I forgive,
Or him, as I would be forgotten by
O be forgiven for salt bites I took.
Who drew me off last, willy-nilly, live
On (darling) free. If we meet, know me by
Your own exempt (I pray) and earthly look.

Sonnets to Chris

[103]

A 'broken heart' . . but *can* a heart break, now?
Lovers have stood bareheaded in love's 'storm'
Three thousand years, changed by their mistress' 'charm',
Fitted their 'torment' to a passive bow,
Suffered the 'darts' under a knitted brow,
And has one heart *broken* for all this 'harm'?
An arm is something definite. My arm
Is acting—I hardly know to tell you how.

It aches . . well, after fifteen minutes of
Serving, I can't serve more, it's not my arm,
A piece of pain joined to me, helpless dumb thing.
After four months of work-destroying love
(An hour, I still don't lift it: I feel real alarm:
Weeks of this,—no doctor finds a thing),
        not much; and not all. Still, this is something.

[104]

A spot of poontang on a five-foot piece,
Diminutive, but room *enough* . . like clay
To finger eager on some torrid day . .
Who'd throw her black hair back, and hang, and tease.
Never, not once in all one's horny lease
To'have had a demi-lay, a pretty, gay,
Snug, slim and supple-breasted girl for play . .
She bats her big, warm eyes, and slides like grease.

And cuff her silly-hot again, mouth hot
And wet her small round writhing—but this screams
Suddenly awake, unreal as alkahest,
My god, this isn't what I *want!*—You tot
The harrow-days you hold me to, black dreams,
The dirty water to get off my chest.

[105]

Three, almost, now into the ass's years,
When hard on burden burden galls my back,
I carry corn feeds others, only crack
Cudgels, kicks on me, mountainous arrears
Worsen—avulse my fiery shirt!—The spheres
May sing with pain, I grieve knee-down, I slack
Deeper in evil . . love's demoniac
Jerquer, who frisked me, hops aside and jeers.

The dog's, and monkey's years—pot's residue,
Growling and toothless, giggling, grimacing—
I hope to miss. Who in my child could see
The adulter and bizarre of thirty-two?—
But I will seem more silent soon . . mire-king.
Time, time that damns, disvexes. Unman me.

[106]

Began with swirling, blind, unstilled oh still,—
The tide had set in toward the western door
And I was working with the tide, I bore
My panful of reflexion firm, until
A voice arrested me,—body, and will,
And panful, wheeled and spilt, tempted nerves tore,
And all uncome time blackened like the core
Of an apple on through man's heart moving still . .

At nine o'clock and thirty Thursday night,
In Nineteen Forty-seven, February
Twice-ten-day, by a doorway in McCosh,
So quietly neither the rip's cold slosh
Nor the meshing of great wheels warned me, unwary,
An enigmatic girl smiled out my sight.

[107]

Darling I wait O in my upstairs box
O for your footfall, O for your footfáll
in the extreme heat—I don't mind at all,
it's silence has me and the movement of clocks
keeping us isolated longer: rocks
did the first martyr and will do to stall
our enemies, I'll get up on the roof of the hall
and heave freely. The University of Soft Knocks

will headlines in the *Times* make: Fellow goes mad,
crowd panics, rhododendrons injured. Slow
will flow the obituaries while the facts get straight,
almost straight. He was in love and he was had.
That was it: he should have stuck to his own mate,
before he went a-conning across the sea-O.

[108]

I owe you, do I not, a roofer: though
My sister-*in*-law and her nephews stayed,
Not I stayed. O kind sister-outlaw, laid
Far off and legally four weeks, stoop low,
For my true thanks are fugitive also
Only to you;—stop off your cant, you jade,
Bend down,—*I* have not ever disobeyed
You; and you will hear what it is I owe.

I owe you thanks for evenings in your house
When . . neither here, nor there, nowhere, were you,
Nights like long knives; . . *two* letters! . . life like a mouse
Cheeseless, but trapt. Another debit to
Your kinder husband. From the country of Choice
Another province chopt,—and they were few.

[109]

Ménage à trois, like Tristan's,—difficult! . .
The convalescent Count; his mistress; fast
The wiry wild arthritic young fantast
In love with her, his genius occult,
His weakness blazing, ugly, an insult
A salutation; in his yacht they assed
Up and down the whole coast six months . . last
It couldn't: . . the pair to Paris. Chaos, result.

Well—but four worse!! . . all four, marvellous friends—
Some horse-shit here, eh?—You admitted it,
Come, you did once . . and we *are friends*, I say.—
'La Cuchiani aima Tristan, mais . . .'
(The biographer says) *unscrupulous* a bit,
Or utterly . . There, of course, the resemblance ends.

[110]

'Ring us up when you want to see us . . .'—'Sure',
Said Moses to the SS woman, smil-
ing hopeless Moses.—Put her whip and file
Away and walked away, strip-murderer,
A svelte Chris, whistling . . Knowing, it's all *your*
(Alas) initiation: *you* I can't: while
We are relationless, 'us'?—Hail, chat: cant, heil!—
Hypocrite-perfect! hoping *I* endure.

A winter-shore is forming in my eye,
The widest river: down to it we dash,
In love, but I am naked, and shake; so,
Uncoloured-thick-oil clad, you nod and cry
'Let's go!' . . white fuzzless limbs you razor flash,
And I am to follow the way you go.

27 August

Sonnets to Chris

[111]

Christian to Try: 'I am so coxed in it,
All I can do is pull, pull without shame,
Backwards,—on the coxswain fall the fiery blame,
I slump free and exhausted.'—'Stop a bit,'
Try studied his sloe gin, 'if you must fit
A trope so, you must hope to quit the game'
Pursued my brown friend with the plausible name
'Before your heart enlarging mucks you. Minute
By minute you pull faster.'—But I too
Am named, though lost . . you learn God's will, give in,
After, and whatever, you sit on, you sit.
Try 'Quit' said 'and be free.' I freeze to you
And I am free now of the fire of this sin
I choose . . I lose, yes . . but then I submit!

[112]

I break my pace now for a sonic boom,
the future's with & in us. I sit fired
but comes on strong with the fire fatigue: I'm tired.
'I'd drive my car across the living-room
if I could get it inside the house.' You loom
less, less than before when your voice choired
into my transept hear I now it, not expired
but half-dead with exhaustion, like Mr Bloom.

Dazzle, before I abandon you, my eyes,
my eyes which I need for journeys difficult
in which case it may be said that I survive you.
Your voice continues, with its lows & highs,
and I am a willing accomplice in the cult
and every word that I   have gasped of you is true.

[113]

'I didn't see anyone else, I just saw Lies'
Anne Frank remorseful from the grave: ah well,
it was a vision of her mother in Hell,
a payment beforehand for rebellion's seize,
whereby she grew up: springing from her knees
she saw her parents level. I ward your spell
away, and I try hard to look at you level
but that is quite unaccustomed to me, Lise.

Months I lookt up, entranced by you up there
like a Goya ceiling which will not come down,
in swirling clouds, until the end is here.
Tetélestai. We steamed in a freighter from Spain
& I will never see those frescoes again
nor need to, having memorized your cloudy gown.

[114]

You come blonde visiting through the black air
knocking on my hinged lawn-level window
and you will come for years, above, below,
& through to interrupt my study where
I'm sweating it out like asterisks: so there,—
you are the text, my work's broken down so
I found, after my grandmother died, slow,
and I had flown far South to her funeral spare

but crowded with relations, I found her last
letter unopened, much less answered: shame
overcame me so far I paused & cried
in my underground study, for all the past
undone & never again to walk tall, lame
at the mercy of your presence to abide.

Sonnets to Chris

[115]

As usual I'm up before the sun
begins to warm this intolerable place
and I have stared all night upon your face
but am not wiser thereby. Everyone
rattles his weakness or his thing undone,
I shake you like a rat. Open disgrace
yawns all before me: have I left a trace,
a spoor? Clouding it over, I look for my gun.

She's hidden it. I won't sing on of that.
Whiskey is bracing. Failures are my speed,
I thrive on ends, the dog is at the door
in heat, the neighbourhood is male except one cat
and they thresh on my stoop. Prevent my need,
Someone, and come & find me on the floor.

[116]

Outlaws claw mostly to a riddled end,
the close of their stories known. The cause of our story
which led us up from Hell to Purgatory,
then again downwards, has been fully penned
and stands mysterious: what lawyer will defend
there hopeless lovers with their eyes set on glory
for whom one tryst a week is satisfactory
but we can't have that, merely. Shall I let it depend

on the weather & her moods, my waking up,
my cycling speed? or let it all go smash
in a welter of despair & suicides?
I stand off. I will the matter to a stop.
After the brightness, on Monday night the trash.
I am a savant of the problem on both sides.

All we were going strong last night this time,
the *mots* were flying & the frozen daiquiris
were downing, supine on the floor lay Lise
listening to Schubert grievous & sublime,
my head was frantic with a following rime:
it was a good evening, an evening to please,
I kissed her in the kitchen—ecstasies—
among so much good we tamped down the crime.

The weather's changing. This morning was cold,
as I made for the grove, without expectation,
some hundred Sonnets in my pocket, old,
to read her if she came. Presently the sun
yellowed the pines & my lady came not
in blue jeans & a sweater. I sat down & wrote.

Judges xvi.22

Sonnets to Chris

HOMAGE TO MISTRESS BRADSTREET

[1 9 5 3]

*[Born 1612 Anne Dudley, married at 16
Simon Bradstreet, a Cambridge man,
steward to the Countess of Warwick &
protégé of her father Thomas Dudley
secretary to the Earl of Lincoln.
Crossed in the Arbella, 1630, under
Governor Winthrop.]*

[1]

The Governor your husband lived so long
moved you not, restless, waiting for him? Still,
you were a patient woman.—
I seem to see you pause here still:
Sylvester, Quarles, in moments odd you pored
before a fire at, bright eyes on the Lord,
all the children still.
'Simon . . .' Simon will listen while you read a Song.

[2]

Outside the New World winters in grand dark
white air lashing high thro' the virgin stands
foxes down foxholes sigh,
surely the English heart quails, stunned.
I doubt if Simon than this blast, that sea,
spares from his rigour for your poetry
more. We are on each other's hands
who care. Both of our worlds unhanded us. Lie stark,

[3]

thy eyes look to me mild. Out of maize & air
your body's made, and moves. I summon, see,
from the centuries it.
I think you won't stay. How do we
linger, diminished, in our lovers' air,
implausibly visible, to whom, a year,
years, over interims; or not;
to a long stranger; or not; shimmer & disappear.

[4]

Jaw-ript, rot with its wisdom, rending then;
then not. When the mouth dies, who misses you?
Your master never died,
Simon ah thirty years past you—
Pockmarkt & westward staring on a haggard deck
it seems I find you, young. I come to check,
I come to stay with you,
and the Governor, & Father, & Simon, & the huddled men.

Homage to Mistress Bradstreet

[5]

By the week we landed we were, most, used up.
Strange ships across us, after a fortnight's winds
unfavouring, frightened us;
bone-sad cold, sleet, scurvy; so were ill
many as one day we could have no sermons;
broils, quelled; a fatherless child unkennelled; vermin
crowding & waiting: waiting.
And the day itself he leapt ashore young Henry Winthrop

[6]

(delivered from the waves; because he found
off their wigwams, sharp-eyed, a lone canoe
across a tidal river,
that water glittered fair & blue
& narrow, none of the other men could swim
and the plantation's prime theft up to him,
shouldered on a glad day
hard on the glorious feasting of thanksgiving) drowned.

[7]

How long with nothing in the ruinous heat,
clams & acorns stomaching, distinction perishing,
at which my heart rose,
with brackish water, we would sing.
When whispers knew the Governor's last bread
was browning in his oven, we were discourag'd.
The Lady Arbella dying—
dyings—at which my heart   rose, but I did submit.

[8]

That beyond the Atlantic wound our woes enlarge
is hard, hard that starvation burnishes our fear,
but I do gloss for You.
Strangers & pilgrims fare we here,
declaring we seek a City. Shall we be deceived?
I know whom I have trusted, & whom I have believed,
and that he is able to
keep   that I have committed to his charge.

[9]

Winter than summer worse, that first, like a file
on a quick, or the poison suck of a thrilled tooth;
and still we may unpack.
Wolves & storms among, uncouth
board-pieces, boxes, barrels vanish, grow
houses, rise. Motes that hop in sunlight slow
indoors, and I am Ruth
away: open my mouth, my eyes wet: I wóuld smile:

[10]

vellum I palm, and dream. Their forest dies
to greensward, privets, elms & towers, whence
a nightingale is throbbing.
Women sleep sound. I was happy once . .
(Something keeps on not happening; I shrink?)
These minutes all their passions & powers sink
and I am not one chance
for an unknown cry or a flicker of unknown eyes.

[11]

Chapped souls ours, by the day Spring's strong winds swelled,
Jack's pulpits arched, more glad. The shawl I pinned
flaps like a shooting soul
might in such weather Heaven send.
Succumbing half, in spirit, to a salmon sash
I prod the nerveless novel succotash—
I must be disciplined,
in arms, against that one, and our dissidents, and myself.

[12]

Versing, I shroud among the dynasties;
quaternion on quaternion, tireless I phrase
anything past, dead, far,
sacred, for a barbarous place.
—To please your wintry father? all this bald
abstract didactic rime I read appalled
harassed for your fame
mistress neither of fiery nor velvet verse, on your knees

[13]

hopeful & shamefast, chaste, laborious, odd,
whom the sea tore. —The damned roar with loss,
so they hug & are mean
with themselves, and I cannot be thus.
Why then do I repine, sick, bad, to long
after what must not be? I lie wrong
once more. For at fourteen
I found my heart more carnal and sitting loose from God,

[14]

vanity & the follies of youth took hold of me;
then the pox blasted, when the Lord returned.
That year for my sorry face
so-much-older Simon burned,
so Father smiled, with love. Their will be done.
He to me ill lingeringly, learning to shun
a bliss, a lightning blood
vouchsafed, what did seem life. I kissed his Mystery.

[15]

Drydust in God's eye the aquavivid skin
of Simon snoring lit with fountaining dawn
when my eyes unlid, sad.
John Cotton shines on Boston's sin—
I ám drawn, in pieties that seem
the weary drizzle of an unremembered dream.
Women have gone mad
at twenty-one. Ambition mines, atrocious, in.

[16]

Food endless, people few, all to be done.
As pippins roast, the question of the wolves
turns & turns.
Fangs of a wolf will keep, the neck
round of a child, that child brave. I remember who
in meeting smiled & was punisht, and I know who
whispered & was stockt.
We lead a thoughtful life. But Boston's cage we shun.

[136

[17]

The winters close, Springs open, no child stirs
under my withering heart, O seasoned heart
God grudged his aid.
All things else soil like a shirt.
Simon is much away. My executive stales.
The town came through for the cartway by the pales,
but my patience is short.
I revolt from, I am like, these savage foresters

[18]

whose passionless dicker in the shade, whose glance
impassive & scant, belie their murderous cries
when quarry seems to show.
Again I must have been wrong, twice.
Unwell in a new way. Can that begin?
God brandishes. O love, O I love. Kin,
gather. My world is strange
and merciful, ingrown months, blessing a swelling trance.

[19]

So squeezed, wince you I scream? I love you & hate
off with you. Ages! *Useless.* Below my waist
he has me in Hell's vise.
Stalling. He let go. Come back: brace
me somewhere. No. No. Yes! everything down
hardens I press with horrible joy down
my back cracks like a wrist
shame I am voiding oh behind it is too late

[20]

hide me forever I work thrust I must free
now I all muscles & bones concentrate
what is living from dying?
Simon I must leave you so untidy
Monster you are killing me Be sure
I'll have you later Women do endure
I can *can* no longer
and it passes the wretched trap whelming and I am me

Homage to Mistress Bradstreet

[21]

drencht & powerful, I did it with my body!
One proud tug greens Heaven. Marvellous,
unforbidding Majesty.
Swell, imperious bells. I fly.
Mountainous, woman not breaks and will bend:
sways God nearby: anguish comes to an end.
Blossomed Sarah, and I
blossom. Is that thing alive? I hear a famisht howl.

[22]

Beloved household, I am Simon's wife,
and the mother of Samuel—whom greedy yet I miss
out of his kicking place.
More in some ways I feel at a loss,
freer. Cantabanks & mummers, nears
longing for you. Our chopping scores my ears,
our costume bores my eyes.
St. George to the good sword, rise! chop-logic's rife

[23]

& fever & Satan & Satan's ancient fere.
Pioneering is not feeling well,
not Indians, beasts.
Not all their riddling can forestall
one leaving. Sam, your uncle has had to
go fróm us to live with God. 'Then Aunt went too?'
Dear, she does wait still.
Stricken: 'Oh. Then he takes   us one by one.' My dear.

[24]

Forswearing it otherwise, they starch their minds.
Folkmoots, & blether, blether. John Cotton rakes
to the synod of Cambridge.
Down from my body my legs flow,
out from it arms wave, on it my head shakes.
Now Mistress Hutchinson rings forth a call—
should she? many creep out at a broken wall—
affirming the Holy Ghost
dwells in one justified. Factioning passion blinds

[25]

all to all her good, all—can she be exiled?
Bitter sister, victim! I miss you.
—I miss you, Anne,
day or night weak as a child,
tender & empty, doomed, quick to no tryst.
—I hear you. Be kind, you who leaguer
my image in the mist.
—Be kind you, to one unchained eager far & wild

[26]

and if, O my love, my heart is breaking, please
neglect my cries and I will spare you. Deep
in Time's grave, Love's, you lie still.
Lie still. —Now? That happy shape
my forehead had under my most long, rare,
ravendark, hidden, soft bodiless hair
you award me still.
You must not love me, but   I do not bid you cease.

[27]

Veiled my eyes, attending. How can it be I?
Moist, with parted lips, I listen, wicked.
I shake in the morning & retch.
Brood I do on myself naked.
A fading world I dust, with fingers new.
—I have earned the right to be alone with you.
—What right can that be?
Convulsing, if you love, enough, like a sweet lie.

[28]

Not that, I know, you can. This cratered skin,
like the crabs & shells of my Palissy ewer, touch!
Oh, you do, you do?
Falls on me what I like a witch,
for lawless holds, annihilations of law
which Time and he and man abhor, foresaw:
sharper than what my Friend
brought me for my revolt when I moved smooth & thin,

Homage to Mistress Bradstreet

[29]

faintings black, rigour, chilling, brown
parching, back, brain burning, the grey pocks
itch, a manic stench
of pustules snapping, pain floods the palm,
sleepless, or a red shaft with a dreadful start
rides at the chapel, like a slipping heart.
My soul strains in one qualm
ah but *this* is not to save me but to throw me down.

[30]

And out of this I lull. It lessens. Kiss me.
That once. As sings out up in sparkling dark
a trail of a star & dies,
while the breath flutters, sounding, mark,
so shorn ought such caresses to us be
who, deserving nothing, flush and flee
the darkness of that light,
a lurching frozen from a warm dream. Talk to me.

[31]

—It is Spring's New England. Pussy willows wedge
up in the wet. Milky crestings, fringed
yellow, in heaven, eyed
by the melting hand-in-hand or mere
desirers single, heavy-footed, rapt,
make surge poor human hearts. Venus is trapt—
the hefty pike shifts, sheer—
in Orion blazing. Warblings, odours, nudge to an edge—

[32]

—Ravishing, ha, what crouches outside ought,
flamboyant, ill, angelic. Often, now,
I am afraid of you.
I am a sobersides; I know.
I *want* to take you for my lover. —Do.
—I hear a madness. Harmless I to you
am not, not I? —No.
—I cannot but be. Sing a concord of our thought.

[33]

—Wan dolls in indigo on gold: refrain
my western lust. I am drowning in this past.
I lose sight of you
who mistress me from air. Unbraced
in delirium of the grand depths, giving away
haunters what kept me, I breathe solid spray.
—I am losing you!
Straiten me on. —I suffered living like a stain:

[34]

I trundle the bodies, on the iron bars,
over that fire backward & forth; they burn;
bits fall. I wonder if
I killed them. Women serve my turn.
—Dreams! You are good. —No. —Dense with hardihood
the wicked are dislodged, and lodged the good.
In green space we are safe.
God awaits us (but I   am yielding) who Hell wars.

[35]

—I cannot feel myself God waits. He flies
nearer a kindly world; or he is flown.
One Saturday's rescue
won't show. Man is entirely alone
may be. I am a man of griefs & fits
trying to be my friend. And the brown smock splits,
down the pale flesh a gash
broadens and Time holds up your heart against my eyes.

[36]

—Hard and divided heaven! creases me. Shame
is failing. My breath is scented, and I throw
hostile glances towards God.
Crumpling plunge of a pestle, bray:
sin cross & opposite, wherein I survive
nightmares of Eden. Reaches foul & live
he for me, this soul
to crunch, a minute tangle of eternal flame.

[37]

I fear Hell's hammer-wind. But fear does wane.
Death's blossoms grain my hair; I cannot live.
A black joy clashes
joy, in twilight. The Devil said
'I will deal toward her softly, and her enchanting cries
will fool the horns of Adam.' Father of lies,
a male great pestle smashes
small women swarming towards the mortar's rim in vain.

[38]

I see the cruel spread Wings black with saints!
Silky my breasts not his, mine, mine, to withhold
or tender, tender.
I am sifting, nervous, and bold.
The light is changing. Surrender this loveliness
you cannot make me do. *But* I will. Yes.
What horror, down stormy air,
warps towards me? My threatening promise faints—

[39]

torture me, Father, lest not I be thine!
Tribunal terrible & pure, my God,
mercy for him and me.
Faces half-fanged, Christ drives abroad,
and though the crop hopes, Jane is so slipshod
I cry. Evil dissolves, & love, like foam;
that love. Prattle of children powers me home,
my heart claps like the swan's
under a frenzy of *who* love me & who shine.

[40]

As a canoe slides by on one strong stroke
hope his hélp not I, who do hardly bear
his gift still. But whisper
I am not utterly. I pare
an apple for my pipsqueak Mercy and
she runs & all need naked apples, fanned
their tinier envies.
Vomitings, trots, rashes. Can be hope a cloak?

[41]

for the man with cropt ears glares. My fingers tighten
my skirt. I pass. Alas! I pity all.
Shy, shy, with mé, Dorothy.
Moonrise, and frightening hoots. 'Mother,
how *long* will I be dead?' Our friend the owl
vanishes, darling, but your homing soul
retires on Heaven, Mercy:
not we one instant die, only our dark does lighten.

[42]

When by me in the dusk my child sits down
I am myself. Simon, if it's that loose,
let me wiggle it out.
You'll get a bigger one there, & bite.
How they loft, how their sizes delight and grate.
The proportioned, spiritless poems accumulate.
And they publish them
away in brutish London, for a hollow crown.

[43]

Father is not himself. He keeps his bed,
and threw a saffron scum Thursday. God-forsaken words
escaped him raving. Save,
Lord, thy servant zealous & just.
Sam he saw back from Harvard. He did scold
his secting enemies. His stomach is cold
while we drip, while
my baby John breaks out. O far from where he bred!

[44]

Bone of moaning: sung Where he has gone
a thousand summers by truth-hallowed souls;
be still. Agh, he is gone!
Where? I know. Beyond the shoal.
Still-all a Christian daughter grinds her teeth
a little. This our land has ghosted with
our dead: I am at home.
Finish, Lord, in me this work thou hast begun.

Homage to Mistress Bradstreet

[45]

And they tower, whom the pear-tree lured
to let them fall, fierce mornings they reclined
down the brook-bank to the east
fishing for shiners with a crookt pin,
wading, dams massing, well, and Sam's to be
a doctor in Boston. After the divisive sea,
and death's first feast,
and the galled effort on the wilderness endured,

[46]

Arminians, and the King bore against us;
of an 'inward light' we hear with horror.
Whose fan is in his hand
and he will throughly purge his floor,
come towards mé. I have what licks the joints
and bites the heart, which winter more appoints.
Iller I, oftener.
Hard at the outset; in the ending thus hard, thus?

[47]

Sacred & unutterable Mind
flashing thorough the universe one thought,
I do wait without peace.
In the article of death I budge.
Eat my sore breath, Black Angel. Let me die.
Body a-drain, when will you be dry
and countenance my speed
to Heaven's springs? lest stricter writhings have me declined.

[48]

'What are those pictures in the air at night,
Mother?' Mercy did ask. Space charged with faces
day & night! I place
a goatskin's fetor, and sweat: fold me
in savoury arms. Something is shaking, wrong.
He smells the musket and lifts it. It is long.
It points at my heart.
Missed he must have. In the gross storm of sunlight

[49]

I sniff a fire burning without outlet,
consuming acrid its own smoke. It's me.
Ruined laughter sounds
outside. Ah but I waken, free.
And so I am about again. I hagged
a fury at the short maid, whom tongues tagged,
and I am sorry. Once
less I was anxious when more passioned to upset

[50]

the mansion & the garden & the beauty of God.
Insectile unreflective busyness
blunts & does amend.
Hangnails, piles, fibs, life's also.
But we are that from which draws back a thumb.
The seasons stream and, somehow, I am become
an old woman. It's so:
I look. I bear to look. Strokes once more his rod.

[51]

My window gives on the graves, in our great new house
(how many burned?) upstairs, among the elms.
I lie, & endure, & wonder.
A haze slips sometimes over my dreams
and holiness on horses' bells shall stand.
Wandering pacemaker, unsteadying friend,
in a redskin calm I wait:
beat when you will our end. Sinkings & droopings drowse.

[52]

They say thro' the fading winter Dorothy fails,
my second, who than I bore one more, nine;
and I see her inearthed. I linger.
Seaborn she wed knelt before Simon;
Simon I, and linger. Black-yellow seething, vast
it lies fróm me, mine: all they look aghast.
It will be a glorious arm.
Docile I watch. My wreckt chest hurts when Simon pales.

Homage to Mistress Bradstreet

[53]

In the yellowing days your faces wholly fail,
at Fall's onset. Solemn voices fade.
I feel no coverlet.
Light notes leap, a beckon, swaying
the tilted, sickening ear within. I'll—I'll—
I am closed & coming. Somewhere! I defile
wide as a cloud, in a cloud,
unfit, desirous, glad—even the singings veil—

[54]

—You are not ready? You áre ready. Pass,
as shadow gathers shadow in the welling night.
Fireflies of childhood torch
you down. We commit our sister down.
One candle mourn by, which a lover gave,
the use's edge and order of her grave.
Quiet? Moisture shoots.
Hungry throngs collect. They sword into the carcass.

[55]

Headstones stagger under great draughts of time
after heads pass out, and their world must reel
speechless, blind in the end
about its chilling star: thrift tuft,
whin cushion—nothing. Already with the wounded flying
dark air fills, I am a closet of secrets dying,
races murder, foxholes hold men,
reactor piles wage slow upon the wet brain rime.

[56]

I must pretend to leave you. Only you draw off
a benevolent phantom. I say you seem to me
drowned towns off England,
featureless as those myriads
who what bequeathed save fire-ash, fossils, burled
in the open river-drifts of the Old World?
Simon lived on for years.
I renounce not even ragged glances, small teeth, nothing,

[57]

O all your ages at the mercy of my loves
together lie at once, forever or
so long as I happen.
In the rain of pain & departure, still
Love has no body and presides the sun,
and elfs from silence melody. I run.
Hover, utter, still,
a sourcing   whom my lost candle like the firefly loves.

NOTES

Stanzas

1–4 The poem is about the woman but this exordium is spoken by the poet, his voice modulating in stanza 4, line 8 [4.8] into hers.

1.1 He was not Governor until after her death.

1.5 Sylvester (the translator of Du Bartas) and Quarles, her favourite poets; unfortunately.

5.4,5 Many details are from quotations in Helen Campbell's biography, the Winthrop papers, narratives, town histories.

8.4ff. Scriptural passages are sometimes ones she used herself, as this in her *Meditation liii*.

11.8 *that one*: the Old One.

12.5–13.2 The poet interrupts.

18.8 Her first child was not born until about 1633.

22.6 *chopping*: disputing, snapping, haggling; axing.

23.1 *fere*: his friend Death.

24.1 Her irony of 22.8 intensifies.

24.2 *rakes*: inclines, as a mast; bows.

25.3 One might say: He is enabled to speak, at last, in the fortune of an echo of her— and when she is loneliest (her former spiritual adviser having deserted Anne Hutchinson, and this her closest friend banished), as if she had summoned him; and only thus, perhaps, is she enabled to hear him. This second section of the poem is a dialogue, his voice however ceasing well before it ends at 39.4, and hers continuing for the whole third part, until the coda (54–57).

29.1–4 Cf. Isa. 1:5.

29.5,6 After a Klee.

33.1 Cf., on Byzantine icons, Frederick Rolfe ('Baron Corvo'): 'Who ever dreams of praying (with expectation of response) for the prayer of a Tintoretto or a Titian, or a Bellini, or a Botticelli? But who can refrain from crying "O Mother!" to these unruffleable wan dolls in indigo on gold?' (quoted from *The Desire and Pursuit of the Whole* by Graham Greene in *The Lost Childhood*).

Homage to Mistress Bradstreet

33.5,6 'Délires des grandes profondeurs,' described by Cousteau and others; a euphoria, sometimes fatal, in which the hallucinated diver offers passing fish his line, helmet, anything.

35.3,4 As of cliffhangers, movie serials wherein each week's episode ends with a train bearing down on the strapped heroine or with the hero dangling over an abyss into which Indians above him peer with satisfaction before they hatchet the rope. *rescue*: forcible recovery (by the owner) of goods distrained.

37.7,8 After an engraving somewhere in Fuchs's collections. *Bray*, above (36.4), puns.

39.5 The stanza is unsettled, like 24, by a middle line, signaling a broad transition.

42.8 *brutish*: her epithet for London in a kindly passage about the Great Fire.

46.1,2 Arminians, rebels against the doctrine of unconditional election. Her husband alone opposed the law condemning Quakers to death.

46.3,4 Matthew 3:12.

46.5,6 Rheumatic fever, after a celebrated French description.

48.2ff. *Space . . . outside*: delirium.

51.5 Cf. Zech. 14:20.

51.6 *Wandering pacemaker*: a disease of the heart, here the heart itself.

52.4 Seaborn Cotton, John's eldest son; Bradstreet being then magistrate.

52.5,6 Dropsical, a complication of the last three years. Line 7 she actually said.

55.4 *thrift*: the plant, also called Our Lady's cushion.

55.8 *wet brain*: edema.

56.5,6 Cf. G. R. Levy, *The Gate of Horn*, p. 5.

HIS THOUGHT MADE POCKETS & THE PLANE BUCKT

[1 9 5 8]

Henry sats in de plane & was gay.
Careful Henry nothing said aloud
but where a virgin out of cloud
to her Mountain dropt in light
his thought made pockets & the plane buckt.
'Parm me, Lady.' 'Orright.'

Venice, 182-

White & blue my breathing lady leans
across me in the first light, so we kiss.
The corners of her eyes are white. I miss,
renew. She means
to smother me thro' years of this.

Hell chill young widows in the heel of night—
perduring loves, melody's thrusting, press
flush with the soft skin, whence they sprung! back. Less
ecstasy might
save us for speech & politeness.

I hear her howl now, and I slam my eyes
against the glowing face. Foul morning-cheese
stands fair compared to love. On waspish knees
our pasts surprise
and plead us livid. Now she frees

a heavy lock was pulling . . I kiss it,
lifting my hopeless lids—and all trace
of passion's vanisht from her eyes & face,
the lip I bit
is bluer, a blackhead at the base

of her smooth nose looks sullenly at me,
we look at each other in entire despair,
her eyes are swimming by mine, and I swear
sobbing quickly
we áre in love. The light hurts. 'There . . . '

Scots Poem

Loversgrove lay
off to the lighthearted south,
chat-south, miles & more miles. Weel,
mot-tive flunks a man's mouth seems full of teeth.

His Thought Made Pockets & the Plane Buckt

Peered at her long
sidewise and would not or could
not say Love will be leaping
hopeless forever, hard on one who stood

near to her long
till she lookt poorly and died.
Braird in the breast evergreen,
grey the fieldgrass though, man's friend. I'm inside.—

—Trumpet shall sound,
angel & archangel cry
'Come forth, Isobel Mitchel,
and meet William Matheson in the sky.'

The Mysteries

(a crazed man calls)

And now you be my guest.
Thinking like wings, solemn with moons & truth,
I accost you on a summit of your honour
Erich Kahler for you shoot like a tooth
Where you grill, if others glare in wonder,
You too have to come out

And now you be my guest.
At the trice of harvest to a middle ground
I ascend and seek the hollow of my tree
Central in a grove and call: cherry sound
Swelling through swart night, near the sea, near sea,
Men aye did charm abroad

And now you be my guest
For peace to peace will not assuage or answer
My goddess at the Cross-ways. Crown the gong!
Rears the first fox, and ducks, and is a dancer!
The stonechat clatters in the bracken! Song
Through flutes shrugs up from bronze

And now you be my guest.
In the sea-green blindness I found Thetis kind
And you will find me with you. I must sing
Passions unended while you are turning, blind,
Great blows thukk in darkness, thickening
Cymbals, a small hand waves,

And so you be my guest
Uncircling, you who were a dancing man
Dance in darkness! Drips off our grapes blood,
They scream, the child is swinging on the fan,
A purpose tightens in the thigh of god
Like your heart in the drums' thunder

And now you be my guest
While leaping mouths rage forward and white eyes,
Coarse night between smooth laurel boles, crowns shove
And crack to be timely at the sacrifice
Where I go to pieces. I am lived by love,
And I am partly dying

And now you be my guest
So we go, one, for wineless ecstasy
And whether will ever either back O turn
Is known, and the snow is hovering over the sea
And the child cries, and worshippers will burn
The sweet lost leaves of my trees.

They Have

A thing O say a sixteenth of an inch
long, with whiskers
& wings it doesn't use, & many legs,
has all this while been wandering in a tiny space
on the black wood table by my burning chair.
I see it has a feeler of some length
it puts out before it.
That must be how it was following the circuit
of the bottom of my wine-glass, vertical: Mâcon: I thought

it smelt & wanted some but couldn't get hold.
Now here's another thing, on my paper, a fluff
of legs, and I blow: my brothers & sisters go away.
But here he's back, & got between the pad
& padback, where I save him and
shift him to my blue shirt, where he is.
The other little one's gone somewhere else.
They have things easy.

The Poet's Final Instructions

Dog-tired, suisired, will now my body down
near Cedar Avenue in Minneap,
when my crime comes. I am blazing with hope.
Do me glory, come the whole way across town.

I couldn't rest from hell just anywhere,
in commonplaces. Choiring & strange my pall!
I might not lie still in the waste of St Paul
or buy DAD's root beer; good signs I forgive.

Drop here, with honour due, my trunk & brain
among the passioning of my countrymen
unable to read, rich, proud of their tags
and proud of me. Assemble all my bags!
Bury me in a hole, and give a cheer,
near Cedar on Lake Street, where the used cars live.

from *The Black Book (i)*

Grandfather, sleepless in a room upstairs,
Seldom came down; so when they tript him down
We wept. The blind light sang about his ears,
Later we heard. Brother had pull. In pairs
He, some, slept upon stone.
Later they stamped him down in mud.
The windlass drew him silly & odd-eyed, blood

Broke from his ears before they quit.
Before they trucked him home they cleaned him up somewhat.

Only the loose eyes' glaze they could not clean
And soon he died. He howled a night and shook
Our teeth before the end; we breathed again
When he stopt. Abraham, what we have seen
Write, I beg, in your Book.
No more the solemn and high bells
Call to our pall; we call or gibber; Hell's
Irritable & treacherous
Despairs here here (not him) reach now to shatter us.

from *The Black Book (ii)*

Luftmenschen dream, the men who live on air,
Of other values, in the blackness watching
Peaceful for gangs or a quick raid,
The ghetto nods a mortal head
Soundless but for a scurry, a sigh, retching,—
No moan of generation fear.
Hands hold each other limper
While the moon lengthens on the sliding river.

Prolong the woolen night—Solomon sang—
And never the soul with its own revenge encumber
But like a cry of cranes dies out,
Ecstatic, faint, a moment float-
ing, flying soul, or flares like August timber
In wild woe vanishing.
Blue grows from grey, towards slaughter.
(An Ashkenazi genius stoned Ivan; a sculptor.)

'Boleslaus brought us here, surnamed the Good,
Whose dust rolls nearly seven hundred years
Towards Sirius: we thank that King
As for the ledge whereto we cling,
Night in the caves under the ruins; stars,
Armbands come off, for which we could

Be glad but the black troops gather.'
So those who kneel in the paling sky & shiver.

*   *   *

Dawn like a rose unfolds—flower of parks—
Alleys of limetrees, villas, ponds, a palace
Down a deserted riverbed,
The Lazienki Gardens' pride,
Monument to a king able and callous
Who far Vienna from the Turks
Bloodily did deliver.
For foreigners, now, a sort of theatre.

One officer in black demarches here
Cupshot, torn collar by a girl unwilling
Native & blond through the debauch
That kept him all night from his couch,
Hurts his head and from the others' howling
Drove him out for morning air.
Brooding over the water
He reddens suddenly. He went back & shot her.

from *The Black Book (iii)*

Lover & child, a little sing.
From long-lockt cattle-cars who grope
Who near a place of showers come
Foul no more, whose murmuring
Grows in a hiss of gas will clear them home:
Away from & toward me: a little soap,
Disrobing, *Achtung!* in a dirty hope,
They shuffle with their haircuts in to die.
Lift them an elegy, poor you and I,
Fair & strengthless as seafoam
Under a deserted sky.

[156

A Sympathy, A Welcome

Feel for your bad fall how could I fail,
poor Paul, who had it so good.
I can offer you only: this world like a knife.
Yet you'll get to know your mother
and humourless as you do look you will laugh
and all the others
will N O T be fierce to you, and loverhood
will swing your soul like a broken bell
deep in a forsaken wood, poor Paul,
whose wild bad father loves you well.

Not to Live

(Jamestown 1957)

It kissed us, soft, to cut our throats, this coast,
like a malice of the lazy King. I hunt,
& hunt! but find here what to kill?—nothing is blunt,
but phantoming uneases I find. Ghost
on ghost precedes of all most scared us, most
we fled. Howls fail upon this secret, far air: grunt,
shaming for food; you must. I love the King
& it was not I who strangled at the toast
but a flux of a free & dying adjutant:
God be with him. He & God be with us all,
for we are not to live. I cannot wring,
like laundry, blue my soul—indecisive thing . .
From undergrowth & over odd birds call
and who would starv'd so survive? God save the King.

American Lights, Seen From Off Abroad

Blue go up & blue go down
to light the lights of Dollartown

His Thought Made Pockets & the Plane Buckt

Nebuchadnezzar had it so good?
wink the lights of Hollywood

I never think, I have so many things,
flash the lights of Palm Springs

I worry like a madwoman over all the world,
affirm the lights, all night, at State

I have no plans, I mean well,
swear the lights of Georgetown

I have the blind staggers
call the lights of Niagara

We shall die in a palace
shout the black lights of Dallas

I couldn't dare less, my favorite son,
fritter the lights of Washington

(I have a brave old So-and-so,
chuckle the lights of Independence, Mo.)

I cast a shadow, what I mean,
blurt the lights of Abilene

Both his sides are all the same
glows his grin with all but shame

'He can do nothing night & day,'
wonder his lovers. So they say.

'Basketball in outer space'
sneers the White New Hampshire House

I'll have a smaller one, later, Mac,
hope the strange lights of Cal Tech

I love you one & all, hate shock,
bleat the lights of Little Rock

I cannot quite focus
cry the lights of Las Vegas

I am a maid of shots & pills,
swivel the lights of Beverly Hills

Proud & odd, you give me vertigo,
fly the lights of San Francisco

I am all satisfied love & chalk,
mutter the great lights of New York

I have lost your way
say the white lights of Boston

Here comes a scandal to blight you to bed.
'Here comes a cropper.' That's what I said.

Lévanto
7 October 1957

Note to Wang Wei

How could you be so happy, now some thousand years
disheveled, puffs of dust?
It leaves me uneasy at last,
your poems teaze me to the verge of tears
and your fate. It makes me think.
It makes me long for mountains & blue waters.
Makes me wonder how much to allow.
(I'm reconfirming, God of bolts & bangs,
of fugues & bucks, whose rocket burns & sings.)
I wish we could meet for a drink
in a 'freedom from ten thousand matters.'
Be dust myself pretty soon; not now.

His Thought Made Pockets & the Plane Buckt

Formal Elegy

[1 9 6 4]

I

A hurdle of water, and O these waters are cold
(warm at outset) in the dirty end.
Murder on murder on murder, where I stagger,
whiten the good land where we have held out.
These kills were not for loot,
however Byzantium hovers in the mind:
were matters of principle—that's worst of all—
& fear & crazed mercy.
Ruby, with his mad claim
he shot to spare the Lady's testifying,
probably is sincere.
No doubt, in his still cell, his mind sits pure.

II

Yes, it looks like a wilderness—pacem appellant.
Honour to Patrolman Tippit. Peace to the rifler's widow.
Seven, I believe, play fatherless.

III

Scuppered the yachts, the choppers, big cars, jets.
Nobody goes anywhere,
lengthened (days) into TV.
I am four feet long, invisibly.
What in the end will be left of us is a stare,
underwater.
If you want me to join you in confident prayer, let's
not.
I sidled in & past, gazing upon it,
the bier.

IV

Too Andean hopes, now angry shade.—
I am an automobile. Into me climb
many, and go their ways. Onto him climbed
a-many and went his way.

Formal Elegy

For a while we seemed to be having a holiday
off from ourselves—ah, but the world is wigs,
as sudden we came to feel
and even hís splendid hair kept not wholly real
fumbling & falsing in & out of the Bay of Pigs,
the bad moment of this excellent man,
suffered by me as a small car can.
Faithful to course we stayed.

V

Some in their places are constrained to weep.
Stunned, more, though.
Black foam. A weaving snake. An invulnerable sleep.
It doing have to come so.
All at once, hurtless, in the tide of applause
& expectation. I write from New York
where except for a paraplegic exterminator—
a gracious & sweet guy—
nobody has done no work
lately

VI

It's odd perhaps that Dallas   cannot after their crimes
criminals protect or Presidents.
Fat Dallas, a fit set.
I would not perhaps have voted for him next time.
Images of Mr Kennedy blue the air,
who is little now, with no chance to grow great,
but who have set his touch across the State,
true-intended, strong

VII

My breath comes heavy, does my breath.
I feel heavy about the President's death.

VIII

I understand I hear I see I read
schoolgirls in Dallas when the white word came
or slammed, cheered in their thoughtful grades,
brought-up to a loving tone.
I do not sicken but somewhat with shame
I shift my head an inch; who are my own.
I have known a loving Texas   woman in parades
and she was boastful & treacherous.
That boringest of words, whereas here I blush,
'education', peters to a nailing of us.

IX

An editor has asked me in my name
what wish or prophecy I'd like to state
for the new year. I am silent on these occasions
steadily, having no love for a fool
(which I keep being) but I break my rule:
I do all-wish the bullets swim astray
sent to the President, and that all around
help, and his heart keep sound.
I have a strange sense
                              he's about to be the best of men.
Amen.

X

It's quiet at Arlington. Rock Creek is quiet.
My prīmers, with Mount Auburn. Everybody should
have his sweet boneyards. Yet let the young not go,
our apprentice King! Alas,
muffled, he must. He seemed good:
brainy in riot, daring, cool.
                              So
let us abandon the scene of disorder. Drop
them shattered bodies into tranquil places,
where moulder as you will. We compose our faces
cold as the cresting waters; ready again.

Formal Elegy

The waters break.
All black & white together, stunned, survive
the final insolence to the head of you;
bow.
Overwhelmed-un, live.
A rifle fact is over, pistol facts
almost entirely are too.
The man of a wise face opened it to speak:
Let us continue.

LOVE & FAME

[1 9 7 1]

Sleep! In your boat brought into the living-room
supreme admirer of the ancient sea

Your mockery of the pretentious great
your self-revelations
constitute still in any sunset sky
a cursing glory

❧ *Part One* ❧

Her & It

I fell in love with a girl.
O and a gash.
I'll bet she now has seven lousy children.
(I've three myself, one being off the record.)

I wish she'd read my book & write to me
from O wherever ah how far she is.
After all, I get letters from anybody.
From hers, I'd tear to the 'phone.

It's not now near at all the end of winter.
I have to fly off East to sing a poem.
Admirers, some, will surge up afterward,
I'll keep an eye out for her.

My tough Songs well in Tokyo & Paris
fall under scrutiny. My publishers
very friendly in New York & London
forward me elephant cheques.

Time magazine yesterday slavered Saul's ass,
they pecked at mine last year. We're going strong!
Photographs all over!
She muttered something in my ear I've forgotten as we danced.

Cadenza on Garnette

'If I had said out passions as they were,'
plain-saying Wordsworth confided down deep age,

'the poems could never have been published.'
Ha! a confrère.

She set up a dazing clamour across this blood
in one of Brooks Hall's little visiting rooms.
In blunt view of whoever might pass by
we fondled each other's wonders.

One night she couldn't come down, she had a cold,
so I took away a talkative friend of hers,
to squirrel together inklings as to Garnette,
any, no matter what, she did, said, was.

O it flowed fuller than the girl herself,
I feasted on Louise.
I all but fell in love with her instead,
so rich with news.

Allen long after, being taxed obscenely
in a news-sheet of Spoleto, international town,
complained to me next day: His aim was tell it all.
Poets! . . Lovers & secrets!

How did we break off, now I come to it,
I puzzle. Did she date somebody else
& I warred with that & she snapped 'You don't own me'
or did the flare just little by little fall?

so that I cut in & was cut in on,
the travelling spotlights coloured, the orchestra gay,
without emphasis finally,
pressing each other's hand as he took over.

Shirley & Auden

O lithest Shirley! & the other worlds

She did not say anything definite; but I twigged
(a word I picked up later in Cambridge, England):

I would not make this one.
No indeed. Alas!

The most flamboyant fag on campus, P W,
frightened me one Socratic evening
by telling me that *anybody*
targeting all attention to the matter

can M A K E anybody—no bar sex or age
or modesty or toilet-training or marriage status.
He'd been thrown out of seven schools, & knew.
He once gave the homosexual howl

on 52nd Street to Noel Coward
himself, who rose up in the rear
of his open-top chauffeured limousine
& flinging their down-flaunt of the hand howled back.

I sometimes still (rarely) think of P W
& I wonder how his beauteous long blond hair
& heavy bright knit ties & camel's-hair topcoat
are making out in this man's world.

Also of G S, a crony of his,
also queer, who had written half a novel
called 'Fish Out of Water' & was a prominent fellow
among our gang on the Fourth Floor of John Jay
that ran the College.

An old-time novelist myself. At twelve
I wrote a half a science-fiction book
about a trip to Neptune & Ee-loro-a'ala
'published' by Helen Justice in two brown-wrappered volumes,

readership limited ah to the eighth grade
at P.S. 69 in Jackson Heights,
Long Island. She was pretty *keen* on me
but too tall for my then romantic image.

Besides I was being faithful to Charlotte Coquet
skating up & down in front of her blue house
passionate in the late afternoon barely to be noticed.
O Charlotte Coquet . .

I was political in my first year; very.
With Tom McGovern & Paul MacCutcheon
we founded an Independent Party
to break the syndicate of the fraternities.

I lost the trivial Vice-Presidency
to a combed void from Kent School, Alpha Delt,
by five bare bitter votes.
In two years we had a majority on Student Council.

I recognized Auden at once as a new master,
I was by then a bit completely with it.
My love for that odd man has never altered
thro' some of his facile bodiless later books.

This place is done for, England & so on.
The poet mourns but clamps it to a symptom
fascinating, obscurely foreseeing
the hectic dancer of your delicious end.

O and Shakespeare seized his daring in both hands
to warn the star of the age, acclaiming but adding
something in a Chorus of *Henry V*
on 'favourites,

made proud by Princes, that advance their pride
against that power that bred it.'

Nobody told the Earl, or if one did
it went unheeded,—from a *poet*? words
to menace action? O I don't think so.
I wonder if Shakespeare trotted to the jostle of his death.

When I flew through *The Orators* first
I felt outstretched, like an archaeologist

Carl Blegen himself with his withered arm
I shook in Cincinnati at Nestor's palace:

'Woe*isme*' (the Channing wail
of ladies young at that ladies' school wailing poetry)
that anyone would put great Auden down.
I'd rather prove inadequate myself.

I vow I poured more thought that Fall into Auden
than into Shirley C
the preternatural dancer from Johnson Hall.
O lithest Shirley,—I wouldn't be up to you now.

But darling, sister, do you yourself ever dance any more?
My heart quails as I put this unbearable question,—
into what faraway air?

Freshman Blues

My intense friend was tall & strongly made,
almost too handsome—& he was afraid
his penis was too small.
We mooted it, we did everything but examine it

whether *in se* or by comparison
to the great red joy a pecker ought to be
to pump a woman ragged. Only kid sisters,
he muttered, want to somersault with me.

Thought much I then on perforated daddy,
daddy boxed in & let down with strong straps,
when I my friends' homes visited, with fathers
universal & intact.

McGovern was critical: I treated my girl *slight*
who was so kind to me I climbed in bed
with her, with our pajamas, an icy morning
when I'd stayed overnight

by her mother's kindness, flustered by my status,
listening then downstairs.
Tom took her over and I ceased to fear
her nervous & carbuncled brother Thornton.

Images of Elspeth

O when I grunted, over lines and her,
my Muse a nymphet & my girl with men
older, of money, continually
lawyers & so, myself a flat-broke Junior.

But the one who made me wild
was who she let take naked photographs
never she showed me but she was proud of.
Unnerving; dire.

My love confused confused with after loves
not ever over time did I outgrow.
Solemn, alone my Muse grew taller.
Rejection slips developed signatures,

many thought Berryman was under weigh,
he wasn't sure himself.
Elspeth became two snapshots in his keeping,
with all her damned clothes on.

She married a Law School dean & flourisheth.
I almost married, with four languages
a ballerina in London, and I should have done.
—Drawing the curtain over fragrant scenes

& interviews malodorous, find me
domestic with my Muse
who had manifested, well, a sense of humour
fatal to bardic pretension.

Dance! from Savannah Garnette with your slur
hypnotic, you'll stay many.

I walked forth to a cold snow to post letters
to a foreign editor & a West Coast critic

wishing I could lay my old hands somewhere on those snapshots.

My Special Fate

I tore it open, by one end, & found
French prose translations, a French estimate.
I dreamt at times in those days of my *name*
blown by adoring winds all over

and once a postcard came from 'Harold Spitz'
a gentleman in Brooklyn, running 'Huh!
You like that stuff? It stinks.'
One of my first fan-letters.

She was eminent at Barnard.
We sat at the Dean's table
during a prom, and I smiled on the Dean
thinking of her protégée's naked photographs,

and shagging with a rangy gay thin girl
(Miss Vaughan) I tore a section of the draperies down.
I wore white buckskin shoes with tails sometimes
& was widely known on Morningside Heights,

a tireless & inventive dancing man.
I left a dance one night with one Clare Reese,
short & pretty, poor teeth, sensual;
we took the subway north to a waste ground

over the Hudson where we tumbled down
under a trembling moon.
Coarse kids collected to jeer down on us
struggling back up into bra, panties, trousers.

At all times loomed for me my special fate,
Elspeth's haggard unsuccessful lover.

Drunks

One night in Albany
on a geology field-trip, in a corridor
upstairs of our hotel
I found McGovern on his hands & knees

heading for his lost room after a bet
which upright I had won.
I read everybody, borrowing their books from Mark,
it took me quite a while to get to Yeats.

I wondered every day about suicide.
Once at South Kent—maybe in the Third Form?—
I lay down on the tracks before a train
& had to be hauled off, the Headmaster was furious.

Once at a New Year's party at Mark Van Doren's
to which I took my Jane & H
cautioning them to behave themselves
the place was crawling with celebrities

poor H got stuck in an upstairs bedroom
with the blonde young wife of a famous critic
a wheel at one of the book clubs
who turned out to have nothing on under her gown

sprawled out half-drunk across her hostess's bed
moaning 'Put it in! Put it in!'
He was terrified.
I passed out & was put in that same bed.

Down & Back

It is supernal what a youth can take
& barely notice or be bothered by
which to him older would work ruin.
Over Atherton I almost lost not only my mind

but my physical well-being!
night on night till 4 till 5 a.m.
intertangled breathless, sweating, on a verge
six or seven nerve-destroying hours

sometimes a foul dawn saw me totter home.
Mental my torment too all that fierce time
she 'loved' me; but she wouldn't quite sleep with me
although each instant brought a burning chance

she suddenly might! O yes: it hung in the air
her living-room was thick with it like smoke
both of us smelt it
blood sludge from a martini

This was during vacation, then my God
she went back to Northampton
& only wrote once or twice a day
in that prize-winning penmanship

I went back to the world sore & chagrined
with a hanging head & no interest
in anything.
It was then I think I flunked my 18th Century

I wrote a strong exam, but since it was Mark
a personal friend, I had to add a note
saying of the 42 books in the bloody course
I'd only read 17.
                        He liked my candour
(he wrote) & had enjoyed the exam
but had no option except to give me F in the course—

costing my scholarship. The Dean was nice
but thought the College & I should part company
at least for a term, to give me 'time to think'
& regroup my forces (if I'd any left).

A *jolt*. And almost worse, I had let Mark down.
I set about to fix the second thing.

I paged the whole century through for five monk's months
keeping an encyclopedic notebook.

I made among other things an abridgement of Locke's *Essay*
down to some hundred pages
preserving all his points & skeleton
but chopping away superfluous exposition.

Mark thought it ought to be published
but we found out there was one in print already.
Anyway he changed my grade retroactively & talked to the Dean.
My scholarship was restored, the Prodigal Son
welcomed with crimson joy.

Two Organs

I remind myself at that time of Plato's uterus—
of the seven really good courses I ever took
one was a seminar with Edman met at night
in his apartment, where we read them all

all the Dialogues, in chronological order, through
so that I got *something* out of Columbia—
Plato's uterus, I say,
an animal passionately longing for children

and, if long unsatisfied after puberty,
prone to range angrily, blocking the air passages
& causing distress & disease.
For 'children' read: big fat fresh original & characteristic poems.

My longing yes was a woman's
She can't know can she *what kind* of a baby
she's going with all the will in the world to produce?
I suffered trouble over this,

I didn't want my next poem to be *exactly* like Yeats
or exactly like Auden

since in that case where the hell was *I*?
but what instead *did* I want it to sound like?

I couldn't sleep at night, I attribute my life-long insomnia
to my uterine struggles. 'You must undress'
a young poet writes to me from Oregon
'the great face of the body.'

The Isolation so, young & now I find older,
American, & other.
While the rest of England was strolling thro' the Crystal Palace
Arnold was gnashing his teeth on a mountain in Sicily.

An eccentric friend, a Renaissance scholar, sixty-odd,
unworldly, he writes limericks in Medieval Latin,
stood up in the rowboat fishing to take a leak
& exclaimed as he was about it with excitement

'I wish my penis was big enough for this whole lake!'
My phantasy precisely at twenty:
to satisfy at once all Barnard & Smith
& have enough left over for Miss Gibbs's girls.

Olympus

In my serpentine researches
I came on a book review in *Poetry*
which began, with sublime assurance,
a comprehensive air of majesty,

'The art of poetry
is amply distinguished from the manufacture of verse
by the animating presence in the poetry
of a fresh idiom: language

so twisted & posed in a form
that it not only expresses the matter in hand
but adds to the stock of available reality.'
I was never altogether the same man after *that*.

I found this new Law-giver all unknown
except in the back numbers of a Cambridge quarterly
Hound & Horn, just defunct.
I haunted on Sixth Avenue until

at 15¢ apiece or 25
I had all 28 numbers
& had fired my followers at Philolexian & Boar's Head
with the merits of this prophet.

My girls suffered during this month or so,
so did my seminars & lectures &
my poetry even. To be a *critic*, ah,
how deeper & more scientific.

I wrote & printed an essay on Yeats's plays
re-deploying all of Blackmur's key terms
& even his sentence-structure wherever I could.
When he answered by hand from Boston my nervous invitation

to come & be honoured at our annual Poetry Reading,
it must have been ten minutes before I could open the envelope.
I got *him* to review Tate's book of essays
& *Mark* to review *The Double Agent*. Olympus!

I have travelled in some high company since
less dizzily.
I have had some rare girls since but never one so philosophical
as that same Spring (my last Spring there) Jean Bennett.

Nowhere

Traitoring *words*,—tearing my thought across
bearing it to foes.
Two men ahead of me in line in the College Study
about the obscurity of my 'Elegy: Hart Crane'.

More comfortable at the Apollo among blacks
than in Hartley Hall where I hung out.

A one named Brooks Johnson, with it in for Negroes,
I told one noon I'd some coon blood myself

and he spread the word wide while the campus laughed.
Magical mourning blues,
Victoria, Bessie. Teagarden. Pine-top Smith
the sightless passionate constructor.

Anti-semitism through the purblind Houses.
News weird out of Germany.
Our envy for any visitor to the Soviet Union.
The shaking incredible transcripts of the Trials.

Cagney's inventions in gesture, the soul-kiss
in *42nd Street*. Coop's little-boy-ness.
Chaplin emerging nonchalant from under the tarpaulin.
Five Dietrich films in a day.

Ping-pong at the Little Carnegie,
the cheapest firstrate date in the Depression city.
A picture of me in *The New York Times*
with a jock-strap on, & socks & shoes,

taken during the Freshman-Sophomore Rush:
face half from the camera, hardly any knew me,
praise God in St Bonaventura's Heaven!
Hours of acedia, pencil on the desk

coffee in a cup, ash-tray flowing
the window closed, the universe unforthcoming,
Being ground to a halt.
Inaccessible unthinkable the childlike enthusiasm

of grand Unamuno setting down his profession
in the Visitors' Book on top of a Spanish mountain:
'A humble man, & a tramp.'
Long after, in a train from Avila

I met a cop who called him Don Miguel;
another of my Sophomore heroes.

And David Hume stood high with me that year
& Kleist, for the 'Puppet-theatre'.

Uncertainties, presentiments.
Piranesi's black & lovely labyrinths, come-ons like a whore's.
Gautier rapt before a staircase at the Alcázar
winding up monumental through the ruin to give out on—nothing.

In & Out

Niceties of symbolism & identification.
The verve I flooded toward in *Don Giovanni*
A shroud, a spade.
Sense of a selfless seeker in this world.

I gave up crew and track after Freshman Spring.
I had my numerals & no more time.
No politics.
I was watching Corbière doomed, John Davidson doomed, their
                                        frantic aplomb.

Shapes of the white ape & his irresistible companions.
My birthday the same as Burroughs',
I had a letter on 'Tarzana' stationery.
He lost his knack later on.

Corridors deep, near water. The surgeon looks over the parapet
& looks straight down in the water. '*Mordserum* sie habe sagen.
Wo ist Doktor Dumartin? Doktor Dumartin
muss Doktor Dumartin *finden!*'

When was I most afraid? Of eerie Wither,
his nonchalance abandoned. Of fragile Elspeth's opinion.
Of a stabbed lady in a drawer at Bellevue
one Saturday afternoon, we peered at Starr Faithful's

stomach in a jar, Exhibit H, avocado-green
Down to the Princeton game with no brakes to speak of

stopping by coasting into cars ahead
I'd never seen such traffic

Princeton had two complete Sophomore backfields
& took us 19–0. But the Brown game,
the last quarter ticking out, 7–0,
a freezing rain on their 2-yard line

& couldn't bull it over
neither Cliff Montgomery nor Al Barabas
my friend with shoulders & bright
who scored the only touchdown at the Rose Bowl.
I still hear from him, wanting me to contribute.

Money? for Columbia?? They use my name
now & then. That's plenty.
I make a high salary & royalties & fees
and brother I need it all.

I sent $100 it's true to Montana
to fund a poetry prize in the name of a girl
I liked in hospital, named Rita Lux,
a suicide, witty & masochistic

who was trying to get her priest to leave the Church
& marry her, she beat a punching bag
with bare fists until her knuckles bled
cursing with every blow 'John Berryman! . . . John Berryman! . . .'

I learnt in one week more about prose from Pascal
than ever from any Englishman I learnt
though from John Aubrey something, Pascal's polar.
I was tickled by Whitman's also.

And the live magazines were gone,
The Dial, Symposium. Where could one pray to publish?
The Criterion's stories & poems were so weak.
Solely *The Southern Review*, not *Partisan* yet.

After my dismal exile at my school
I made at Columbia a point of being popular,
by mid-November already I knew by name
most of the nearly 500 men in my class,

including commuters, touchingly pleased
to have a soul recognize them.
I liked them, a man of the world, I felt like them,
barring my inordinate desire.

Morose and slovenly, Zander thought like a tank
the only man in college who understood Hegel
agile enough too for the *Tractatus*
I used to stop by his room, which he never left.

Vistas ahead of what must be endured,
cold girls, fear, thoughtless books . .

'Dear Mr C, A reviewer in *The Times*
considering 200 poems of yours
produced over a period of fifteen years
adjudged them "crushingly dull"; my view too,

though you won't suppose of course I read them all.
Sir, you are trivial.
Pray do not write to me again. Pitch defileth.
Yours faithfully, Henry.'

The Heroes

For all his vehemence & hydraulic opinions
Pound seemed feline, zeroing in on feelings,
hovering up to them, putting his tongue in their ear,
delicately modulating them in & out of each other.

Almost supernatural crafter; maybe unhappy,
disappointed continually,
not fated like his protégé Tom or drunky Jim
or hard-headed Willie for imperial sway.

How I maneuvered in my mind their rôles
of administration for the modern soul
in English, now one, now ahead another,
for this or that special strength, wilful & sovereign.

I had, from my beginning, to adore heroes
& I elected that they witness to,
show forth, transfigure: life-suffering & pure heart
& hardly definable but central weaknesses

for which they were to be enthroned & forgiven by me.
They had to come on like revolutionaries,
enemies throughout to accident & chance,
relentless travellers, long used to failure

in tasks that but for them would sit like hanging judges
on faithless & by no means up to it Man.
Humility & complex pride their badges,
every 'third thought' their grave.

These gathering reflexions, against young women
against seven courses in my final term,
I couldn't sculpt into my helpless verse yet.
I wrote mostly about death.

Crisis

My offended contempt for the mental & stylistic workings of
                                        Ruskin & Carlyle
extended to their advocate,
who also mouthed at me Wordsworth in Hamilton Hall
holding up my appreciation of that great poet

for more than eighteen months.
Later he wrote a book on E. A. Robinson,
a favourite of mine (not interesting metrically
but with the gist of it in him)

which I went into with Schadenfreude
gratified to find it insensitive & unworthy.
O I come here to a tricky old scandalous affair!
He tried to keep me from *graduating*.

I may explain that this man had come to hate me personally.
Not only did I give him hell in class:
I saw my nine friends did. With ironic questions
& all but insolent comment & actual interruptions

we made Professor N wish he was elsewhere
rather than in English 163.
I must further explain: I needed a B,
I didn't need an A, as in my other six courses,

but the extra credits accruing from those A's
would fail to accrue if I'd any mark under B.
The bastard knew this,
as indeed my predicament was well known

through both my major Departments. Under the risk I ran
with N, I took care to keep an elaborate notebook
on all the readings Romantic & Victorian
to flourish if he got funny. He got very funny,—

leaving instructions not to post his marks
till the last stated day, he sailed for Italy,
and I found myself with a C,
squarely in the middle of Hell.

Luckily the Dean was down there with me,
along with Mark & my advisor Gutmann
& the whole senior staff of the English Department,
because I *had* to graduate:

not only had they put me in Phi Beta Kappa,
they'd given me their major Fellowship
for two years in England
& the disgrace if I couldn't take it up

would be general: only embarrassing
but very that: a plague. But what could they do?
I showed my notebook around & pointed out
the Apollinaire-like implausibility of my C

considering all my A's & my magisterial notebook.
I didn't have to mention personal spite.
They held unhappy meetings for two days.
To change the mark of a colleague in his absence?

Finally, a command decision:
they'd give me a second exam, invented by themselves,
& judge it, & if my paper justified,
they'd elevate the highly irrational mark.

I took it—it was fair, hard—& I killed it.
I never knew what I got, but the course-grade
cranked upward to a B. I graduated.
In my immediate section of the Commencement line

we were mostly Phi Betes, & the normal guys would have
                              nothing to do with us.

I collected my first installment, more dead than alive
from over-work & poetic theory & practice & Miss Jean B—
a thousand dollars it was—and took off for Canada,
to nurse my dark wounds & prepare my psyche for Cambridge,

a still more foreign scene.

Recovery

I don't know what the hell happened all that summer.
I was done in, mentally. I wrote nothing, I read nothing.
I spent a pot of money, not being used to money,
I forget on what, now. I felt dazed.

After some wandering days in Montreal
I went to a little town where Dr Locke

cured any & everything with foot 'adjustments',
on hundreds of patients daily from all over North America

outdoors in a hardwood grove in front of his clinic.
I made vague friends with a couple, the brother in a wheel-chair,
his pleasant sister looking after him.
They were dull & very poor. I gave them tea,

we talked about what young people talk about.
Weeks somehow went by. All this time my art was in escrow,
I vegetated, I didn't even miss Jean,
without interest in what I was, what I might become

never came up, as day by day
I stood in line for the Doctor & gave them tea.
I didn't think much of the nothing I knew of Canada,
half British-oriented, half-French, half-American;

no literature, painting, architecture,
music, philosophy, scholarship . .
(McLuhan & Frye unthinkable ahead).
I wasn't unhappy, I wasn't anything,
until I pulled myself reluctantly together at last

& bowed goodbye to my lame ducks
& headed for Pier 42—where my nervous system
as I teetered across the gang-plank
sprang back into expectation. I kissed Jean

& Mother & shook hands with old Halliday
and I mounted to the *Britannic*'s topmost deck
O a young American poet, not yet good,
off to the strange Old World to pick their brains
& visit by hook or crook with W. B. Yeats.

[188

❧ *Part Two* ☙

Away

Ah! so very slowly
the jammed dock slides away backward,
I'm on my way to Bumpus' & the Cam,
haunts of old masters where I may improve.

Now we're swinging round, tugs hoot,
I don't think I was ever better pleased
with the outspread opening world & even myself
O when *The Nation* took my epitaph.

In fifteen minutes I have made a friend
a *caricaturiste* for *Vendredi*
who has been covering the elections
& a young tall Haitian doctor joins us now

It beats the Staten Island ferry hollow
I used to take to Clinton Dangerfield
to type out from dictation her pulp Westerns
I'm impressed by the *bulk* of the ship

Yeats, Yeats, I'm coming! it's me. Faber & Faber,
you'll have to publish me some day with éclat
I haven't quite got the hang of the stuff yet
but I swamp with possibility

My God, we're in open water
I feel like Jacob with his father's blessing
set forth to con the world too, only *I* plan
to do it with simple work & with my ear

First Night at Sea

I'm at a table with Canadians
He translates Villon. Villon! What Canadian
could English make of those abject bravura laments?
He says he'll give me a copy.

We walk the top deck in dark, Pedro Donga & I,
the Haitian proved a narcissist & we evade him.
He sings me a Basque folk-song, his father was Basque
passing through, his mother a Spanish lady

married, staying there. He ran away
at nine, with gypsies. At the University of Lyon
he assisted with experiments in resuscitation,
he says the Russians are ahead of us in this field.

He sang then for a night-club in Berlin
& got 50 sexual offers a week.
With Memel, the Belgian composer
he went to the Congo to collect tribal tunes.

I listened with three ears.

Now he lives a bachelor in Paris
thirty-three & he has to shave twice a day,
short, muscular.
We trade quotations of Lorca's ballads,

grave news of the Loyalists' fight to hold Madrid.
I have felt happy
before but not in the flying wind like this.
He says come see him at Christmas.

London

I hardly slept across the North Atlantic.
We talked. His panoramas,

plus my anticipations, made me new.
He drew large cartoons of me

reclining in my bunk; needing a shave.
(Dean Hawkes had said to me at the end,
about the British differences & my behaviour in Cambridge,
'And, listen, for God's sake, Berryman, sometimes shave.')

Mr Wharton did give me his sad volume
of the medieval genius thief in Canadian.
I told his wife I didn't know how to play bridge,
which (against my principles) was a lie.

Donga debarked at Southampton, tenoring 'Christmas!'
I made up a brief rapprochement with the pouting Haitian
(when *girls* pout, I used to be available)
and then we docked, south of London.

I took with my luggage a cab to the 'Cumberland Hotel, sir,'
near Marble Arch, the only hotel I'd heard of
& near Bumpus' in Oxford Street:
we arrived & I looked at the entrance

reminding me of the Hotel Pennsylvania
no place for me, not yet met Bhain, not yet met Saul, O my
                                                    brothers,
& said in American 'Let's move on,
I want a small cheap hotel near here, let's go.'

In half an hour, alive after crossing Oxford Street,
that bloody lefthand traffic,
I was downstairs in Bumpus', O paradiso
where I grabbed the Oxford collection of Keats's letters
& the Sloss & Wallis edition of Blake's *Prophetic Books*.

I went to feel the Elgin marbles, I fed at Simpson's.
Ignoring whores, I walked to a naked night-club
off Piccadilly, leaving early,
& took a 9:06 train up to Cambridge.

The Other Cambridge

Tom Grumbold's bridge has balusters set diagonally
('subtle & very effective')
& a pie-slice of granite is gone from one globe,—God knows how,—
upon this exquisite famous by-me-crossed-six-times-daily bridge.

Clare itself in 1359; by Edward I's granddaughter.
It's not a distinguished college: Trinity
or John's or Magdalene, or King's;
but it *is* rather old. It burned & burned.

My Court is brand-new, named for the War dead,
M4 my number. My rooms look as if they had never been inhabited.
My bedder is Mrs Mizzen, pronounced 'zed' as she laughed with me.
My gyp: There are no stories about these rooms or this staircase or this
Court.

Anecdotes I collected, inspired by Aubrey;
especially death-words & sayings in crisis.
At the trial of the Earls
ten years of venom flared forth in six words:

when the great Ralegh rose to testify,
Essex called out 'What boots it swear The Fox?'
I liked documents, letters, Herndon's *Lincoln*
for the study of one of the most interesting men since Christ.

Spires, gateways; bells. I like this town:
its bookshops, Heffer's above all and Bowes & Bowes
but Galloway & Porter too, & Deighton Bell
& sparkling Gordon Fraser's in Portugal Place

for days outranked for me the supernatural glass in King's Chapel,
the Entrance Gateway of John's, the Great Court of Trinity.
Slowly, as rapidly my books assembled every afternoon,
I strolled to look & see, & browsed, & began to feel.

Mother of Newton & Wordsworth! Milton & lazy Gray;
imperious Bentley, Porson wittier than Byron,
'Yes, Mr Southey is indeed a wonderful poet.
He will be read when Homer & Virgil are forgotten.'

(Byron always spoiled it by adding 'But not till then.')
Drunks for six centuries while the towers flew
skyward & tranquil punts poled under tranquil bridges:
David's forever new bookstall in Market Hill

where for shillings I bought folios
of Abraham Cowley of O delectable 'The Chronicle':
the 1594 Prayer Book by twelve Cambridge men
& one outlander: Peterhouse' formal garden:

Queens' Wooden Bridge which Newton put together
without a bolt or nail (at last rot began,
they took it down & couldn't put it back,
now it's all bolts & nails, so much for Progress):

Cloisters & the Fellows' Buildings, the Combination Rooms
where wine o'erflows weak-noddled dons: Caius' Gate of Honour.
Anthony Eden passed within ten feet of me
in a Chancellorship procession; a film star!

Images, memories, of a lonely & ambitious young alien.
Buildings, buildings & their spaces & decorations,
are death-words & sayings in crisis.
Old masters of old Cambridge, I am listening.

Friendless

Friendless in Clare, except Brian Boydell
a Dubliner with no hair
an expressive tenor speaking voice
who introduced me to the music of Peter Warlock

who had just knocked himself off, fearing the return
of his other personality, Philip Heseltine.

Brian used to play *The Curlew* with the lights out,
voice of a lost soul moving.

These men don't know our poets.
I'm asked to read; I read Wallace Stevens & Hart Crane
in Sidney Sussex & Cat's.
The worthy young gentlemen are baffled. I explain,

but the idiom is too much for them.
The Dilettante Society here in Clare
asked me to lecture to them on Yeats
& misspelt his name on the invitations.

Black hours over an unclean line.
Fear. Of failure, or, worse, *insignificance*.
Solitudes, sometimes, of an alien country
no book after all will ever read me into.

I gorge on Peek Freans & brood.
I don't do a damned thing but read & write.
I wish I were back in New York!
I feel old, yet I don't understand.

Monkhood

I don't show my work to anybody, I am quite alone.
The only souls I feel toward are Henry Vaughan & Wordsworth.
This guy Dylan Thomas though is hotter than anyone we have
                                                    in America
        & hardly at all like Auden.

Pat's reading Conrad through for the second time
'to see if I was right,' my new companion,
with 35/-a week from his solicitors.
I buy him *breakfast* at the Dorothy

& we dawdle over it discussing suicide.
He only has two things left (his wife *took* him),

a carmine sports car & a large-paper set of Conrad.
Maybe I better add

an all but preternatural ability at darts
which keeps him in drink.
He is sleeping with both his landlady & his landlady's daughter,
one on the ground floor & one upstairs,

he hates to go on across there back at night.
And I think in my unwilling monkhood *I* have problems!
He's studying with Wittgenstein & borrowing Kafka.
A hulking sly depressed attractive talker.

      *   *   *

I never went to see Wittgenstein or Broad,
I suffered a little from shyness, which was just arrogance
not even inverted.
I refused to meet Eliot, on two occasions,

I knew I wasn't with it yet
& would not meet my superiors. Screw them.
Along with my hero-worship & wish for comradeship
went my pride, my 'Satanic pride',

as Delmore later, when we were preaching at Harvard
together as kids, he far superior then to me,
put it to my *pleasure* one day
out of his gentle heart & high understanding

of both the strengths & cripplings of men.
Did even Eileen ever understand me sharper?
Many write of me these days & some with insight
but I think of Delmore's remark that afternoon.

Even Cervantes' judgment has not yet wholly overcome me.

Will I ever write properly, with passion & exactness,
of the damned strange demeanours of my flagrant heart?
& be by anyone anywhere undertaken?
One *more* unanswerable question.

Love & Fame

Views of Myself

Another old friend, long afterward,
in the *Advocate* devoted to my jazz
put it differently:
he called it my 'bloody-mindedness'.

I will also roar you as 'twere any sucking dove
these twilight days
but I was hell young.
I did not censor anything I said

& what I said I said with force & wit
which crushed some no doubt decent & by me now would be spared

human personalities with shoes on.
I stand ashamed of myself;
yes, but I stand. Take my vices alike

with some my virtues, if you can find any.
I stick up like Coriolanus with my scars
for mob inspection.
Only, dear, I am not running in any election

I am not my gifted egomaniacal ally N. Mailer

The *sorrows* of the Hero, Alexander's.
The terrors of the Saint,—
most people feel okay! Thoreau was *wrong*,
he judged by himself.

When I was fiddling later with every wife
on the Eastern seaboard
I longed to climb into a pulpit & confess.
Tear me to pieces!

Lincoln once wrote to a friend 'I bite my lip & am quiet.'

Transit

O a little lonely in Cambridge that first Fall
of fogs & buying books & London on Thursday for plays
& visiting Rylands in his posh rooms at King's
one late afternoon a week.

He was kind to me stranded, & even to an evening party
he invited me, where Keynes & Auden
sat on the floor in the hubbub trading stories
out of their Oxbridge wealth of folklore.

I joined in desperation the Clare ping-pong team
& was assigned to a Sikh in a bright yellow sweater
with a beard so gorgeous I could hardly serve;
his turban too won for him.

I went to the Cosmo, which showed Continental films
& for weeks only Marx Brothers films,
& a short about Oxford was greeted one evening
with loud cunning highly articulate disdain.

Then I got into talk with Gordon Fraser
& he took me home with him out to Mill Lane
to meet his wife Katharine, a witty girl
with strange eyes, from Chicago.

The news from Spain got worse. The President of my Form
at South Kent turned up at Clare, one of the last let out of Madrid.
He designed the Chapel the School later built
& killed himself, I never heard why
or just how, it was something to do with a bridge.

Meeting

One luncheon party in Andy's rooms in Magdalene
was dominated by a sort of a beauty of a queen

Love & Fame

whose charm the company kept enchanted to center on
whose voice & carriage seemed perhaps those of an actress

Indeed I caught on: the most passionate & versatile actress in
    Cambridge

famous for Good Deeds in *Everyman*
famous for Cordelia & the Duchess of Malfi
overwhelming in *Heartbreak House*
with a ballet career behind her in Italy

reading Modern Languages now at Newnham
& working up Katharine in *Love's Labours Lost*
for a Garden production at Lord Horder's place
down near Southampton's old estate in the Spring.

I don't think I said a word, although I knew
(as probably no one else there did)
the chance is good he wrote *Love's Labours*
for the Earl & his friends down there in '93.

I couldn't drink my sherry, I couldn't eat.
I looked; I listened.
I don't know how I made it home to Memorial Court.
I never expected to meet her again.

But Cambridge is a small place, & a few days later
she was almost out of Portugal Place wheeling her bike
as I was wheeling mine in. *She greeted me.*
With heartburn I asked her to tea. She smiled, & accepted.

Tea

O! I had my gyp *prepare* that tea.
But she wasn't hungry or thirsty, she wanted to talk.
She had not met an American before,
to *talk* with; much less an American *poet*.

I told her honestly I wasn't much of one yet but probably would be.
She preferred Racine to Shakespeare; I said I'd fix that
& read her the King's cadenzas in *All's Well*
about that jerk Bertram's father.

We mooted ancestry: she English-Jewish-Belgian;
me mostly English, traces of Irish-Scotch & so on
but long ago, before the Revolution.
Her father is an expert on sleep: praised, pioneered

by Aldous Huxley. Lives by counselling in London.
By six-fifteen she had promised to stop seeing 'the other man'.
I may have heard better news but I don't know when.
Then—I think—then I stood up, & we kissed.

She skipped dinner at Newnham.

❧ *Part Three* ❧

The Search

I wondered ever too what my fate would be,
women & after-fame become *quite* unavailable,
or at best unimportant. For a tooth-extraction
gassed once, by a Russian woman in Detroit,

I dreamed a dream to end dreams, even my dreams:
I had died—no problem: but a mighty hand
was after my works too, feeling here & there,
& finding them, bit by bit.
At last he found the final of all one, & pulled *it* away, & said 'There!'

I began the historical study of the Gospel
indebted above all to Guignebert

& Goguel & McNeile
& Bultmann even & later Archbishop Carrington.

The Miracles were a stumbling-block;
until I read Karl Heim, trained in natural science;
until I had sufficiently attended to
The Transfiguration & The Ecstasy.

I was weak on the Fourth Gospel. I still am,
in places; I plan to amend that.
Wellisch on *Isaac & Oedipus*
supplements for me Kierkegaard.

Luther on *Galatians* (his grand joy)
I laid aside until I was older & wiser.
Bishop Andrewes' account of the Resurrection-appearances
in 1609 seemed to me, seems to me, it.

I studied Titian's remarks on The Tribute-Money.
Bishop Westcott's analysis (it took him 25 years)
of the first eighteen verses of *St. John*
struck me as of a cunning like Odysseus'.

And other systems, high & primitive,
ancient & surviving, did I not neglect,
sky-gods & trickster-gods, gods impotent,
the malice & force of the dead.

When at twelve Einstein lost belief in God
he said to himself at once (as he put it later)
'Similarly motivated men, both of the past & of the present,
together with their achieved insights,
waren die unverlierbaren Freunde'—the unloseable friends.

Message

Amplitude,—voltage,—the one friend calls for the one,
the other for the other, in my work;

in verse & prose. Well, hell.
I am not writing an autobiography-in-verse, my friends.

Impressions, structures, tales, from Columbia in the Thirties
& the Michaelmas term at Cambridge in '36,
followed by some later. It's not my life.
That's occluded & lost.

That consisted of lectures on St Paul,
scrimmages with women, singular moments
of getting certain things absolutely right.
Laziness, liquor, bad dreams.

That consisted of three wives & many friends,
whims & emergencies, discoveries, losses.
It's been a long trip. Would I make it again?
But once a Polish belle bared me out & was kind to it.

I don't remember why I sent this message.
Children! children! form the point of all.
Children & high art.
Money in the bank is also something.

We will all die, & the evidence
is: Nothing after that.
Honey, we don't rejoin.
The thing meanwhile, I suppose, is to be courageous & kind.

Relations

I feel congruity, feel colleagueship
with few even of my fine contemporaries
Cal, Saul, Elizabeth,
modester Meredith, not yet quite good Deneen Peckinpah

inditing a dirty novel in Montreal.
Bhain Campbell was extracted from me
in dolour, yellow as a second sheet
& I have not since tried to resume the same.

Losses! as Randall observed
who walked into a speeding car
under a culvert at night in Carolina
having just called his wife to make plans for the children.

Woe quotidian, woe a crony
glowing on the pillow, talkative.
But dividends too:
Miss Bishop, who wields a mean lyric

since Emily Dickinson only Miss Moore is adroiter,
addressed me in her first letter to me as 'John'
saying 'Surely I may? as if we were friends.
I wrote you a fan-letter twenty years ago.'

Among a-many other   letters never came.

Antitheses

Dawdling into glory;
or with hammer-strokes.
Our friends have taken both ways.
I'll put the first way first.

Mooning, wishers,
unable to make up our mind like a practical man
about *anything*.
The first time I saw Wystan Auden his socks didn't match.

Only—the other path—we are *hard-headed*.
Victor Hugo (not one of my favourite authors,
except for, in *Les Orientales*, 'Les Djinns')
wrote down each night to the end of his passionate life
the exact sums he paid Joséphine & Héloise.

So: we moon; we tough.
Nobody can make head or tail of us.
Plato threw us *out*.
Freud threw out a hint about Leonardo . .

International art: . . I feel *friendly* to the idea
but skeptical.
I live at 33 Arthur Ave. S.E.
& mostly write from here.

My rocking-chair is dark blue, it's in one corner
& swivels, as my thought drifts.
My wife's more expensive patchquilt rocker
is five feet away & does not swivel.

Have a Genuine American Horror-&-Mist on the Rocks

(14,500 six-ton concrete-&-steel vaults of nerve-gas rockets, lethal)

The terrible trains crawl seaward thro' the South,
where TV teams quiz small-town citizens:
'Waal . . . if the Army says it's safe, it's okay with me.
Ah've got a boy in Veetnam.'

All this mad stuff has been there fifteen years!
leaking its coffins. Had the Chinese come
down in Korea, who knows? then or now knows?
Nobody *knows anything*

but somewhere up in the murky constellation
of Government & the scientists & the military
responsible to no-one someone knows
that he too doesn't know anything

and can't say what would then have happened or will 'now' *happen*
on the Atlantic bottom in the long dark
of decades of ecology to come
while the 20th Century flies insanely on.

To a Woman

The problem is urgent, yes, for this hot light
we so love may not last.
Man seems to be darkening himself;
you must still for some & the other depend on him,
but perhaps essentially now it is your turn.

Your three sons, your political career,
your husband's legal work & fervency in bed,
your story-writing, your great bodily freshness
at thirty-one now, yes, for the problem is urgent
as a spasm of diarrhoea.

You must perhaps both pray for & abandon
your peculiar strength of patience,
daring daily more or all.
Oddly crowned with a solitary ailanthus,
the tortured red hills to this hot light swell with pride.

A Huddle of Need

I wondered about their things. Were they large or small?
Sensitive, or not?
Reddish, or otherwise?
Then I undertook research in this subject.

No woman I ever came on was satisfied with them.
Too large! Too small!
'They're not interesting.'
But O my thin small darling, they are yours.

Woe the Toltecs, & everything is forgotten
almost but stately terraces. I think so, and
the terrors of the knife.
Maybe the sex of the knife made a difference.

I will say: I have been wrong.
And God settled the Jews in Odessa
when he might have put them in Jerusalem
I go now this far, in the Book of Babel.

I seldom now go out. She's out of town.
After all has been said, and all *has* been said,
Man is a huddle of need.
Having explained so much, I close my mouth.

Damned

Damned. Lost & *damned*. And I find I'm pregnant.
It must have been in a shuffle of disrobing
or shortly after.
I confess: I don't know what to do.

She wept steadily all thro' the performance.
As soon as I tucked it in she burst into tears.
She had a small mustache but was otherwise gifted,
riding, & crying her heart out.

(She had been married two years) I was amazed.
(Her first adultery) I was scared & guilty.
I said 'What are you crying for, darling? *Don't*.'
She stuttered something & wept on.

She came again & again, twice ejecting me
over her heaving. I turned my head aside
to avoid her goddamned tears,
getting in my beard.

I am busy tired mad lonely & old.
O this has been a long long night of wrest.

I saw her once again: on a busy sidewalk
outside a grocery store
& she was big & I did *not* say 'Is it mine?'
I congratulated her.

Brighter it waxeth; it's almost seven.

Of Suicide

Reflexions on suicide, & on my father, possess me.
I drink too much. My wife threatens separation.
She won't 'nurse' me. She feels 'inadequate'.
We don't mix together.

It's an hour later in the East.
I could call up Mother in Washington, D.C.
But could she help me?
And all this postal adulation & reproach?

A basis rock-like of love & friendship
for all this world-wide madness seems to be needed.
Epictetus is in some ways my favourite philosopher.
Happy men have died earlier.

I still plan to go to Mexico this summer.
The Olmec images! Chichén Itzá!
D. H. Lawrence has a wild dream of it.
Malcolm Lowry's book when it came out I taught to my precept
                                        at Princeton.

I don't entirely resign. I may teach the Third Gospel
this afternoon. I haven't made up my mind.
It seems to me sometimes that others have easier jobs
& do them worse.

Well, we must labour & dream. Gogol was impotent,
somebody in Pittsburgh told me.
I said: At what age? They couldn't answer.
That is a damned serious matter.

Rembrandt was sober. There we differ. Sober.
Terrors came on him. To us too they come.
Of suicide I continually think.
Apparently he didn't. I'll teach Luke.

Dante's Tomb

A tired banana & an empty mind
at 7 a.m. My world offends my eyes
bleary as an envelope cried-over
after the letter's lost.

In spite of it all, both it & me,
I'll chip away at the mystery.
There's a Toltec warrior in Minneapolis
with narrow eyes, reclining.

The head raised & facing you;
larger than life-size, in tan granite.
The cult perished.
The empty city welcomed the monkeys.

We don't *know*. Hundreds & hundreds of little poems
rolled up & tied with ribbons
over the virgin years, 'unwanted love'.
And Miss Bishop's friend has died,

and I will die and one day in Ravenna
I visited his tomb. A domed affair,
forbidding & tight shut.
'Dantis Poetae Sepulchrum.'

She said to me, half-strangled, 'Do that again.
And then do the other thing.'
Sunlight flooded the old room
& I was both sleepy & hungry.

Despair

It seems to be DARK all the time.
I have difficulty walking.
I can remember what to say to my seminar
but I don't know that I want to.

I said in a Song once: I am unusually tired.
I repeat that & increase it.
I'm vomiting.
I broke down today in the slow movement of K.365.

I certainly don't think I'll last much longer.
I wrote: 'There may be horribles.'
I increase that.
(I think she took her little breasts away.)

I am in love with my excellent baby.
Crackles! in darkness HOPE; & disappears.
Lost arts.
Vanishings.

Walt! We're downstairs,
even you don't comfort me
but I join your risk my dear friend & go with you.
There are no matches

Utter, His Father, one word

The Hell Poem

Hospital racket, nurses' iron smiles.
Jill & Eddie Jane are the souls.
I like nearly all the rest of them too
except for when they feed me paraldehyde.

Tyson has been here three heavy months;
heroin. We have the same doctor: She's improving,
let out on pass tonight for her first time.
A madonna's oval face with wide dark eyes.

Everybody is jolly, patients, nurses,
orderlies, some psychiatrists. Anguishes;
gnawings. Protractions of return
to the now desired but frightful outer world.

Young Tyson hasn't eaten since coming back.
She went to a wedding, her mother harangued her
it was all much too much for her
she sipped wine with a girl-friend, she fled here.

Many file down for shock & can't say after
whether they ate breakfast. Dazed till four.
One word is: the memory will come back.
Ah, weeks or months. Maybe.

Behind the locked door, called 'back there',
the worse victims.
Apathy or ungovernable fear
cause them not to watch through the window starlight.

They can't have matches, or telephone. They slob food.
Tantrums, & the suicidal, are put back there.
Sometimes one is promoted here. We are ecstatic.
Sometimes one has to go back.

It's all girls this time. The elderly, the men,
of my former stays have given way to girls,
fourteen to forty, raucous, racing the halls,
cursing their paramours & angry husbands.

Nights of witches: I dreamt a headless child.
Sobbings, a scream, a slam.
Will day glow again to these tossers, and to me?
I am staying days.

Death Ballad

('I don't care')

Tyson & Jo, Tyson & Jo
became convinced it was no go
& decided to end it all
at nineteen,—on the psychiatric ward.

Trouble is, Tyson was on the locked ward,
Jo for some reason on the open
and they were forbidden to communicate
either their love or their hate.

Heroin & the cops were Tyson's bit
I don't know just what Jo's was, ah but it
was more self-destructive still.
She tried to tear a window & screen out.

United in their feel of worthlessness
& rage, they stood like sisters in their way
blocking their path. They made a list
of the lies of Society & glared: 'We don't exist.'

The charismatic quality of these charming & sensitive girls
smiled thro' their vices; all were fond of them
& wished them well.
They sneered: 'We prefer Hell.'

What will their fates be? Put their heads together,
in their present mental weather,
no power can prevent their dying. That is so.
Only, Jo & Tyson, Tyson & Jo,

take up, outside your blocked selves, some small thing
that is moving
& wants to keep on moving
& needs therefore, Tyson, Jo, your loving.

'*I* Know'

Revelations every two hours on the Lounge.
So Hilary 17 tried suicide.
She goes barefooted & quizzically laughs.
There seems nothing wrong with her.

Her father found her. At the hospital they shot her several
times in the hip.

A bottle and a half of sleeping pills.
She came out of it, not even nauseated;
'I have a tough stomach.'

O Tyson: 'I don't *think* any more. I *know*.'

And Bertrand Russell's little improbable son
said to his teacher, a friend of ours at Princeton,
when they came to 'two plus two equals four'
piped up 'My *father* isn't sure of that.'

Ah at all levels. Many of the sane
walking the streets like trees
are weirder than my mournful fellow-patients;
they hide it better.

Laana's husband's lawyer served papers this afternoon.
That excellent & even noble woman cried as we sat on the Lounge.
The architecture of the locked ward leaves much to be desired.
A private conversation with mad Tyson
infeasible. Jeff, 6′4″, 18, paws my right arm, & cries.

Purgatory

The days are over, I leave after breakfast
with fifteen hundred things to do at home;
I made just now my new priority list.
Who will I miss?

Paul Bauer at 3 a.m. with his fine-going story
I cover over with him word by word
controlling the reader to do half the work
but forcing each sentence-series interesting?

Marcia, 15, tall, with her sweet shy grin
& low-voiced question
'Do you think I belong here like the others?'
against the piano, the pool- & ping-pong tables?

Greg who wandered into my room at midnight
& rehearsed to me (exhausted)
with finite iteration & wild pauses
his life-story? He retired two years ago
& hasn't had a good day or a good night since.

Some of the rest? Yes, yes! except for the black lady
who told us on Wednesday morning in the Group
she was going to suicide between 62 and 67.
Arrogant, touchy, vain, self-pitying, & insolent:

I haven't been spoken to so for thirteen years.
In print of course they insult you, & who cares? But in person?
O no I won't miss *her*. But Mrs Massey,
long widowed, long retired, toothpick-thin,

grew bored, & manages, with a withered smile
for each sole patient, our downstairs dining-room
at the evening eat. We have been friends for years
on my returnings, her survival. Late in a dinner
she stops by whatever table I am at

& bends over: 'Mr Berryman, was everything all right?'
Tonight though she touched my elbow afterward
as I was bearing my cleared tray to the rack:
'It gives me honour to serve a man like you,

would you sometime write me out a verse or two & sign it?'
O my brave dear lady, yes I will.
This is it.
I certainly will miss at 6:25 p.m. you.

And if *you* can carry on so, so maybe can I.

Heaven

Free! while in the cathedral at Seville
a Cardinal is singing. I bowed my face

& licked the monument. Aged women
waited behind me. Free! to lick & believe,

Free free! on an Easter afternoon
I almost said I loved her, we held hands
in the cemetery. Choirs came down on us,
St Anselm bothered his ecstatic repose to chide.

Ambrose interpreted: I was in love with her,
she was half with me. Among the tombs.
She married before she died,
a lissom light-haired alluring phantastic young lady.

Fly by, spirits of Night, her cenotaph
& forgive my survival with one shoe.
She forgave me that golden day whatever yen—
but what might forgive her loss?

Allow her exalted kind forbidding voice
a place in the *Lachrymosa*.
Let her sing on.
O lucky spirits to sing on with her.

Then *a capella*: mourning, barely heard,
across the Venetian waters: louder, dear,
I have a 15% hearing loss from a childhood illness,
louder, my darling, over at San Giorgio.

The Home Ballad

We must work & play and John Jacob Niles
will sing our souls to rest
(in his earlier-78 recordings).
Tomorrow we'll do our best, our best,
tomorrow we'll do our best.

The income tax is done, is done,
and three full weeks before
& it's going to be O very bad

but the medical expenses are more, are more,
the medical & support are more.

I left the place with one cracked toe,
at noon I packed in haste
out of that hospital O to go
they wanted me to stay, to stay
for an X-ray. I said 'Doctors, pray

the thing's not dislocated or broken O
any damned thing beside—
if it is, you're helpless—if it's not, you're a bore'
O I left that ward on my right foot
lurching on my left toe.

It hurt like hell, but never mind—
I hobbled on to free
swinging my typescript book like a bee
with honey back to the comb, the comb,
bringing my lovelies home.

The postal strike will end, will end,
I sent that Nixon a wire
because my ex-wife said I should—
I always do what she says, she says,
because my son sets me on fire.

It's home to my daughter I am come
with verses & stories true,
which I would also share with you,
my dear, my dear,
only you are not my daughter.

Now my book will go to friends—
women & men of wit—
Xerox'd before we publish it, it,
the limited edition & the public it,
before we publish it.

It's *Love & Fame* called, honey Kate,
you read it from the start
and sometimes I reel when you praise my art
my honey almost hopeless angry art,
which was both our Fate—

❦ *Part Four* ❧

Eleven Addresses to the Lord

1

Master of beauty, craftsman of the snowflake,
inimitable contriver,
endower of Earth so gorgeous & different from the boring Moon,
thank you for such as it is my gift.

I have made up a morning prayer to you
containing with precision everything that most matters.
'According to Thy will' the thing begins.
It took me off & on two days. It does not aim at eloquence.

You have come to my rescue again & again
in my impassable, sometimes despairing years.
You have allowed my brilliant friends to destroy themselves
and I am still here, severely damaged, but functioning.

Unknowable, as I am unknown to my guinea pigs:
how can I 'love' you?
I only as far as gratitude & awe
confidently & absolutely go.

I have no idea whether we live again.
It doesn't seem likely

from either the scientific or the philosophical point of view
but certainly all things are possible to you,

and I believe as fixedly in the Resurrection-appearances to Peter and
to Paul
as I believe I sit in this blue chair.
Only that may have been a special case
to establish their initiatory faith.

Whatever your end may be, accept my amazement.
May I stand until death forever at attention
for any your least instruction or enlightenment.
I even feel sure you will assist me again, Master of insight & beauty.

2

Holy, as I suppose I dare to call you
without pretending to know anything about you
but infinite capacity everywhere & always
& in particular certain goodness to me.

Yours is the crumpling, to my sister-in-law terrifying thunder,
yours the candelabra buds sticky in Spring,
Christ's mercy,
the gloomy wisdom of godless Freud:

yours the lost souls in ill-attended wards,
those agonized thro' the world
at this instant of time, all evil men,
Belsen, Omaha Beach,—

incomprehensible to man your ways.
May be the Devil after all exists.
'I don't try to reconcile anything' said the poet at eighty,
'This is a damned strange world.'

Man is ruining the pleasant earth & man.
What at last, my Lord, will you allow?

Postpone till after my children's deaths your doom
if it be thy ineffable, inevitable will.

I say 'Thy kingdom come,' it means nothing to me.
Hast Thou prepared astonishments for man?
One sudden Coming? Many so believe.
So not, without knowing anything, do I.

3

Sole watchman of the flying stars, guard me
against my flicker of impulse lust: teach me
to see them as sisters & daughters. Sustain
my grand endeavours: husbandship & crafting.

Forsake me not when my wild hours come;
grant me sleep nightly, grace soften my dreams;
achieve in me patience till the thing be done,
a careful view of my achievement come.

Make me from time to time the gift of the shoulder.
When all hurt nerves whine shut away the whiskey.
Empty my heart toward Thee.
Let me pace without fear the common path of death.

Cross am I sometimes with my little daughter:
fill her eyes with tears. Forgive me, Lord.
Unite my various soul,
sole watchman of the wide & single stars.

4

If I say Thy name, art Thou there? It may be so.
Thou art not absent-minded, as I am.
I am so much so I had to give up driving.
You attend, I feel, to the matters of man.

Across the ages certain blessings swarm,
horrors accumulate, the best men fail:

Socrates, Lincoln, Christ mysterious.
Who can search Thee out?

except Isaiah & Pascal, who saw.
I dare not ask that vision, though a piece of it
at last in crisis was vouchsafèd me.
I altered then for good, to become yours.

Caretaker! take care, for we run in straits.
Daily, by night, we walk naked to storm,
some threat of wholesale loss, to ruinous fear.
Gift us with long cloaks & adrenaline.

Who haunt the avenues of Angkor Wat
recalling all that prayer, that glory dispersed,
haunt me at the corner of Fifth & Hennepin.
Shield & fresh fountain! Manifester! Even mine.

5

Holy, & holy. The damned are said to say
'We never thought we would come into this place.'
I'm fairly clear, my Friend, there's no such place
ordained for inappropriate & evil man.

Surely they fall dull, & forget. We too,
the more or less just, I feel fall asleep
dreamless forever while the worlds hurl out.
Rest may be your ultimate gift.

Rest or transfiguration! come & come
whenever Thou wilt. My daughter & my son
fend will without me, when my work is done
in Your opinion.

Strengthen my widow, let her dream on me
thro' tranquil hours less & down to less.
Abrupt elsewhere her heart, I sharply hope.
I leave her in wise Hands.

6

Under new management, Your Majesty:
Thine. I have solo'd mine since childhood, since
my father's blow-it-all when I was twelve
blew out my most bright candle faith, and look at me.

I served at Mass six dawns a week from five,
adoring Father Boniface & you,
memorizing the Latin he explained.
Mostly we worked alone. One or two women.

Then my poor father frantic. Confusions & afflictions
followed my days. Wives left me.
Bankrupt I closed my doors. You pierced the roof
twice & again. Finally you opened my eyes.

My double nature fused in that point of time
three weeks ago day before yesterday.
Now, brooding thro' a history of the early Church,
I identify with everybody, even the heresiarchs.

7

After a Stoic, a Peripatetic, a Pythagorean,
Justin Martyr studied the words of the Saviour,
finding them short, precise, terrible, & full of refreshment.
I am tickled to learn this.

Let one day desolate Sherry, fair, thin, tall,
at 29 today her life the Sahara Desert,
who never has once enjoyed a significant relation,
so find His lightning words.

8

A Prayer for the Self

Who am I worthless that You spent such pains
and take may pains again?

I do not understand; but I believe.
Jonquils respond with wit to the teasing breeze.

Induct me down my secrets. Stiffen this heart
to stand their horrifying cries, O cushion
the first the second shocks, will to a halt
in mid-air there demons who would be at me.

May fade before, sweet morning on sweet morning,
I wake my dreams, my fan-mail go astray,
and do me little goods I have not thought of,
ingenious & beneficial Father.

Ease in their passing my beloved friends,
all others too I have cared for in a travelling life,
anyone anywhere indeed. Lift up
sober toward truth a scared self-estimate.

9

Surprise me on some ordinary day
with a blessing gratuitous. Even I've done good
beyond their expectations. What count we then
upon Your bounty?

Interminable: an old theologian
asserts that even to say You exist is misleading.
Uh-huh. I buy that Second-century fellow.
I press his withered glorifying hand.

You certainly do not as I exist,
impersonating as well the meteorite
& flaring in your sun your waterfall
or blind in caves pallid fishes.

Bear in mind me, Who have forgotten nothing,
& Who continues. I may not foreknow
& fail much to remember. You sustain
imperial desuetudes, at the kerb a widow.

10

Fearful I peer upon the mountain path
where once Your shadow passed, Limner of the clouds
up their phantastic guesses. I am afraid,
I never until now confessed.

I fell back in love with you, Father, for two reasons:
You were good to me, & a delicious author,
rational & passionate. Come on me again,
as twice you came to Azarias & Misael.

President of the brethren, our mild assemblies
inspire, & bother the priest not to be dull;
keep us week-long in order; love my children,
my mother far & ill, far brother, my spouse.

Oil all my turbulence as at Thy dictation
I sweat out my wayward works.
Father Hopkins said the only true literary critic is Christ.
Let me lie down exhausted, content with that.

11

Germanicus leapt upon the wild lion in Smyrna,
wishing to pass quickly from a lawless life.
The crowd shook the stadium.
The proconsul marvelled.

'Eighty & six years have I been his servant,
and he has done me no harm.
How can I blaspheme my King who saved me?'
Polycarp, John's pupil, facing the fire.

Make too me acceptable at the end of time
in my degree, which then Thou wilt award.
Cancer, senility, mania,
I pray I may be ready with my witness.

DELUSIONS *etc*

of John Berryman

[1 9 7 2]

We haue piped vnto you, and ye haue not danced:
wee haue mourned vnto you, and ye haue not lamented.

On parle toujours de 'l'art réligieux'. L'art est réligieux.

And indeed if Eugène Irténev was mentally deranged
everyone is in the same case; the most mentally deranged
people are certainly those who see in others indications
of insanity they do not notice in themselves.

Feu! feu! feu!

Than longen folk to goon on pilgrimages

❧ I ❧

OPUS DEI

(a layman's winter mockup, wherein moreover
the Offices are not within one day said
but thro' their hours at intervals
over many weeks—such being the World)

Lord, have mercy on my son: for he is lunatick,
and sore vexed: for ofttimes he falleth into
the fire, and oft into the water.

And he did evil, because he prepared not
his heart to seek the Lord.

Lauds

Let us rejoice on our cots, for His nocturnal miracles
antique outside the Local Group & within it
& within our hearts in it, and for quotidian miracles
parsecs-off yielding to the Hale reflector.

Oh He is potent in the corners. Men
with Him are potent: quasars we intuit,
and sequent to sufficient discipline
we perceive this glow keeping His winter out.

My marvellous black new brim-rolled felt is both stuffy & raffish,
I hit my summit with it, in firelight.
Maybe I only got a Yuletide tie
(increasing sixty) & some writing-paper

but ha (ha*ha*) I've bought myself a hat!
Plus-strokes from position zero! Its feathers sprout.
Thank you, Your Benevolence!
permissive, smiling on   our silliness You forged.

Matins

Thou hard. I will be blunt: Like widening
blossoms again glad toward Your soothe of sun
& solar drawing forth, I find meself
little this bitter morning, Lord, tonight.

Less were you tranquil to me in my dark
just now than tyrannous. O some bore down
sore with enticements—One abandoned me—
half I swelled up toward—till I crash awake.

However, lo, across what wilderness
in vincible ignorance past forty years
lost to (as now I see) Your sorrowing
I strayed abhorrent, blazing with my Self.

I thought I was in private with the Devil
hounding me upon Daddy's cowardice
(trustless in stir the freeze: 'Do your own time').
Intertangled all—choking, groping bodies.

'Behold, thou art taken in thy mischief,
because thou art a bloody man' with horror
loud down from Heaven did I not then hear,
but sudden' was received,—appointed even

poor scotographer, far here from Court,
humming over goodnatured Handel's Te Deum.
I waxed, upon surrender, strenuous
ah almost able service to devise.

I am like your sun, Dear, in a state of shear—
parts of my surface are continually slipping past others,

not You, not You. O I may, even, wave
in crisis like a skew Wolf-Rayet star.

Seas and hills, the high lakes, Superior,
accomplish your blue or emerald donations—
manifest too your soft forbearance, hard
& flint for fierce man hardly to take in.

I take that in. Yes. Just now. I read that.

Hop foot to foot, hurl the white pillows about,
jubilant brothers: He is our overlord,
holding up yet with crimson flags the Sun
whom He'll embark soon mounting fluent day!

Prime

Occludes wild dawn. Up thro' green ragged clouds
one sun is tearing, beset alders sway
weary under swollen sudden drops
and February winds shudder our doors,

Lord, as thou knowest. What fits me today
which work I can? I've to poor minimum
pared my commitments; still I'm sure to err
grievous & frequent before Evensong

and both I long toward & abhor that coming.
Yet *if* You and I make a majority
(as old Claudel encouraged) what sharp law
can pass this morning?—upon which, I take heart.

Also: 'The specific gravity of iron
is one and one-half times the size of Switzerland.'
Zany enlivens. People, pipe with pipes:
the least of us is back on contract, even

unto myself succeeding in sunrise
all over again!

All customary blessings,
anathemas of the date (post-Lupercal,
and sure The Baby was my valentine),

I'm not Your beaver, here disabled, still
it is an honour, where some have achieved,
to limp behind along, humming, & keen
again upon what blue trumps, hazy, vainless glory.

In Alexandria, O Saint Julian
gouty, chair-borne, displayed then on a camel
thorough the insufferable city, and burned.
In other places, many other holy

bishops, confessors, and martyrs. Thanks be to God.

Interstitial Office

Bitter upon conviction
(even of the seven women jurors
several wept) I will not kneel just now,
Father. I know I must

but being black & galled for these young men,
sick with their savage Judge
('we felt we had no alternative,
since all their evidence was ordered stricken')—

deep fatigue.
Conducting his own defence: 'men do pass laws
that usurp God's power . . .
I hope you'll try in your own way to speak peace.

God guide you.' Grim the prosecutor:
'He's trying to weasel his way out of it.'
Draft records here would have gone up in fire.
Peasant ladies & poupies there   went up go up in fire.

Who sat thro' all three trials tells me the juror in blue
looked inconsolably sad, and hid her eyes,
when one propped up on his table a little hand-lettered sign
WE LOVE YOU.

The judge is called P N.
This is of record. Where slept then Your lightning?
Loafed Your torque.
Well. Help us all! Yes—yes—I kneel.

Terce

Oh half as fearful for the yawning day
where full the Enemy's paratus and
I clearly may
wholly from prime time fail, as yet from yesterday

with good heart grateful having gone no more
(under what gentle tempting You knew I bore)
than what occurred astray,
I almost at a loss now genuflect and pray:

Twice, thrice each day five weeks at 'as we forgive
those who trespass against us' I have thought
ah his envenomed & most insolent missive
and I have *done* it!—and I damn him still

odd times & unawares catch myself at it:
I'm not a good man, I won't ever be,
there's no health in here. You expect too much.
This pseudo-monk is all but at despair.

My blustering & whining & *ill* will
versus His will—Forgive my insolence,
since when I was a fervent child to You
and Father Boniface each 5 a.m.

But this world that was not. Lavender & oval,
lilac, dissolve into one's saying hurriedly

'In sex my husband is brutal, beating, dirty, and drunk.'
Has this become Thy will, Thou Reconciler?

I seem to hear Retreat blast thro' bleared air
back to an unassailable redoubt,
even old Nile-sounds, where 'tears' & 'men' sound the same
and 'not to be' & 'be complete' are one.

Ugh. What the *hell* quail I perplexed about?
Christ Jesus. Gethsemane & Calvary
& the Emmaus road, hardly propose
(someone was saying) most of us are lost.

Sext

High noon has me pitchblack, so in hope out,
slipping thro' stasis, my heart skeps a beat
actuellement,
reflecting on the subtler menace of decline.

Who mentioned in his middle age 'Great Death
wars in us living which will have us all'
caused choreographers to tinker maps
pointing a new domestic capital

and put before Self-Preservation '1)'.
We do not know, deep now the dire age on,
if it's so, or mere a nightmare of one dark one,
Mani's by no means ultimate disciple.

I personally call it: outmoded biology,
of even mutation ignorant,
and in that, that a bare one in 100 is benevolent.

I wish You would clear this up. Moreover, I know
it may extend millennia, or ever, till
you tell somebody to. Meantime: Okay.
Now hear this programme for   my remnant of today.

Corpuscle-Donor, to the dizzy tune
of half a hundred thousand while I blink
losing that horrid same
scarlet amount and reel intact ahead:

so of rare Heart repair my fracturing heart
obedient to disobedience
minutely, wholesale, that come midnight neither
my mortal sin nor thought upon it lose me.

Nones

Problem. I cannot come among Your saints,
it's not in me—'Velle' eh?—I will, and fail.
But I would rather not be lost from You—
if I could hear of a middle ground, I'd opt:

a decent if minute salvation, sort of, on some fringe.
I am afraid, afraid. Brothers, who if
you are afraid are my brothers—veterans of fear—
pray with me now in the hour of our living.

It's Eleseus' grave makes the demons tremble,
I forget under what judge he conquered the world,
we're not alone here. Hearing Mark viii, though,
I'm sure to be ashamed of by. I am ashamed.

Riotous doubt assailed me on the stair,
I paused numb. Not much troubled with doubt,
not used to it. In a twinkling can man be lost?
Deep then in thought, and thought brought no relief.

But praying after, and somewhat after prayer
on no occasion fear had gone away!
I was alone with You again: 'the iron did swim.'
It has been proved to me again & again

He does *not* want me to be lost. Who does? The other.
But 'a man's shaliach is as it were himself':
I am Your person.

I have done this & that which I should do,
and given, and attended, and been still,
but why I do so I cannot be sure,
I am suspicious of myself. Help me!

I am olding & ignorant, and the work is great,
daylight is long, will ever I be done,
for the work is not for man, but the Lord God.
Now I have prepared with all my might for it

and mine O shrinks a micro-micro-minor
post-ministry, and of Thine own to Thee I have given,
and there is none abiding but woe or Heaven,
teste the pundits. Me I'm grounded for peace.

Flimsy between cloth, what may I attain
who slither in my garments? there's not enough of me,
Master, for virtue. I'm loose, at a loss.

Lo, where in this whirlpool sheltered in bone,
only less whirlpool bone, envisaging,
a sixtieth of an ounce to every pint,
sugar to blood, or coma or convulsion,

I hit a hundred and twenty notes a second
as many as I may to the glory of confronting—
unstable man, man torn by blast & gale—
Your figure, adamantly frontal.

Vespers

Vanity! hog-vanity, ape-lust
slimed half my blue day, interspersed
solely almost with conversation feared,
difficult, dear, leaned forward toward & savoured,

surivaling between. I have not done well.
Contempt—if even the man be judged sincere—
verging on horror, top a proper portion,
of the poor man in paracme, greeding still.

That's nothing, nothing! For his great commands
have reached me here—to love my enemy
as I love me—which is quite out of the question!
and worse still, to love You *with my whole mind*—

insufferable & creative addition to Deuteronomy 6—

Shift! Shift!
                Frantic I cast about abroad
for avenues of out: Who really this this?
Can *all* be lost, then? (But some do these things . .
I flinch from some horrible saints half the happy mornings—

so that's blocked off.) Maybe it's not God's voice
only Christ's only. (But our Lord is our Lord.
No vent there.) If more's demanded of man than can
man summon, You're unjust. Suppose not. See Jewish history,

tormented & redeemed, millennia later
in Freud & Einstein forcing us sorry & free,
Jerusalem Israeli! flames Anne Frank
a beacon to the Gentiles weltering.

With so great power bitter, so marvellous mild even mercy?
It's not conformable. It must be so,
but I am lost in it, dire Friend. Only I remember
of Solomon's cherubim 'their faces were inward.'

And thro' that veil of blue, & crimson, & linen,
& blue, You brood across forgiveness and
the house fills with a cloud, so that the priests
cannot stand to minister   by reason of the cloud.

Compline

I would at this late hour as little as may be
(in-negligent Father) plead. Not that I'm not attending,
only I kneel here spelled
under a mystery of one midnight

un-numbing now toward sorting in & out
I've got to get as little as possible wrong
O like Josiah then I heard with horror
instructions ancient as for the prime time

I am the king's son who squat down in rags
declared unfit by wise friends to inherit
and nothing of me left but skull & feet
& bloody among their dogs the palms of my hands.

Adorns my crossbar Your high frenzied Son,
mute over catcalls. How to conduct myself?
Does 'l'affabilité, l'humilité'
drift hither from the Jesuit wilderness,

a programme so ambitious? I am ambitious
but I have always stood content with towers
& traffic quashing thro' my canyons wild,
gunfire & riot fan thro' new Detroit.

Lord, long the day done—lapse, & by bootstraps,
oaths & toads, tranquil microseconds,
memory engulphing, odor of bacon burning
again—phantasmagoria prolix—

a rapture, though, of the Kingdom here here now
in the heart of a child—not far, nor hard to come by,
but natural as water falling, cupped
& lapped & slaking the child's dusty thirst!

If He for me as I feel for my daughter,
being His son, I'll sweat no more tonight

but happy snore & drowse. I have got it made,
and so have all we of contrition, for

if He loves me He must love everybody
and Origen was right & Hell is empty
or will be at apocatastasis.
Sinners, sin on. We'll suffer now & later

but not forever, dear friends & brothers! Moreover:
my old Black freshman friend's mild formula
for the quarter-mile, 'I run the first 220
as fast as possible, to get out in front.

Then I run the second 220 even faster,
to stay out in front.' So may I run for You,
less laggard lately, less deluded man
of oxblood expectation
with fiery little resiny aftertastes.

Heard sapphire flutings. The winter will end. I remember You.
The sky was red. My pillow's cold & blanched.
There are no fair bells in this city. This fireless house
lies down at Your disposal as usual! Amen!

ৡ II ৯

Washington in Love

I

Rectitude, and the terrible upstanding member

II

The music of our musketry (my first) is: *beautiful*

III

Intolerable Sally, loved in vain

IV

Mr John Adams of Massachusetts . . I accept, gentlemen.

* * *

V

Aloes. Adders. Roman gratitude.

VI

My porch elevation from the Potomac in 174′ 7½″.

VII

Bring the wounded, Martha! BRING THE WOUNDED, MEN.

Beethoven Triumphant

1

Dooms menace from tumults. Who's immune
among our mightier of headed men?
Chary with his loins
womanward, he begot us an enigma.

2

Often pretended he was absentminded
whenas he couldn't hear; and often was.

'. . . always *he*, he everywhere, as one says of Napoleon'
(Sir John Russell in '21 hearing a Trio)

3

O migratory rooms, the unworthy brothers, the worthless nephew!
One time his landlord tipped a hat to him;
Beethoven moved. Awkward & plangent
charged to the Archduke's foot,—who told his court 'Leave him alone.'

4

My unpretending love's the B flat major
by the old Budapest done. Schnabel did record
the Diabelli varia. I can't get a copy.
Then there's Casals I have, 101, both parts.

5

Moments are, early on in the 4th Piano Concerto
show him at his unrivalled middle best.
It does go up and up, and down lingeringly.
Miser & Timon-giving, by queer turns.

6

They wanted him London, partout. 'Too late', 'Too late'
he muttered, and mimicked piano-playing.
Prodigious, so he never knew his age
his father'd lied about.

7

Whatever his kindness to Rossini and contempt for Italians,
if down he sat a while in an exquisite chair
it had to be thrown out (five witnesses,
none of whom says quite why).

8

O did he sleep sound? Heavy, heavy that.
Waked at 3:30 not by some sonata
but by a botched rehearsal of the Eighth
where all thing has to go right

(Koussevitzky will make it, Master; lie back down)

9

Lies of his fluency from Betty von Arnim
to eager Goethe, who'd not met the man.
Fact is, he stumbled at the start
and in the sequence, stumbled in the middle,

10

often unsure at the end—shown by his wilderness
on-sketchings encrusted like Tolstoy (not Mozart:
who'd, ripping napkins, the whole strict in mind
before notes serried; limitationless, unlike you).

11

Inundations out from ground zero.
Back from an over-wealth, the simplification of Necessity.
When brother Johann signed 'Real Estate Owner', you: 'Brain owner'.
And what, among fumbling notes, in the nights, did you read?

12

Coffee and tallow spot your *Odyssey*
though, and when Schindler was an arse to ask
your drift in Opus 31 and the Appassionata
you uttered at him, cheerful, 'Just read *The Tempest*.'

13

Thinking presides, some think now,—only presides—
at the debate of the Instincts; but presides,
over powers, over love, hurt-back.
You grumbled: 'Religion and Figured Bass are closed concepts.
Don't argue.'

14

To disabuse the 'Heiligerdankgesang'?
Men up to now sometimes weep openly.
Tortured your surly star to sing impossibly
against the whole (small) thwarting orchestra.
One chord thrusts, as it must

15

find allies, foes, resolve, in subdued crescendo.
Unfazed, you built-in the improbable.
You clowned. You made throats swallow
and shivered the backs of necks.
You made quiver with glee, at will; not long.
This world is of male energy male pain.

16

Softnesses, also, yours, which become us.
What stayed your chosen instrument? The 'cello?
At two points. At others, the forte-piano.
At others, the fiddles & viola & 'cello.

17

I'm hard to you, odd nights. I bulge my brain,
my shut chest already suffers,—so I play blues
and Haydn whom you—both the which touch but they don't ache me.
I'm less inured in your disaster corner,
Master. You interfere.
                    O yes we interfere

or we're mere sweetening: what? the alkali lives
around and after ours. Sleeking down nerves
Passing time dreaming. And you did do that   too.
       There hover Things cannot be banned by you;
damned few.
                 If we take our head in our ears and listen
Ears! Ears! the Devil paddled in you

18

heard not a hill flute or a shepherd sing!
tensing your vision onto an alarm
of gravid measures, sequent to demure,
all we fall, absently foreknowing . .
You force a blurt: Who was I?
Am I these tutti, am I this rallentando?
This entrance of the oboe?
                          I am all these
the sane man makes reply on the locked ward.

19

Did ever you more than (clearly) cope odd women?
save clumsy uncommitted overtures
au moins à Joséphine? save the world-famous unsent
or when retrieved and past-death-treasured letter?

20

Deception spared. No doubt he took one look:
'Not mine; I can't make a kroner there.'
Straightforward staves, dark bars,
late motions toward the illegible. Musical thighs,

21

spared deep age. Out at prime, in a storm
inaudible thunder he went, upon his height.
The other day I called our chief prose-writer

at home a thousand miles off and began
'How are you, Sir?'   out of three decades' amity

22

'I'm OLD,' he said. Neither of us laughed.
Spared deep age, Beethoven. I wish you'd caught
young Schubert's last chamberworks and the Winterreise
you could have read through, puffing.

23

Ah but the indignities you flew free from,
your self-abasements even would increase
together with your temper, evil already,
'some person of bad character, churlish & eccentric'
For refusing to scribble a word of introduction:
'He is an unlicked bear'—almost Sam Johnson.

24

An entertainer, a Molière, in the onset
under too nearly Mozart's aegis,
the mysteries of Oedipus old were not beyond you.
Islands of suffering & disenchantment & enchantment.

25

But the brother charged the dying brother board & lodging.
Bedbugs biting, stench, unquenchable thirst,
ungovernable swelling. Then the great Malfatti
gave up on, and accorded frozen punch ad lib.

26

Your body-filth flowed on to the middle of the floor
'I shall, no doubt, soon be going above'
sweat beading you, gasping of Shakespeare,
knocking over the picture of Haydn's birthplace.

27

They said you died.   '20,000 persons of every class'
clashed at the gates of the house of mourning, till they locked them.
Franz Schubert stalked the five hundred feet to the church.
It's a lie! You're all over my wall!

You march and chant around here! I hear your thighs.

Your Birthday in Wisconsin You Are 140

'One of the wits of the school' your chum would say—
Hot diggity!—   What the *hell* went wrong for you,
Miss Emily,—besides the 'pure & terrible' Congressman
your paralyzing papa,—and Mr Humphrey's dying
        & Benjamin's (the other reader)? . .

Fantastic at 32 outpour, uproar, 'terror
since September, I could tell to none'
after your 'Master' moved his family West
and timidly to Mr Higginson:
        'say if my verse is alive.'

Now you wore only white, now you did not appear,
till frantic 50 when you hurled your heart
down before Otis, who would none of it
thro' five years for 'Squire Dickinson's cracked daughter'
        awful by months, by hours . .

Well. Thursday afternoon, I'm in W————
drinking your ditties, and (dear) *they* are *alive*,—
more so than (bless her) Mrs F who teaches
farmers' red daughters & their beaux *my* ditties
        and yours & yours & yours!
        Hot diggity!

Drugs Alcohol Little Sister

(1887–1914)

When I peered out, he had nine nights to spare
after his gun was man-handled from him
while the dying in his care
mountained and the weakened mind gave way.

So far off to my flatland flew no moan
who'd fail to focus yet for silly weeks.
I shoot him, though, a fellow agony
then I could hardly coo now I must speak

(back from this *schwartze Verwesung* whose white arms
lean subtle over ivories & blacks
and I am sweating, her blind scent subdues
ordure & the hiss of souls escaping)

for let us not all together in such pain
dumb apart pale into oblivion—no!
Trakl, con the male nurse.
Surmounted by carrion, cry out   and overdose & go.

In Memoriam (1914–1953)

I

Took my leave (last) five times before the end
and even past these precautions lost the end.
Oh, I *was* highlone in the corridor
      fifteen feet from his bed

where no other hovered, nurse or staff or friend,
and only the terrible breathing ever took place,
but trembling nearer after some small time
      I came on the tent collapsed

and silence—O unable to say when.
I stopped panicked a nurse, she a doctor
in twenty seconds, he pulled the plasticine,
    bent over, and shook his head at me.

Tubes all over, useless versus coma,
on the third day his principal physician
told me to pray he'd die, brain damage such.
    His bare stub feet stuck out.

II

So much for the age's prodigy, born one day
before I surfaced—when this fact emerged
Dylan grew stuffy and would puff all up
    rearing his head back and roar

'A little more—more—*respect* there, Berryman!'
Ah he had thát,—so far ahead of me,
I half-adored him for his intricate booms & indecent tales
    almost entirely untrue.

Scorn bottomless for elders: we were twenty-three
but Yeats I worshipped: he was amused by this,
all day the day set for my tea with the Great Man
    he plotted to turn me up drunk.

Downing me daily at shove-ha'penny
with *English* on the thing. C—— would slump there
plump as a lump for hours, my word how that changed!
    Hard on her widowhood—

III

Apart a dozen years, sober in Seattle
'After many a summer' he intoned
putting out a fat hand. We shook hands.
    How very shook to see him.

His talk, one told me, clung latterly to Eden,
again & again of the Garden & the Garden's flowers,
not ever the Creator, only of that creation
    with a radiant will to go there.

I have sat hard for twenty years on this
mid potpals' yapping, and O I sit still still
though I quit crying that same afternoon
    of the winter of his going.

Scribbled me once, it's around somewhere or other,
word of their 'Edna Millay cottage' at Laugharne
saying come down to and disarm a while
    and down a many few.

O down a many few, old friend,
and down a many few.

୧ III ୨

Gislebertus' Eve

Most men are not wicked. . . . They
are sleep-walkers, not evildoers.
KAFKA TO G JANOUCH

Eve & her envy roving slammed me down
prone in discrepancy: I can't get things right:
the passion for secrets the passion worst of all,
the ultimate human, from Leonardo & Darwin

to the austere Viennese with the cigar
and Bohr a-musing: 'The opposite of a true

statement is a false statement. But the opposite
of a profound truth may be another profound truth.'

So now we see where we are, which is all-over
we're nowhere, son, and suffering we know it,
rapt in delusion, where weird particles
frantic & Ditheletic orbit our

revolutionary natures. She snaked out a soft
small willing hand, curved her ivory fingers on
a new taste sensation, in reverie over
something other,
sank her teeth in, and offered him a bite.

I too find it delicious.

Scholars at the Orchid Pavilion

1

Sozzled, Mo-tsu, after a silence, vouchsafed
a word alarming: 'We must love them all!'
Affronted, the fathers jumped.
'Yes' he went madly on and waved in quest
of his own dreadful subject 'O the fathers'
he cried 'must not be all!'
Whereat upon consent we broke up for the day.

2

The bamboo's bending power formed our theme
next dawn, under a splendid wind. The water
flapped to our tender gaze.
Girls came & crouched with tea. Great Wu pinched one,
forgetting his later nature. How the wind howled,
tranquil was our pavilion,
watching & reflecting, fingering bamboo.

3

'Wild geese & bamboo' muttered Ch'en Hung-shou
'block out our boundaries of fearful wind.
Neither requires shelter.
I shelter among painters, doing bamboo.
The young shoots unaffected by the wind
mock our love for their elders.'
Mo-tsu opened his mouth & closed it to again.

4

'The bamboo of the Ten Halls,' went on Ch'en
'of my time, are excellently made.
I cannot find so well
ensorcelled those of later or former time.
Let us apply the highest praise, pure wind,
to those surpassing masters;—
having done things, a thing, along that line myself.'

Tampa Stomp

The first signs of the death of the boom came in the summer,
early, and everything went like snow in the sun.
Out of their office windows. There was miasma,
a weight beyond enduring, the city reeked of failure.

The eerie, faraway scream of a Florida panther,
gu-roomp of a bull-frog. One broker we knew
drunk-driving down from Tarpon Springs flew free
when it spiralled over & was dead without one mark on him.

The Lord fled that forlorn peninsula
of fine sunlight and millions of fishes & moccasins
& Spanish moss & the Cuban bit my father
bedded & would abandon Mother for.

Ah, an antiquity, a chatter of ghosts.
Half the fish now in half the time

since those blue days died. We're running out
of time & fathers, sore, artless about it.

Old Man Goes South Again Alone

O parakeets & avocets, O immortelles
& ibis, scarlet under that stunning sun,
deliciously & tired I come
toward you in orbit, Trinidad!—albeit without the one

I would bring with me to those isles & seas,
leaving her airborne westward thro' great snows
whilst I lapse on your beaches
sandy with dancing, dark   moist eyes among my toes.

The Handshake, The Entrance

'You've got to cross that lonesome valley' and
'You've got to cross it by yourself.'
'Ain't no one gwine cross it for you,
You've got to cross it by yourself.'
Some say John was a baptist, some say John was a Jew,
some say John was just a natural man

addin' he's a preacher too?

'You've got to cross that lonesome valley,'
Friends & lovers, link you and depart.
This one is strictly for me.
I shod myself & said goodbye to Sally
Murmurs of other farewells half broke my heart
I set out sore indeed.

The High King failed to blossom on my enterprise.
Solely the wonderful sun shone down like lead.
Through the ridges I endured,
down in no simple valley I opened my eyes,

[248

with my strong walk down in the vales & dealt with death.
I increased my stride, cured.

Lines to Mr Frost

Felled in my tracks by your tremendous horse
slain in its tracks by the angel of good God,
I wonder toward your marvellous tall art
warning away maybe in that same morning

you squandered afternoon of your great age
on my good gravid wife & me, with tales
gay of your cunning & colossal fame
& awful character, and—Christ—I see

I know & can do nothing, and don't mind—
you're talking about American power and how
somehow we've got to be got to give it up—
so help me, in my poverty-stricken way

I said the same goddamn thing yesterday
to my thirty kids, so I was almost ready
to hear you from the grave with these passionate grave
last words, and frankly Sir you fill me with joy.

He Resigns

Age, and the deaths, and the ghosts.
Her having gone away
in spirit from me. Hosts
of regrets come & find me empty.

I don't feel this will change.
I don't want any thing
or person, familiar or strange.
I don't think I will sing

any more just now;
ever. I must start
to sit with a blind brow
above an empty heart.

No

She says: *Seek help!* Ha-ha Ha-ha & Christ.
Gall in every direction, putrid olives,
stench of the Jersey flats, the greasy clasp
crones in black doorways afford their violent clients

A physicist's lovely wife grinned to me in Cambridge
she only liked, apart from getting gamblers hot
& stalk out on them, a wino for the night
in a room off Scollay Square, a bottle, his efforts

Dust in my sore mouth, this deafening wind,
frightful spaces down from all sides, I'm pale
I faint for some soft & solid & sudden way out
as quiet as hemlock in that Attic prose

with comprehending friends attending—
a certain reluctance but desire here too,
the sweet cold numbing upward from my burning feet,
a last & calm request, which will be granted.

The Form

Mutinous & free I drifted off
unsightly. I did not see the creatures watch.
I had forgotten about the creatures, which
were kind and whether any of them was mine.

I am a daemon. Ah, when Mother was ill
a Sister took me into their little chapel
to admire the plaster angels: 'Mine are real,'
I said, 'and fly around the chapel on *my* farm.'

O torso hurled high in great 'planes from town
down on convulsing town, brainsick applause
thick to sick ear, thro' sixteen panicked nights
a trail of tilted bottles. I had no gun,

and neither Wednesday nor Thursday did buy one
but Friday and I put it in my bag
and bought a wide-eyed & high-yaller whore
for company of darkness. Deep in dream

I saw myself upreared like William the Silent
over his tomb in Delft, armoured & impotent;
she shook me screaming. In another place
I shuddered as I combed & saw my face.

Swallowing, I felt myself deranged
and would be ever so. He has spewed me out.
I wandered, for some reason, raging, home
where then I really hurt. All that life ahead alone

vised me from midnight. I prepared for dawn.
An odd slight thought like a key slid somewhere:
'Only tomorrow.' Wondering, I said: 'Oh.
It's possible, then.'
                    My light terrible body unlocked, I leaned upon
                                                              You.

Ecce Homo

Long long with wonder I thought you human,
almost beyond humanity but not.
Once, years ago, only in a high bare hall
of the great Catalan museum over Barcelona,
     I thought you might be more—

a Pantocrator glares down, from San Clemente de Tahull,
making me feel you probably were divine,
but not human, thro' that majestic image.

Now I've come on something where you seem both—
    a photograph of it only—

Burgundian, of painted & gilt wood,
life-size almost (not that we know your Semitic stature),
attenuated, your dead head bent forward sideways,
your long feet hanging, your thin long arms out
    in unconquerable beseeching—

A Prayer After All

Father, Father, I am overwhelmed.
I cannot speak tonight.
Do you receive me back into Your sight?
It seems it must be so, for

strangely the Virgin came into my mind
as I stood beside my bed—
whom I not only have not worshippéd
since childhood, but also

harsh words have said of, that she pushed her Son
before his time was come
which he rebuked her for, and leaving home
repudiated hers & her—

and for no reason, standing in the dark
before I had knelt down
(as is my custom) to speak with You, I found
my tongue feeling its way

thro' the Hail Mary, trying phrase by phrase
its strangeness, for the unwelcome
to my far mind estranged, awaiting some
unacceptable sense, and

Father I was amazed I could *find none*
and I have walked downstairs

to sit & wonder: You must have been Theirs
all these years, and They Yours,

and now I suppose I have prayed to You after all
and Her and I suppose she is the Queen of Heaven
under Your greater glory, even
more incomprehensible but forgiving glory.

Back

I was out of your Church for 43 years, my Dear;
adopted back in, welling blood.
Admire the techniques of your ministers
I must, succeeding, but could not enjoy them

during the rite: for the man in fury,
possessed by his own tumultuous & burning energy,
to bring to a halt is hard as tungsten carbide
and crook his knees is harder than to die.

Exceptional, singular, & mysterious,
ochered, forbidden to utter,
the revolted novice & veteran thro' cold night
vigilant in the forest, a caring beast,

becoming sacral, perforates his nose
at first glow, in honour of the Mother.
Whose coming to be is constant,
Thou hast caused her coming-to-be in beauty.

Hello

Hel*lo* there, Biscuit! You're a better-looking broad
by much than, and your sister's dancing up & down.
'I just gave one mighty Push'
your mother says, and we are all in business.

I thought your mother might powder my knuckles
gript at one point, with wild eyes on my tie
'Don't move!' and then the screams began,
they wheeled her off, and we are all in business.

I wish I knew what business (son) we're in
I can't wait seven weeks to see her grin
I'm not myself, we are all changing here
direction *and* velocity, to   accommodate you, dear.

❦ IV *Scherzo* ❧

Navajo Setting the Record Straight

'Warrior Who Went With a Crowd, my sand-painter grandfather,'
said Axel no-middle-initial Mankey Jr
to the Marine sarge, 'served at Fort Wingate
as a sergeant-major scout, and he was buried

with full military honors in Arlington.
So screw you, Sergeant, *and* your Greek accent.
Moreover, from the black world into the blue
came The First People, to the yellow world,

and finally into the present sick white world
thro' a giant reed,—which may be seen to this day
near Silverton, Colorado. Yah-ah-teh.'
His unbound black locks wind-flared as back at Left & Right Mittens
motherless next to the earth-covered log hogan of Mrs Hetty Rye.

Henry By Night

Henry's nocturnal habits were the terror of his women.
First it appears he snored, lying on his back.
Then he thrashed & tossed,
changing position like a task fleet. Then, inhuman,
he woke every hour or so—they couldn't keep track
of mobile Henry, lost

at 3 a.m., off for more drugs or a cigarette,
reading old mail, writing new letters, scribbling
excessive Songs;
back then to bed, to the old tune or get set
for a stercoraceous cough, without quibbling
death-like. His women's wrongs

they hoarded & forgave, mysterious, sweet;
but you'll admit it was no way to live
or even keep alive.
I won't mention the dreams I won't repeat
sweating & shaking: something's gotta give:
up for good at five.

Henry's Understanding

He was reading late, at Richard's, down in Maine,
aged 32? Richard & Helen long in bed,
my good wife long in bed.
All I had to do was strip & get into my bed,
putting the marker in the book, & sleep,
& wake to a hot breakfast.

Off the coast was an island, P'tit Manaan,
the bluff from Richard's lawn was almost sheer.
A chill at four o'clock.
It only takes a few minutes to make a man.

A concentration upon now & here.
Suddenly, unlike Bach,

& horribly, unlike Bach, it occurred to me
that *one* night, instead of warm pajamas,
I'd take off all my clothes
& cross the damp cold lawn & down the bluff
into the terrible water & walk forever
under it out toward the island.

Defensio in Extremis

I said: Mighty men have encamped against me,
and they have questioned not only the depth of my defences
but my sincerity.
Now, Father, let them have it.

Thou knowest, however their outcry & roar,
in a study of stillness I read my single heart
after my collapsed returning.
Oh even A, great E, & tender M

splinter at my immusical procedures & crude loves.
Surely some spiritual life is not what it might be?
Surely they are half-ful of it?
Tell them to leave me damned well alone with my misunderstood
                                                                orders.

Damn You, Jim D., You Woke Me Up

I thought I'd say a thing to please myself
& why not him, about his talent, to him
or to some friend who'd maybe pass it on
because he printed a sweet thing about me
a long long time ago, & because of gladness
to see a good guy *get out* of the advertising racket
& suddenly make like the Great Chicago Fire—
yes that was it, fine, fine—(this was a dream

woke me just now)—I'll get a pen & paper
at once & put that down, I thought, and I went
away from where I was, up left thro' a garden
in the direction of the Avenue
but got caught on a smart kid's escalator
going uphill against it, got entangled,
a girl was right behind me in the dark,
they hoisted up some cart and we climbed on
& over the top & *down*, thinking Jesus
I'll break my arse but a parked car broke the fall
I landed softly there in the dark street
having forgotten all about   the Great Chicago Fire!

Somber Prayer

O my Lord, I am not eloquent
neither heretofore, nor since Thou hast spoken . .
but I am slow of speech, of a dim tongue.
He mentions, here, Thy 'counsel and dominion';

so I will borrow Newton's mouth. Spare me
Uccello's ark-locked lurid deluge, I'm
the brutal oaf from the barrel stuck mid-scene,—
or ghost me past the waters . . Miriam . .

A twelve-year-old all solemn, sorry-faced,
described himself lately as 'a lifetime prick'.
Me too. Maladaptive devices.
At fifty-five, half-effective, I still feel rotten about myself.

Panicky weekdays, I pray hard,
not worth.

Sucking, clinging, following, crying, smiling,
I come Your child to You.

Unknowable? perhaps not altogether

I dare interpret: Adonai of rescue.
Whatever and ever other I have lain skew over
however O little else around You know
I doubt I'm wrong on this.
Augustine and Pascal swore the same strange.

Yet young men young men in the paddies rescue.

Add Sway omnicompetent, add pergalactic Intellect,
forbearance invisible, a tumbling thunder of laughter
(or whence our so alert pizzazz & laughter?),
an imagination of the queens of Chartres the kings there, if these only,
                                                                    still
we're trans-acting with You.

Minnesota Thanksgiving

For that free Grace bringing us past great risks
& thro' great griefs surviving to this feast
sober & still, with the children unborn and born,
among brave friends, Lord, we stand again in debt
and find ourselves in the glad position: Gratitude.

We praise our ancestors who delivered us here
within warm walls all safe, aware of music,
likely toward ample & attractive meat
with whatever accompaniment
Kate in her kind ingenuity has seen fit to devise,

and we hope—across the most strange year to come—
continually to do them and You not sufficient honour
but such as we become able to devise

out of a decent or joyful *conscience* & thanksgiving.
Yippee!
          Bless then, as Thou wilt, this wilderness board.

A Usual Prayer

According to Thy will: That this day only
I may avoid the vile
and baritone away in a broader chorus
of to each other decent forbearance & even aid.

Merely sensational let's have today,
lacking mostly thinking,—
men's thinking being eighteen-tenths deluded.
Did I get this figure out of St Isaac of Syria?

For fun: find me among   my self-indulgent artbooks
a new drawing by Ingres!
For discipline, two self-denying minus-strokes
and my wonted isometrics, barbells, & antiphons.

Lord of happenings, & little things,
muster me westward fitter to my end—
which has got to be Your strange end for me—
and toughen me effective to the tribes en route.

Overseas Prayer

Good evening. At the feet of the king, my Lord,
I fall seven & yet seven times.
Behold what insult has Your servant suffered
from Shuwardata and Milkiln & his ilk.

Put them under saws, & under harrows of iron,
& under axes of iron, make them pass thro' the brick-kiln
lest upon any time they flirt at me again.
Enjoin them to the blurred & breathless dead.

The Valley of the Cheesemakers has disappeared
also, my Lord. Your precincts are in ruin,
your revenues ungathered. Minarets
blot our horizon as I pen, my Lord.

I feel myself a deep & old objection.
You gave me not a very able tho' of integrity father,
joyless at last, Lord, and sometimes I hardly
(thinking on him) perform my duty to you.

Ah then I mutter 'Forty-odd years past.
Do I yet repine?' and go about your business,—
a fair wind and the honey lights of home
being all I beg this wind-torn foreign evening.

Amos

For three insane things evil, and for four,
vex will I Pekin in the latter days,
their ancestors shall suffer for their children
in turbid horror; thus saith the Lord.

For three insane things evil, and for four,
grieve will I Kremlin present', & the Urals
& dachas, and I will tear their leaderhood
that many may fly home; saith the Lord.

For three insane things evil, and for four,
baffle will I with victory Hanoi
& gross pretenders, the black megaphone
of doctrine over the tribe's hills; saith the Lord.

For three insane things evil, and for four,
sustain will I puny & greedy Thieu
the potent client—harrowing that people on,
and I will have no pity, saith the Lord.

For three insane things evil, and for four,
torment will I the North & South & East

& West with understanding, where they stand,
and I will unman & de-parent them
and will deprive them; thus saith the Lord.

Certainty Before Lunch

Ninety percent of the mass of the Universe
(90%!) may be gone in collapsars,
pulseless, lightless, forever—if they exist.
My friends the probability man & I

& his wife the lawyer are taking a country walk
in the flowerless April snow in exactly two hours
and maybe won't come back. Finite & unbounded
the massive spirals absolutely fly

distinctly apart, by math *and* observation,
current math, this morning's telescopes
& inference. My wife is six months gone
so won't be coming. That mass must be somewhere!

or not? just barely possibly *may not*
B E anywhere? My Lord, I'm glad we don't
on x or y depend for Your being there.
I know You are there. The sweat is, I am here.

The Prayer of the Middle-Aged Man

Amid the doctors in the Temple at twelve, between
mother & host at Cana implored too soon,
in the middle of disciples, the midst of the mob,
between the High Priest and the Procurator,
          among the occupiers,

between the malefactors, and 'stetit in medio,
et dixit, Pax vobis' and 'ascensit ad medium
Personarum et caelorum,' dear my Lord,

mercy a sinner nailed dead-centre too,
        pray not implored too late,—

for also Ezra stood between the seven & the six,
        restoring the new Law.

'How Do You Do, Dr Berryman, Sir?'

Edgy, perhaps. *Not* on the point of bursting-forth,
but toward that latitude,—I think? *Not* 'shout loud & march straight.'
Each lacks something in some direction. I
am not entirely at the mercy of.

The tearing of hair no.

Pickt up pre-dawn & tortured and detained,
Mr Tan Mam and many other students
sit tight but vocal in illegal cells
and as for Henry Pussycat   he'd just as soon be dead

(on the Promise of—I know it sounds incredible—
if can he muster penitence enough—
he can't though—
glory

The Facts & Issues

I really believe He's here all over this room
in a motor hotel in Wallace Stevens' town.
I admit it's weird; and *could*—or could it?—not be so;
but frankly I don't think there's a molecular chance of that.
It doesn't seem hypothesis. Thank heavens
millions agree with me, or mostly do,
and have done ages of our human time,
among whom were & still are some very sharp cookies.
I don't exactly feel missionary about it,
though it's *very* true I wonder if I should.

I regard the boys who don't buy this as deluded.
Of course they regard me no doubt as deluded.
Okay with me! And not the hell with them
at *all*—no!—I feel *dubious* on Hell—
it's here, all right, but elsewhere, after? Screw that,
I feel pretty sure that evil simply ends
for the doer (having wiped him out,
by the way, usually) where good goes on,
or good *may* drop dead too: I don't think so:
I can't say I have hopes in that department
myself, I lack ambition just just there,
I know that Presence says it's mild, and it's mild,
but being what I am I wouldn't care
to dare go nearer. Happy to be here
and to have been here, with such lovely ones
so infinitely better, but to me
even in their suffering infinitely kind
& blessing. I am a greedy man, of course,
but I wouldn't want that kind of luck continued,—
or even *increased* (for Christ's sake), & *forever*?
Let me be clear about this. It is plain to me
Christ underwent man & treachery & socks
& lashes, thirst, exhaustion, the bit, for *my* pathetic & disgusting vices,
to make this filthy fact of particular, long-after,
far-away, five-foot-ten & moribund
human being happy. Well, he has!
I am so happy I could scream!
It's *enough*! I can't BEAR ANY MORE.
Let this be it. I've *had* it. I can't wait.

King David Dances

Aware to the dry throat of the wide hell in the world
O trampling empires, and mine one of them,
and mine one gross desire against His sight
slaughter devising there,
some good behind, ambiguous ahead,
revolted sons, a pierced son, bound to bear,

mid hypocrites amongst idolaters,
mockt in abysm by one shallow wife,
with the ponder both of priesthood & of State
heavy upon me, yea,
all the black same I dance my blue head off!

EARLY POEMS

from "Twenty Poems" in
Five Young American Poets [1940]

Song from "Cleopatra"

From Pharos I have seen her white
Standing with Pompey while the moon
Twice turned and made a silver noon
Upon the Alexandrian night.
When air was olive, she but young,
Ambition died into delight.

A bird there was that died and then
Struck from its ashes into life.
Resentment got continual strife
And blood upon the marsh and fen.
Limp in the antique arms of one
She learnt her hatred for all men.

That Queen insulted Cicero,
Lucan and Horace threw a gibe,
But Antony and all his tribe
Cut out the hearts that called her so.
Wandering upon her terrace
They go and ask not where they go.

What symbol of degraded death
Will now sustain what she has been?
Not a Tanagra figurine
From out the tumult and the wrath.
Perhaps the sensual eye, the pride
That spent itself before her breath.

Early Poems

The Apparition

Frequently when the night
Binds Austria and England in
One indiscriminate place,
Staring I see between
A familiar chair and the slight
Smile of a fresco god your face.

Which from the advancing eye
Withdraws, miles in an instant,
Is quite gone, and the god
Resumes his banishment
To curtain mathematics: dry
And bitter the brain is in my head.

Could I suspend sight where
It met you, could I command
Instinct be still, blood still,
I fancy you might stand
And your eyes, even your hair
Stay to reward that skill.

Tonight I will do: patience
Rule my long love and guide
The wild nerves when they start.
But something will have died
From me if I look once
There and restrain my heart.

Cambridge
1937

Meditation

I

The clouds before the sun when the sun rose
Perform their thoughtless promise, summer rain
Filling the morning falls about the house.
River's resentment to its natural gain
Is reconciled; communications close
To the town, muffled, and the sentinel strain
Of solitude is taken by the ground
Together with half of light and all of sound:
Asylum thus for memory and praise.

II

Uncircumscribed in an August prison
The eye of the mind travels among its past,
Seeing an anxious now; this without plan
But perfect apprehension. Being chaste
It finds simple and strange mostly the moon
Directing loss, generation into waste
Four hundred miles hence and the fluent blood
That never knew an evil from a good
Or heard among the springing corn the sun.

III

Elegy that way. The intelligent eye
Is tourist here and passes on, pausing
Now with delight upon the symmetry
And energetic poise of a grey wing
In Channel flight against a heavy sky,
Bearing like feathers the weight and end of Spring
To scattered home, indicating but this:
The texture of grey flight, analysis
Left dazzled on the shore hungry and dry.

IV

Next remains to the mind, of all those loud
Merciless laughing boys but one who knows
Too the continual drive of craft. The crowd
In classroom and on field, time cannot choose
But give a humorous aspect; we allowed
Last night however in our distant news
No compromise, five years and sea apart.
I thought upon, with sickness at my heart,
The many foundered and a few the proud.

V

And now the eye breaks out to open light
Beyond cloud, where the source it can maintain:
That constant sensibility which by night
Exerts content upon my head, my brain
Invests with careful patience and my sight
By day teaches a singular discipline.
Hers is the obscure laurel, the steady love
Which will not qualify before the grave,
Hers integral and passionate delight.

VI

The uncontrollable eye spins in the year,
A curious harvest brings. Pieces of bread
At twilight on a Dublin quay, and fear;
The clenched lip, a wrinkle on the forehead
Of hanging Christ; the eye sees everywhere
Indestructible evidence of dread,
In apples as in smiles, horrible both.
But generosity upon her mouth
Levels all torment in an actual tear.

VII

Million kaleidoscope: gesture of hand
Whose white invisible hairs are dangerous

Men, whose wrist intends frontier assault and
Rapture; the rain silent beyond the house;
The kernel being stripped of its tough rind
Bitters in air; deserted walls for us
One afternoon a lovely shelter, soft
Grass where a floor had been, and when she laughed
The sound could make a shelter for the mind.

VIII

Items to make a history. Most I stare
Upon the sign of our precaution, now
Symbol of some defeat. For a career
Before it began ends; and she, although
She wanted nothing, wants in the young air
New breath for heritage we have let go.
Her secret loss assures that he is dead
Who could not know his dark restricted bed
And what horizons have been tested there.

Cambridge
13 August 1937

Sanctuary

An evening faultless interval when
Blood ran crescendo in the brain
And time lay as a poem clear
Falls from me now; a friend is gone
Who taught my anger opaque air,
Is all but lost in time; few things remain.

The insolent look a woman gave
Casually from a door one day
Leaves me not, on the other hand;
Strange stigmata to our grave,
Indiscriminate as the wind,
We carry, with our bones they will decay.

The sky and sea are one in the night,
No eye can make distinction where
Eye is contained, eye subject is
To eyelid, even the pawn of light:
But panthers explain parenthesis
Upon their prey and sate all hunger there.

Certainty shall not touch my tongue.
And yet I hold, I have in mind
That this our love will stay for us:
Instructed by the years, belong
Obdurate and anonymous
A sanctuary eye among the blind.

The Trial

The oxen gone, the house is fallen where
Our sons stood, and the wine is spilt, and skew
Among the broken walls the servants are

Except who comes across the scorching field
Historian. But where the wind is from
That struck the mansion, great storms having failed,

No man can say. What wilderness remains?
Prosperous generations, scythe in hand,
Mapped the continents, murdered, built latrines.

Intellectual sores raven among
The faithful organs, corrupting from within;
To scrape them but the fastidious tongue.

Perforce we sit among the ashes, not
By will. We have no friends who come to pray,
Cannot discover what disaster brought:

Ignorant who commanded grass to burn
Like Spanish altars, we can scarcely say
Let the day perish wherein we were born.

1937

Night and the City

Two men sat by a stone in what dim place
Ravelled with flares in darkness they could find,
Considering death. The older man's face
Hollowed the hope out in the young man's mind,

Ribbed it with constant agony and pause
Where conversation multiplied. The air,
Ironic, took their talk of time and cause
Up to indifferent walls and left it there.

Political grammarians gave this
Their scrupulous attention but they saw
Terms dwindle from the eye and emphasis
Whistle on wind: they stared upon the law

While worms in books held carnival and ate
And slept and spurred their nightmares to the post.
Speechless murderous men abroad on great
Thoroughfares found the virgin and the lost.

Night now was ever upon the world-city.
Dogs struck as from inhuman dawn, they fled
Down arrogant apartments to the sea
And soon forgot among the swollen dead

Their genuine excitement when the rush
And rack of their masters fell into dance,
Ignorant sleep but a skeleton hush,
A sterile choreography for penance.

These also they discussed by the flat stone
Where sacrifice had failed; and where were those
Who in the first hysterical days had gone,
Where Matthew and where Alan, where the pose

John Grahame set against a vicious tide,
Or if they were at all still. And slim peace
Preserved the two a time but all their pride
Shrivelled in these abstract civilities.

The barriers were down, they fell afraid
On knees could not remember any smile
For godhead, their teeth appeared and they prayed
Desperate to eventual stars while

Technicians in high windows parried the dark.
They blinked and said 'Supreme predicament
Justifies our despair, but the dogs bark.'
Under the lights their colour came and went:

Mexican subtlety glittered in the cheek
And Roman distance sentried in their eyes,
A sun on arid plains lifted that bleak
Black bridge of nose, historical blood cries

Faster in the spinning veins, faster for some
Inscrutable haven from the willed light,
The lips for a dignity to be dumb,
The antique heart finally for the night.

Nineteen Thirty-Eight

Across the frontiers of the helpless world
The great planes swarm, the carriers of death,
Germs in the healthy body of the air,
And blast our cities where we stand in talk
    By doomed and comfortable fires.

In Asia famous tombs were opened so
And celebrated ancestors walked out
Into the carnage of the Rising Sun,
That horrible light upon a daughter cast,
    The new language in the torn streets.

There was a city where the people danced,
Simple and generous, traditional.
Suddenly the music stopped. Shooting
Began. Some of the living call the dead
    Of the Third Reich the lucky ones.

Terror accumulated in September
Until the island Dove divided up
A southern ally for the Eagle's feast,
And trembled as the Eagle fed, knowing
    The gratitude of appetite.

What was a civil war this year but strangers
Overhead, guns at sea, and foreign guns
And foreign squadrons in the plundered town?
A Spaniard learnt that any time is time
    For German or Italian doom.

Survivors, lean and daring and black men,
Lurked in the hills. The villages were gone,
The land given to rape and colonists.
They slept with hunger in the hills and got
    Legends of their deliverance.

The winter sky is fatal wings. What voice
Will spare the aged and the dying year?
His blood is on all thresholds, bodies found
Swollen in swollen rivers point their fingers:
    Criminal, to stand as warning.

The Curse

Cedars and the westward sun.
The darkening sky. A man alone
Watches beside the fallen wall
The evening multitudes of sin
Crowd in upon us all.
For when the light fails they begin
Nocturnal sabotage among

The outcast and the loose of tongue,
The lax in walk, the murderers:
Our twilight universal curse.

Children are faultless in the wood,
Untouched. If they are later made
Scandal and index to their time,
It is that twilight brings for bread
The faculty of crime.
Only the idiot and the dead
Stand by, while who were young before
Wage insolent and guilty war
By night within that ancient house,
Immense, black, damned, anonymous.

Ceremony and Vision

I

The weather in the drawing-room
I left at that time and came into
A region of exceptional clarity.

Sea was the way. Wind took away
The odour of their trained and railway talk
And several varieties of julep.

Sea was the way. Going, I forgot
Of large brown bodies on the bankrupt sand
The quarrels. I forgot them all

And how a summer foaming by
Will surf our footing out, where are
No records, where the winter tides begin.

II

Their papers were complete. Nevertheless
Blue progression could terrify
Cartographers upon the beach.

Depending on that magnanimity
As web and flies, the elder learnt
Water takes down away its débris.

For with what skill who can transport
Around or through the fabulous windows
Of the skull their tall machines?

He paced and could not get aboard
Whose footprints are his shame
When the salt lapse uncovers them like crime.

III

That country is not famous for its clouds
Although its clouds are famous.
They pass among the swans and pride.

Too they are white capitals,
The pilgrim architecture coming in
Tenderly on that shore.

Sea was the way without history
But depth. The sea's surpassing surfaces
An amateur saw curl and saw return

Constellation. Among whose despair
Moves a delicate legend, as in grass
The antelope who soon will lie and die there.

Early Poems

from Poems [1942]

TO BHAIN CAMPBELL
1911–1940

I told a lie once in a verse. I said
I said I said I said 'The heart will mend,
Body will break and mend, the foam replace
For even the unconsolable his taken friend.'
This is a lie. I had not been here then.

The Dangerous Year

Thus far, to March, into the dangerous year
We have come safely with our children, friends,
Parents, the unfamiliar crowd, and stare
To make out the intentions of that man
     Who is our Man of Fear.

We have come safely. In a frontier brawl
A few men coughed who will not cough again,
Slaughter goes on in China, refugees call
For aid; but these things are remote, they can
     Touch us scarcely at all.

We are secure behind the Northern Ocean.
Whatever folly we commit is blest
Beforehand by the god Exaggeration
Who is our genius—the advancing good
     Simply to be in motion.

Strangers we do not trust, or wish would leave.
Communication has not made us one
As yet, we hope, with foreigners who live

Upon their nerves, perpetually ready
    To triumph or to grieve.

Our factories and homes, the man next door,
Our dear upholstered memories, are safe,
We think. The situation is a bore,
But we have the Atlantic to safeguard us:
    No plane can reach our shore.

The car is still upon the road, we say.
What road? Where will you sleep tomorrow night?
Where are the maps that you had yesterday?
By whose direction are you moving now?
    The light is thin and grey.

It's time to see the frontiers as they are,
Fiction, but a fiction meaning blood,
Meaning a one world and a violent car.
It's time to think about the weekend, think
    Whether the road is war.

Time to forget the crimson and the green
Tinsel upon the Christmas tree, the lake
Shining with summer friends where you have been.
Let all that fade, for you are come upon
    The shifting of the scene.

Forget the crass hope of a world restored
To dignity and unearned dividends.
Admit, admit that now the ancient horde
Loosed from the labyrinth of your desire
    Is coming as you feared.

Courage is not enough, but you must find
Courage, or nothing else can do you good.
It's time to see how far you have been blind
And try to prop your lids apart before
    The midnight of the mind.

New York
1 March 1939

Early Poems

River Rouge, 1932

Snow on the ground. A day in March.
Uncomprehending faces move
Toward the machines by which they live,
Locked; not in anger but in hunger march.
Who gave the order on the wall?
Women are there but not in love.
Who was the first to fall?

Their simple question and their need
Ignored, men on their shoulders lift
The loudest man on the night shift
To shout into the plant their winter need.
Who gave the order on the wall?
The barbed wire and the guns aloft.
Who was the first to fall?

Snow on the bloody ground. Men break
And run and women scream as though
They dreamt a dream human snow
And human audience, but now they wake.
Who gave the order on the wall?
Remember a day in March and snow.
Who was the first to fall?

Communist

'O tell me of the Russians, Communist, my son!
Tell me of the Russians, my honest young man!'
'They are moving for the people, mother; let me alone,
For I'm worn out with reading and want to lie down.'

'But what of the Pact, the Pact, Communist, my son?
What of the Pact, the Pact, my honest young man?'

'It was necessary, mother; let me alone,
For I'm worn out with reading and want to lie down.'

'Why are they now in Poland, Communist, my son?
Why are they now in Poland, my honest young man?'
'For the people of Poland, mother; let me alone,
For I'm worn out with reading and want to lie down.'

'But what of the Baltic States, Communist, my son?
What of the Baltic States, my honest young man?'
'Nothing can be proven, mother; let me alone,
For I'm worn out with reading and want to lie down.'

'O I fear for your future, Communist, my son!
I fear for your future, my honest young man!'
'I cannot speak or think, mother; let me alone,
For I'm sick at my heart and I want to lie down.'

October 1939

Thanksgiving: Detroit

Lockout. The seventh week. Men in the Square
Idle, but the men are standing as they stood.
Thanksgiving is tomorrow. Shall Labour
Rejoice? Or curse? Shall Labour spit that turkey?
In an elaborate spot on Six Mile Road
The men at the bar and the women on the couches
Are dancing, drinking, singing vainly.

Thanksgiving. Shall the Liberal rejoice?
Shall the pieces of the Liberal give praise?
The Liberal is moving left, or rather
The conflagration and the guns move right
As the fuel and the ammunition blaze.
The men at the bar and the women on the couches
Are dancing, drinking, singing vainly.

Thanksgiving, and more than turkeys underground.
Opinion underground. Who shall be glad?
Finks and goons in the streets of the city, cops
Clubbing and watching the clubbing of men, men hide.
The standing men are determined and sad.
The men at the bar and the women on the couches
Are dancing, drinking, singing—vainly.

Epilogue

He died in December. He must descend
Somewhere, vague and cold, the spirit and seal,
The gift descend, and all that insight fail
Somewhere. Imagination one's one friend
Cannot see there. Both of us at the end.
Nouns, verbs do not exist for what I feel.

Appendices

Berryman's Published Prefaces, Notes, and Dedications

"TWENTY POEMS," *Five Young American Poets* [1940]

A NOTE ON POETRY

None of the extant definitions of poetry is very useful; certainly none is adequate; and I do not propose to invent a new one. I should like to suggest what I understand the nature and working of poetry to be by studying one of the poems in this selection. It is not that I assume any poem of mine will serve as a satisfactory example of the art; but one's special familiarity with one's own work is an advantage too considerable, for this analysis, to be forgone. Perhaps the most direct approach is the approach by paraphrase. I propose to paraphrase the poem called "On the London Train"* and examine some of the differences between the methods of prose and of verse, hoping that the examination will illustrate what it is that a poem does in being a poem.

"(I am leaving Cambridge; it is April, 1938; I am on the London train.) Although the face of the man across the compartment from me, on the seat opposite, has a look which I take to express loneliness (there are economic reasons for the loneliness of unmarried men at present in their twenties), no doubt many women, or certain women, are lonely also, on his account. Daily, as they are afflicted with his image or his presence, the possibilities of union daze them and glaze their eyes. They glaze their eyes; their absorption is in part voluntary. They are subject to fantasy: each imagines herself in his embrace, embracing him in a romantic place where water is running, having him secure. (Nor is the desire of these women desire only; it is need, and their traditional need for protection, for maintenance.)

"(But nothing will come of this. Whether or not the man is aware of their desires—probably he is not—he will not, because he can not, satisfy one of them:) he is himself in love. (Nor is his desire simple: he requires a wife to cook, to mend, to counsel, to admire him; he wants children.) Desiring another woman, who is unsatisfied also, incomplete, he is sleepless at night, he endures an exis-

* *Editor's Note: The page number of "On the London Train" in 20P is given here.*

tence of day and night without differentiation or end, since day and night form a setting for love which is not enacted. He says to himself that he would undergo any humiliation, any pain—he would walk on his bare knees, voluntarily blind, eastward to humorous and frozen Tomsk or westward to the sweltering cities of California—if in the end she would let him enter her; or (he is content with less) if she would take him into her house and care for his wounds; or (he would be content with anything) if she would display any merely human interest in the suffering which is his devotion—would recognize it even. (But he is without hope.)

"This situation, the situation of unrequited love, is unfortunate, but it is not singular; it is common in this time and it is usual in history. If you could summon a lover from a former time, or summon John Donne from his grave (a man who experienced or imagined this in all its complex distress), he would confirm most solemnly the testimony of men who have described the unpleasant ordeal, and the ordeal which above all others is humiliating, of loving without return—until the permanent bedroom is attained. And with union the lover's exasperations do not cease. Consider that even Zeus—a god, the most powerful, the most amorous of gods, and (farther back in time than Donne) a Greek—was tormented by jealousy.

"(The cause and the contrast occur to me together.) The sea-shell, undemonstrative and chaste, under the sea where it is protected from movement and desire, can puzzle its Maker, can amaze the course of things. For the shell alone seems to be exempt from the necessities of living creatures—under enormous difficulties, at their wits' end, to win a mate, to breed, to achieve security. That this evidence of defeat should trouble the Maker who has plagued us, abstractly we are glad; but, out of the security of the sea, who suffer on the shore, nothing for our pain can be sufficient recompense."

It is true that this paraphrase is not complete—at almost any point it can be elaborated—and that it cannot pretend to be definitive. But it does at least state rather fully the principal subject; and I think the most casual comparison will show its substantial and technical inferiority to the poem. If to be direct, concrete, compact, is a virtue for the subject as it is here conceived, the verse has the advantage. In the process of translation the particular irony and wit escaped; the abruptness of juxtaposition and the violence were lost. What is easy and perhaps rich in the verse demands cumbersome expansion in the prose: compare the two versions of the passage beginning "If she'd but let him in." These effects in the verse are consequences of form, of craft. One employs verse in order to be able to attain them, for they are unobtainable in prose. In the third stanza, for example, occurs the first serious conflict between syntax and verse-form: "most / Embarrassing" and "this side / Satisfaction" are split in successive lines. The resulting impression of strain, torsion, is useful to the subject. "Satisfaction" is allowed to stand alone, as no other word in the poem does, because it represents a climax. But a third conflict at the end of its line ("green / Difficulties") recalls, as it should recall for the subject, the ordeal which but seemed to end with "Satisfaction." None of these things can be done in prose, and to the extent that they assist in presentation, they are valuable.

This may be put in another way. One of the reasons for writing verse is delight in craftsmanship—rarely for its own sake, mainly as it seizes and makes visible its subject. Versification, rime, stanza-form, trope, are the tools. They provide the means by which the writer can shape from an experience in itself usually vague, a mere feeling or phrase, something that is coherent, directed, intelligible. They permit one to say things that would not otherwise be said at all; it may be said, even, that they permit one to feel things that would not otherwise be felt. Two instances of this shaping occur also in the third stanza. The first line of each of the preceding stanzas runs into the second; but "So it is and has been."—a full stop. A resource of verse-form makes the generalization possible. And after the four weak endings which precede it, the heavy regular final line of the stanza takes up the metrical accumulation and acts, again, as generalization, moving from the earth into mythology—for such a fable as this, the absolute.

Poetry provides its readers, then, with what we may call a language of experience, an idiom, of which the unit may be an entire complicated emotion or incident. The language is not the language of prose. It requires a different kind of reading and a different process of sensibility, and probably the most relevant questions raised for a reader by any poems have to do with the approach toward an ideal of reading. I hope it will be so with the following poems; it is to these questions that my note has tried to suggest answers.

POEMS [1942]

Dedication:
TO BHAIN CAMPBELL (1911–1940)*

The poems, although an arbitrary brief selection from work done during 1939 and 1940, are printed here in the order of composition. Most of them appeared first in *The Kenyon Review, New Poems 1940,* and *New Directions 1941.* "The Statue," first published in *Partisan Review,* was reprinted in *Five Young American Poets* (1940).

* *Editor's Note: The dedicatory poem to Bhain Campbell is included in the text of CP.*

THE DISPOSSESSED [1948]

NOTE

With exceptions for a thematic reason, affecting Section One, the poems stand in what was roughly their order of writing. I have to thank the editors of *Partisan Review*, *The Southern Review*, *The Kenyon Review*, *Accent*, *The Nation*, *The New Republic*, *The Sewanee Review*, *Chimera*, *Poetry*, *The Commonweal*, and the *New Directions* (edited by James Laughlin) and *New Poems* series (edited by Oscar Williams), in whose pages most of the poems, often in earlier versions, originally appeared. Eleven of them were reprinted in the first *Five Young American Poets* (1940), and five others are from a pamphlet *Poems* (1942), both published by New Directions. The first line of "Desires of Men and Women" varies a line by Delmore Schwartz. Parts of "Young Woman's Song" are based on a published journal I once read. "Sweet when the lost arrive" in "A Winter-Piece to a Friend Away" is from the great mad poem of Smart. If there are other obligations that should be mentioned, let the present acknowledgment stand for them. I have felt tempted to add some notes, remarking, for instance, that the subject of "Winter Landscape" is not really the painting by the elder Breughel to which from start to finish the poem refers, that "The Good Life's founded upon L. s. d." (a translation of a refrain by Brecht) is alluded to in my line "The good life's founded upon LST" (LST is Landing Ship, Tanks), that the opening line of "The Dispossessed" occurs in Pirandello's *Six Characters*, even that "The Enemies of the Angels" depends in part on Genesis xix, and so on; but I believe readers dislike notes. One word about "Narcissus Moving"*: it is very early morning; the poet, upstairs in a house across the way, sometimes hears, sometimes watches, the young man's departure, except in the second stanza where he generalizes; the speeches are the young man's, overheard.—N.B. In the general dedication, exception is made for poems dedicated in 1942 to the memory of Bhain Campbell, and for others: "Winter Landscape" is dedicated to Beryl Eeman, "The Animal Trainer" to Mark Van Doren, "Boston Common" to Lieutenant F. B. Boyden, the "Nervous Songs" to my brother, Jefferson, and "Canto Amor" and "The Lightning" to my wife, Eileen.

---

* *Editor's Note: The page number of "Narcissus Moving" in* TD *is given here.*

HOMAGE TO MISTRESS BRADSTREET [1956]

Acknowledgments: The author wishes to record his deep gratefulness to Mr Moe and others for the Guggenheim fellowship which let this work be finished; and to friends; acknowledgment is made also to the editors of *Partisan Review* where it first appeared, and to a correspondent who supplied some of the notes at the end.*

HIS THOUGHT MADE POCKETS & THE PLANE BUCKT [1958]

Dedication:

TO ANN

Acknowledgement is made to the editors of *Partisan Review, Poetry, American Letters, The New Yorker,* and *The Virginia Quarterly Review,* where some of these poems first appeared. "The Mysteries" was made for the festschrift published on the sixtyfifth anniversary of Erich Kahler's birth. None of my work in progress is included except some pieces of an old poem called "The Black Book."

BERRYMAN'S SONNETS [1967]

Dedication:

TO ROBERT GIROUX

NOTE

These Sonnets, which were written many years ago, have nothing to do, of course, with my long poem in progress, *The Dream Songs.* Sonnet 25 appeared in the fortieth-anniversary number of *Poetry;* the others are unprinted.

Ballsbridge, Dublin
October 8th, 1966

---

* *Editor's Note: Berryman's "Notes" to* Homage *follow the text of the poem in* CP.

Appendices

LOVE & FAME [1971], *Faber and Faber edition (England)*

Dedication:
To the memory of
the suffering lover & young Breton master
who called himself 'Tristan Corbière'

(I wish I versed with his bite)*

AFTERWORD

The initial American public reception of this book, whether hostile, cool, or hot, was so uncomprehending that I wondered whether I had wasted my time, until a letter came from Stanford seeing that it is—however uneven—a whole, each of the four movements criticizing backward the preceding, until Part IV wipes out altogether all earlier presentations of the 'love' and 'fame' of the ironic title. Professor Gelpi was in a good technical position to take in what I was up to, being the ablest critic Emily Dickinson has ever had, since my lyric form here had its genesis in a study of hers. But the attack on these two notions begins in the opening poem, and little as I like to show my hand, I pass on to anyone interested some of the readings of it that occurred to me in two minutes when it surfaced from a reverie in hospital one evening last Fall, many months after its composition.

1. Even this distasteful Braggart (Famous Poet & Scandal—note his bastard) *is human* (= weak) like us: he did (once anyway) genuinely love and can genuinely regret.

2. He is more convincing than he knows: his insecurity about his fame (over-brandishing) matches his insecurity over this 'true' (exposed as false by his repeated infidelity to it) love he is so proud of, and we have pathetic before us an existential man, wishing to be (twice—cf. title) what is impossible to quick-silver (Luther's word for man's heart) Man. Our affect: recognition and pity for his unhappiness.

3. Even this apparently genuine love is of course slipping from him (last line), as his apparently genuine fame will do too—which maybe the poor guy really doesn't know, whistling in the dark, thumping his chest. Even I (me vigorous Reader) am superior to *him*.

4. This guy is *unreal*, dreaming of an unchanged re[-e]ncounter after long years, when he can convince her of his success in life (which it does not seem he has

* *Editor's Note: The dedicatory poem to Corbière is included in the text of CP.*

[290

very well convinced himself of). Just one more doomed oldfashioned* type (for all his paraphernalia of modernity—flouting morality & national borders, etc.): The Romantic.

5. Memory failing, clutching at frantic data of life-achievement, obsessed with a vanishing past of happiness in his present loneliness & age, he moves us after all. Maybe we too, in the end—

6. Current noisy psuedo-world-figure fixated on a local ancient unidentifiable whisper.

    Other readings will occur to anybody listening. 'Gash' is sexual slang, of course; the photographs might connect backward with ll.3–4; 'all over' might be taken in a secondary sense and the poem read as a Freudian dream culminating in the exclamations, with detumescence (waking) in the final line. And so on.

    None of this has anything to say about the poem's merit—if it has any merit beyond conciseness, a certain explosive feeling, a certain administrative rhythm-set; and I may add that its weirdness is probably a product of two opposite circumstances: lack of practice (it was the first short poem I had written, almost, in 22 years) and veteran expertize** in an allied medium, the long poem (five of those years were spent on one, thirteen on another), where complexity of this sort, though uncommon, is not unexpected.

Minneapolis
20 June 1971

Editor's Note: Most of the "Afterword" to the FF edition of *Love & Fame* appears as "Scholia to Second Edition" in the earlier FSG second edition, revised, dated 25 January 1971. The concluding sentence of the penultimate paragraph of "Scholia," but not in the FF edition, is "I have killed some of the worst poems in the first edition." The last paragraph, which follows, is substantially different from the last paragraph in the "Afterword" of the FF edition:

None of this has anything to say about the poem's merit, if it has any. I notice it makes play with an obsession that ruled 'The Ball Poem' of 1942 as well as later, *Homage to Mistress Bradstreet* (1948–1953) and *The Dream Songs* (1955–1968): namely, the dissolving of one personality into another without relinquishing the original—here, that of the mature poet omnipotent and that of the aging man deprived and powerless. In the very long poem, of

* *Editor's Note: Berryman spelled "oldfashioned" as it appears.*
** *Editor's Note: Berryman spelled "expertize" as it appears.*

course, many personalities shift, reify, dissolve, survive, project—remaining one.

DELUSIONS Etc. [1972]

Dedication:
TO MARTHA B,
passion & awe

Editor's Notes, Guidelines, and Procedures

Besides *Homage to Mistress Bradstreet*, published in *Partisan Review* in 1953 and as a single volume in 1956, the collections Berryman selected and arranged are:

"Twenty Poems" in *Five Young American Poets* (1940)
Poems (1942)
The Dispossessed (1948)
His Thought Made Pockets & the Plane Buckt (1958)
Berryman's Sonnets (1967)
Love & Fame (first American edition, 1970; British revised edition, 1971; American second edition, revised 1972)
Delusions Etc. (1972, published posthumously but selected and arranged by Berryman)

The three collections Berryman selected from the above volumes include: *Homage to Mistress Bradstreet and Other Poems* (British edition, 1959; American edition, 1968); *Short Poems* (American edition, 1967); and *Selected Poems (1938–1968)* (British edition, 1972). "Formal Elegy" in *Short Poems*, now collected in *CP*, is the only work that did not appear in his previous collections.

For *CP*, I have chosen, as a general guideline, the author's corrected galleys and page proofs as the base texts. I have not incorporated the substantive changes that appear in at least thirty poems in Berryman's later selected collections because I believe that each revised poem represents but *one* version of it. Even though his revisions of selected poems may postdate the first publication of them, one may speak only of the point at which he abandoned a poem and not, in my view, of his "final" intentions. *Love & Fame*, based on Berryman's revised British edition; *Berryman's Sonnets*, based on his original TS; and *Delusions Etc.*, based on a combination of the printer's MS and Berryman's last revisions, must be, for reasons I explain in *Copy-Texts and Variants*, exceptions to my galley-proofs guideline.

The Dispossessed (1948) is placed first in *CP* because it was his first major collection. Since *TD* incorporated over half the poems in "Twenty Poems" (1940) and *Poems* (1942), it reflects, I believe, the best complete overview of Berryman's early poetry. As for the two early collections, only those poems not collected in *TD* are included in this new edition; both are appropriately accounted for in "Early Poems," the last section of *CP*. (A list of the poems that appeared in "Twenty Poems" and *Poems* and again in *TD* may be found in Appendix B.) My arrangement of the collections is different from the order of publication in one other respect: *Berryman's Sonnets* (now *Sonnets to Chris*), substantially completed by October 1947, follows *TD*. Berryman's prefaces and dedications, however, are arranged in order of publication.

Guidelines and Procedures: My first major task was to choose the texts (i.e., the copy-texts) *CP* would follow. I photocopied not only the extant galley and page proofs but also Berryman's handwritten and typed manuscripts of each poem and collection. Most of these documents are at the University of Minnesota in Minneapolis; others are at Columbia University, Harvard University, and Washington University in St. Louis.

In order to determine the historical relationship of the composition, transmission, and publication of each collection, I arranged the photocopied texts in chronological order. Berryman dated many of the texts, some to the day and hour, but in some cases I returned to the originals to attempt to determine the date of composition or typing. Since the chronology of composition may be obscured by photocopies (that is, correctives obliterated or the types and age of paper leveled to uniformity), I compared my arrangement of the photocopies with the original manuscripts and proofs at Minnesota and Columbia. Berryman's handwriting, the typeface and paper, and the relationship of all these to other dated manuscripts helped determine an approximate dating of some of the poems. I did not travel to Harvard and Washington Universities to see the galleys and printer's typescripts of *Poems* and *Thought* because I did not believe the originals, in these cases, would reveal more than the photocopies. I did, however, examine the originals of all other HW and TS versions of the two collections at the University of Minnesota Archives. Berryman's correspondence with his publishers before, during, and after the publication of a collection was helpful in determining the chronology of some texts. In four cases—*Homage, Sonnets, L&F,* and *De*—Berryman's correspondence was available to me. In the remaining four—*20P, Poems, TD,* and *Thought*—his letters to his publishers could not be found.

After I chose the copy-texts, I established the variants between them and the first editions, and, taking into account my editorial guidelines in spelling and mechanics, I removed inadvertent errors, where evidence existed, that were created by typesetting, printing, and proofing. My arguments for the selection of the copy-text for each collection are presented in Copy-Texts and Variants, but, briefly, I relied upon the following sources:

"Twenty Poems" and *Poems*: the first editions

The Dispossessed: the page proofs with reference to Berryman's corrected galleys

Berryman's Sonnets (now *Sonnets to Chris*): Berryman's original typescripts with handwritten changes that were completed in 1947 and the typescripts of his additional 1966 sonnets

Homage to Mistress Bradstreet: Berryman's corrected page proofs for *Partisan Review* (1953)

His Thought Made Pockets & the Plane Buckt: Berryman's corrected galley proofs

Love & Fame: Berryman's corrected page proofs for the British edition (1971), with some reference to the American second edition, revised

Delusions Etc. (now *Delusions etc of John Berryman*): a combination of the printer's copy and Berryman's TS that postdates the printer's copy

My selection of most of the copy-texts of Berryman's collections creates only a few variants in *20P, Poems, TD, Homage,* and *Thought*. In the new text of *Sonnets,* however, there are just over two hundred variants. Likewise, *L&F* and *De* each show approximately fifty-five variants.

I began editing *CP* with the hope of arriving at a set of editorial principles that would give a sort of scientific credibility to my selection of the copy-text. But whatever principles I determined—none could be absolute, I quickly learned—all seemed to point to the question of Berryman's final intentions. Although Berryman's final intentions for the selection and arrangement of the poems in each collection did not seem in doubt, his final intentions for the texts of certain revised poems, and therefore his intentions for the text of whole collections, are open to question. The copy-texts for *Berryman's Sonnets*, published twenty years after they were written, and *Delusions Etc.*, not proofed and corrected by Berryman, in particular called for a thorough investigation of the context of their composition and publication. His final intentions for the two volumes, as well as several revised poems in *TD*, were uncertain.

Authorities on editing—W. W. Greg, Fredson Bowers, James Thorpe, Jerome J. McGann, William Proctor Williams, and Craig S. Abbott—confirmed that while I might attempt to divine Berryman's "final" intentions, I would come closest to determining an accurate text by tracking the entire process of bringing each poem and each collection into print. The selection of the copy-text for his collected works depends, of course, on whether or not he would have preserved the historically accurate text, or the text that incorporated his subsequent revisions, or, as might very well have been the case, the revisions he would have made in bringing together his collected poems.

The history of the texts of his three collections of "selected poems" strongly suggests that, for an edition of his collected poems, he would have as likely published the collections as they first appeared as he would have incorporated his later revisions. In one telling instance, he did not carry forward most of his revisions of the selected poems in *Homage to Mistress Bradstreet and Other Poems* (1959) to the same poems in the later *Short Poems* (1967). Except for a few variables in the punctuation in the poem *Homage to Mistress Bradstreet*, the substantive changes in *HomageAOP* are limited to the selected poems from *TD*. Of the fifty poems in the first edition of *TD*, thirty-nine are collected in *HomageAOP*, and twenty-four of the thirty-nine poems show some fifty-five substantive changes and variables. And yet in the later selection of *Short Poems*, which includes all poems from the 1948 edition of *TD*, there are only twelve variants. Half the variants in *Short Poems* appear to be printing errors; the remaining six are changes and variables that also appear in *HomageAOP* (three word changes and three in punctuation). That Berryman did not carry forward all of his numerous 1959 changes in *HomageAOP* to *Short Poems* eight years later suggests that he was mostly satisfied, at least in 1967, with the text of the first edition of *TD*.

For his *Selected Poems* (1972), Berryman chose thirteen poems from *The Dispossessed*, the texts of which are the revised poems in *HomageAOP*. And yet, for example, in "Whether There Is Sorrow in the Demons" in *Selected Poems*, the word "screams" (l. 2), as it appears in both *TD* and *HomageAOP*, is emended to "creams." This may be a printing error, but this is not the case in the deletion of the last two stanzas in the same poem. Such important variables do not strongly recommend the changes in *Selected Poems* as representing Berryman's final intentions. And, too, if one observes the artistic integrity of *TD* as a whole, there are not enough poems (thirteen out of fifty) to make a case for carrying forward *only* these changes to his collected poems.

Berryman's intentions for a collection at the time it was completed appear to be as final—more so because each constitutes a whole—as the later changes he made in individual poems. Since he revised only selected poems, one may not speak authoritatively of his final intentions for a whole collection. His collections have their own artistic integrity; he selected and arranged each with some principle in mind—thematic, or chronological in order of composition, or a combination of both. In observing the artistic integrity of his collections as they were first published, one is not forced to create a fiction of the texts he might have chosen for his collected works (in Berryman's case, his revisions of a selection of poems rather than his rethinking of a collection as a whole).

Editorial guidelines on mechanics and spelling: "I am a monoglot of English / (American version)," Henry observes, "and, say pieces from / a baker's dozen others" (Dream Song 48). Like Henry, Berryman delighted in the play and undercurrents of foreign and rarely used words, and he drew upon a baker's dozen of English, American, French, German, Italian, and Latin spellings, phrases, and usages. As Richard Eberhart observed in a review of *The Dispossessed*, Berryman's use of language has an "intensity of perception newly, shortly, deftly placed, spaced and 'estopped.' Berryman is a man who can use the word estop. Estop is 'Rare.' " One of the functions of the poet, Berryman believed, is to disrupt our expectations of language so that we are given a new angle of perception. Berryman's spelling and mechanics are a part of the history of his newly, shortly, and deftly placed language. And yet some of his spelling and mechanics suggests arbitrary, as opposed to deftly placed, usage. In most instances, one cannot speak with absolute authority about whether or not his usage is arbitrary, but his punctuation of quotations and ellipsis points do appear to be so. Had he consistently preferred a certain style of ellipsis points and quotation marks in one period of his writing and a different style, say, twenty years later, it would be appropriate in his collected poems to be faithful to his change of preference. But that is not the case; he simply was inconsistent, sometimes in the same poem, in his use of quotation marks and ellipsis points.

Ellipsis: As early as 1936, Berryman began writing in a nervous idiom ("mutter my verses," he wrote in his 1947 notes on *Sonnets*). His personae speak haltingly and his syntax is disrupted. He indicated abrupt shifts in speech and thought with dashes, parentheses, and accent marks, but he favored ellipses most, at least up to about 1948. Thereafter, he dropped ellipses almost entirely (some appear in his subsequent collections) and indicated pauses and shifts with a double or triple blank space. In editorial usage, the three-point ellipsis (four points at the end of the sentence) indicates the writer's intentional omission of words, usually in a quotation. The three-point ellipsis also signifies an abrupt change of thought, or a lapse of time, or an incomplete expression. I have adopted Berryman's most common habit of a two-point ellipsis to indicate pauses and shifts, but in his quotations (punctuated as such), I have used three points to indicate omissions and incomplete expressions. Berryman was also inconsistent in his spacing of ellipsis points. In his typescripts, particularly those of *TD* and *Sonnets*, he most frequently indicated a two-point ellipsis without spacing (that is, ".."), but he did not change the galley or page proofs of either *TD* or *Sonnets* when the spacing followed house style of a spacing between the two points. Sometimes, too, he indicated a space after an ellipsis, as in the TS of Sonnet 5: "Laught.. Well, *etc.*" (l.12). When the line was published in both the American and British editions, the extra spacing was not indicated: "Laught . . Well, *etc.*" This change might also have been a matter of house style, but for *Collected Poems* I have observed spacing not only between the points but also, where Berryman indicated a space in his typescript, after them, as in "Laught . .   Well, *etc.*"

Quotation marks: In his prose, as early as 1931, Berryman adopted the British use of single quotation marks, or inverted commas. During his study in England (1936–38), the usage appears in his poetry. From that time through his last poems in 1971, he most frequently preferred single quotation marks; in a few instances, arbitrarily it appears, he used double quotation marks. Likewise, his use of commas and periods at the end of a quotation, especially in *Love & Fame* and *Delusions Etc.*, seems arbitrary—sometimes inside, sometimes outside the marks. I have regularized his quotation marks to conform to his most frequent preference: single quotes with the comma and period inside the closing mark and all other punctuation outside, except the exclamation point and question mark that belong in the quotation. I have, nevertheless, followed Berryman's habit of placing the comma and the period outside the single quotation mark in short phrases and single words, as in " 'genocide'." ("New Year's Eve").

Capitalization: Throughout his writing, Berryman capitalized words, primarily nouns, to personify or emphasize a concept or action, as in "Consternation and Hope war" ("A Point of Age"), "Bone of moaning: sung Where he has gone" (*Homage*), and "Add Sway omnicompetent, add pergalactic Intellect" ("Unknowable? perhaps not altogether"). These authorial capitalizations do not, of course, raise the question of whether or not to regularize them. But some of Berryman's inconsistent capitalizations do raise the question; in "Fare Well," for example, "Mother" is capitalized, but in "Song of the Tortured Girl," it is not. Similarly, in his later addresses and prayers to God, he was inconsistent in the conventional capitalization of the pronoun referring to God. In Number 9 of his "Eleven Addresses to the Lord," he capitalized the pronoun in the second stanza—"even to say You exist is misleading"—but in the next he did not—"flaring in your sun your waterfall." I thought that perhaps Berryman might have been consistent in not capitalizing the possessive pronoun, but in "Interstitial Office" in the "Opus Dei" poems, one finds "Your lightning" and "Your torque." Since I could not be certain that Berryman's usage was arbitrary, I have not regularized his inconsistent capitalization.

Foreign words and phrases: Berryman frequently quoted foreign words and phrases as though they belong to colloquial English and American usage. For the most part, throughout his writing, he did not italicize foreign words and phrases: in his early poems, "Che si cruccia" ("Parting as Descent") and "peine forte et dure" ("The Long Home"); in his later poems, "Handel's Te Deum" ("Matins") and "actuellement" ("Sext"). And yet, for no apparent reason other than, perhaps, emphasis, he did italicize some foreign words and phrases: *"on m'analyse"* ("New Year's Eve"), *waren die unverlierbaren Freunde* ("The Search"), and " *'Mord-serum* sie haben sagen. / Wo ist Doktor Dumartin? Doktor Dumartin / muss Doktor Dumartin *finden!*' " ("In & Out"). Since I cannot be certain that Berryman did not have a purpose in mind in his eclectic use of italics, I have not attempted to regularize his usage.

Other punctuation: In keeping with his nervous idiom, Berryman elided syllables, as in "squat' " ("1 September 1939") for "squatted" and "sweat' " (Sonnet 53) for "sweated." In a few instances, he indicated the elision of two words, as in "[t]o-'have" (Sonnet 104). In at least one instance he experimented with the spacing of a colon in "New Year's Eve": "(Great evils grieve beneath : eye Caesar's coin)." All of these usages, whether conventional or unconventional, have been allowed to stand. To indicate the pronunciation of a syllable normally elided in speech, he favored the acute accent rather than the conventional grave, as in "learnéd" ("Conversation") and "filteréd" (Sonnet 47). I find only one instance of his using the grave accent in "vouchsafèd" ("Eleven Addresses," #4). I have not emended his use of the acute accent; "vouchsafèd" I have allowed because in a more formal prayer, and word, he probably wished to use the traditional mark.

Spelling: Berryman's spelling is a baker's dozen of British, American, and some French. He often favored the French spelling of a word, as in "trobador" (Sonnet 40) rather than the Anglicized "troubador," and he retained the accent or circumflex that is usually dropped in English and American usage, as in "débris"

("Ceremony and Vision"), "régime" (Sonnet 57), and "rôle" ("The Heroes"). He particularly favored British spelling, and his most consistent usage was the "-our" ending, as in "honour," "harbour," "labour," and "colour." He was also consistent in the British spellings of "grey," "cheque," "kerb," and "programme," but for some words he preferred American spelling, as in "skeptical" ("Antitheses") rather than the chiefly British "sceptical"; "maneuvered" ("The Heroes") rather than the British "manoeuvered"; and "mustaches" ("The Dispossessed" and "Damned") rather than the British "moustaches." He did not adopt the common "-ise" British spelling, as in "civilise." He consistently preferred the American "z" rather than the British "s," as in "immortalized" ("The Statue"), "demoralize" ("World-Tele-gram"), and "unrecognizable" ("The Long Home"). Berryman seemed to change his mind about the spelling of some words. In his early collections, for example, he chose the American spelling of "fantasy" ("Letter to his Brother" and "Farewell to Miles") and "reflections" ("The Possessed"); twenty years later, he used the British spelling, "phantasy" ("Two Organs") and "reflexions" ("The Heroes" and "Of Suicide"). Several words, for whatever reason, are spelled two different ways; for example, "centre" ("World-Telegram") and "center" ("Meeting"); "blond" ("Narcissus Moving" and Sonnet 1) and "blonde" (Sonnets 5 and 22). These in-consistencies have been allowed to stand.

Some of Berryman's spellings are uncertain, for example, "synchrisis" (Sonnet 27), "an-crazy" (Sonnet 53), "vize" (Sonnet 70), "hopelets" (Sonnet 89), "teaze" ("Note to Wang Wei"), and "half-ful" ("Defensio In Extremis"). Most of his un-certain spellings occur in *Sonnets*, the collection in which he experimented most with language and syntax, but he liked to coin words throughout his writing. Some of his coinages are clearly puns, such as "synchrisis" (i.e., "syncrisis") which is meant to pun on "Chris," the woman to whom *Sonnets* are addressed. Some, such as "vize" in Sonnet 70, are more obscure. ("Vize" is a dialectical variation of "vice" meaning "counsel," but it may be, in the context of Sonnet 70, that "vize" is meant to combine "vise" and "vizor.") Unless Berryman either overlooked a misprint or clearly misspelled a word, as he did in the typescript of Sonnet 89 ("deseccation" instead of "desiccation") and in "On the London Train" ("recom-pence" instead of "recompense"), his uncertain spellings have been followed.

Copy-Texts and Variants

Unless otherwise noted, all references to the MSS, TSS, CTSS,* galleys, and page proofs are taken from the John Berryman Papers (JBP) at the University of Minnesota Archives, Minneapolis. For all variants in editions prior to *Collected Poems 1937–1971* see Ernest C. Stefanik, Jr.'s *John Berryman: A Descriptive Bibliography*, University of Pittsburgh Press, 1974.

Variants are separated by a lemma, that is, the emblem]. Left of the lemma, in bold print, is the text for *CP*; right of the lemma is the previously published text, usually the first edition.

THE DISPOSSESSED (1948)

The Copy-Text of TD *for* CP: *The Dispossessed* was published by William Sloane Associates of New York on May 10, 1948. Three months earlier, Berryman had corrected the galleys, dated February 23; the page proofs, completed by March 12, are faithful to his corrections and changes. The printer's TS of *TD* is lost, but the CTS—on which Berryman noted nearly all of the changes he made in the galleys—is complete except for the poem "At Chinese Checkers." The CTS, though, has been marginally helpful in editing *TD* for *CP*: The author's page proofs, with some reference to the corrected galleys, has been my primary copy-text.

Except for a single carbon copy (dated March 20, 1947), Berryman's correspondence with Helen Stewart, the editor at Sloane responsible for overseeing the publication of *TD*, cannot be found. But his notes on scraps of paper, written during the proofing of the galleys, suggest that he instructed Stewart to make several changes in the page proofs.

While the page proofs are faithful to Berryman's corrections and changes in the galleys, several variants are not noted in the galleys. Where the page proofs are different from the galleys (in all, eight variants I assume Berryman instructed in a letter), I have accepted the page proof version with one exception, noted

Editor's Note: See the "Editor's Note" following the Contents for a list of the abbreviations used in CP.

below, in "The Song of the Bridegroom." I have also corrected the two spelling errors in "On the London Train" and "Narcissus Moving."

VARIANTS: left of the] indicates the *CP* version; right of the] indicates the page proof version of *TD*.

"On the London Train"

1.31: recompense] recompence (*Editor's Note*: Neither the Latin and French derivatives nor the English and American spellings suggest "recompence," as Berryman spells it in both the CTS and the page proofs of *TD*. Although the title of the poem might indicate the possibility of a pun on "pence," the English currency, the poem itself, particularly the universal statement in the last stanza where "recompense" appears, does not seem to suggest a local reference. Furthermore, "recompense" is spelt correctly in the *20P* version of "On the London Train." I have emended the apparent misspelling.)

"Farewell to Miles"

> *Editor's Note*: On the CTS of this poem, Berryman wrote the following: "Note: Since Lieutenant Theodore Miles was lost at sea off Leyte on [blank space], I should explain that the poem was written in 1940 on the occasion of his leaving Wayne University, where we were teaching, to complete his doctoral studies at University of Chicago. Harvard is named simply as a type-goal of academic life,—this was before I taught there myself or thought of doing so, and the allusion is not, as it would be if I made it now, ironic. Miles married and was happy before he died."

"Boston Common"

1.59: river:] river, (*Editor's Note*: Although Berryman did not indicate in the galleys that the comma after "river" should be changed to a period, the page proofs show a period. One of his HW notes, written while he was correcting either the galleys or the page proofs, indicates the change. The CTS confirms that a period should follow "river.")

1.114: Tse-tung] Tse-Tung

"The Song of the Bridegroom"

1.9: window.] window, (*Editor's Note*: The comma after "window" in the galleys is so faint that it appears to be a period rather than a comma. Although the page proof shows a comma, I have not accepted it because Berryman apparently saw the comma as a period when he proofed the galleys. The CTS shows a period as well.)

"The Pacifist's Song"

1.9: not . . . Your ill from evil comes . . . Bear] not . . Your ill from evil comes . . Bear (*Editor's Note*: I have added extra points because the ellipses appear in a quotation.)

Appendices

"The Long Home"

> *Editor's Note*: In Berryman's HW notes, made while he was correcting the galleys, he wrote: "I am v[ery] pleased with the printer's faithfulness to my 'accidents'—inadvertent errors aside, & caesuras in *Long Home*." The galleys show that he instructed the printer to make nine emendations to "The Long Home," all of which appear in the page proofs. The variants listed below, however, are not noted in the galleys—perhaps some of the "inadvertent errors" he refers to in his notes—but do appear in the page proofs. Left of the] is the page proof version that is accepted for *CP*; right of the] is the galley version:

> > 1.3: **still,**] still.
> > 1.5: **beside   the**] beside the
> > 1.23: **to   amaze**] to amaze
> > 1.71: **cold   bright**] cold bright
> > 1.77: **come.**] come,

"A Winter-Piece to a Friend Away"

1.38: *Editor's Note*: Berryman did not indicate the emendation of "landscapes" to "landscape" in the galleys, but the "s" is deleted in the proofs. I have assumed he instructed the change.

"New Year's Eve"

1.18: *Editor's Note*: Although Berryman did not indicate the comma between "fate" and the dash in the galleys, it does appear in the page proofs. The emendation is consistent with his punctuation in similar instances, as in the preceding poem "A Winter-Piece to a Friend Away" in ll. 46 and 47: "same,—" and "delays,—".

"Narcissus Moving"

1.25: **pavane**] pavanne (*Editor's Note*: Neither the French nor the Anglicized spelling is "pavanne," as Berryman spells it in both the CTS and the page proofs. I have emended the misspelling.)

1.30: *Editor's Note*: Although Berryman did not indicate the change of "one" to "once" in the galleys, the page proofs show the change, which I assume he instructed.

1.36: **Un**] Une (*Editor's Note*: Berryman corrected the feminine of *silence* in *HomageAOP* to the correct masculine, which is accepted for *CP*.)

"The Dispossessed"

1.1: **that . . . that**] that . . that (*Editor's Note*: I have added an extra point because the ellipsis appears in a quotation.)

SONNETS TO CHRIS (1947, 1966)

TS-1:   The original typescript of *Sonnets* that consists of: the title page (typed on the title page is *Sonnets to Chris* and "John Berryman" with the HW date 1947); a HW index of sonnets 1–100; ribbon TS of sonnets 1–24, 26–105, 110 (now 106 in *CP*), 112–14 (now 108–10 in *CP*); and an epilogue page on which "Judges xvi.22" appears in the center. Some seventy-two emendations in Berryman's HW appear throughout the TS, probably done in late 1947 or early 1948. TS-1 is now in JBP.

CTS-C: The carbon typescript, with the exception of one TS, of the original typescript (TS-1) with Berryman's thirty-two HW changes in black ink; CTS-C consists of: CTSS of sonnets 1–106 and 108–11 and a TS of 107; no title page. Berryman made nearly all the HW changes on the CTS-C in 1966 (only two were done in 1947–48). The CTS-C was the printer's copy-text, now at Columbia University, New York City, for the FSG edition of *Berryman's Sonnets* (1967).

The Copy-Texts of Sonnets *for* CP: Berryman wrote and revised nearly all of *Sonnets* during an intense five- to seven-month period in 1947. The first draft of Sonnet 1, the extant HW MSS indicate, was written on April 26; the last (107 in both *CP* and the FSG edition) was revised on September 30. In late 1947 or early 1948, he typed, with a carbon, the 110 sonnets he considered complete, and, about the same time, he penciled in some seventy-two changes on the TS, two of which were transferred to the CTS. Both MSS were apparently laid aside for nearly twenty years; only Sonnet 25—published in *Poetry* magazine in 1952 and again in *Thought* in 1958—gave a clue that the sonnets existed.

In August 1966, for reasons I shall present below in the "Publication History," Berryman decided to publish *Sonnets*. During the same month, he wrote seven new ones (107 and 112–17 in *CP*) and the prefatory poem in Dream Song stanza form. But the copy-text he sent FSG was not the original TS (TS-1) with his 1947 HW emendations; he chose, instead, the carbon copy (CTS-C). As though he were creating a Joycean puzzle for future editors, he made some thirty-two changes in August 1966 in the CTS-C—the principal characters' names (not his own, however, in Sonnet 84); the places and street names; the date in Sonnet 106; and several words. None of the 1966 changes was based on his HW changes in the original TS.

The outcome of these three separate histories—the writing, revising, typing, and editing in 1947; the writing of the new sonnets; and the revising of the CTS in 1966—was to create three primary texts, each with its own artistic integrity:

1. The original TS with numerous HW changes (1947)
2. The CTS (1947) with HW changes done in 1966
3. The prefatory Dream Song and seven new sonnets (1966), two of which (now Sonnets 115 and 116 in *CP*) were not included in *Berryman's Sonnets*

because they were sent to the publisher after the collection was in press When Berryman decided to publish *Sonnets* in August 1966, he was not—perhaps could not be—true to his final intentions of 1947, and it is his final intentions of 1947, regardless of his intentions of 1966, that should, I believe, dictate the primary copy-text for his collected works.

My choosing the 1947 TS with HW changes restores the artistic integrity of the original *Sonnets* and untangles them from both Berryman's 1966 exigences and the seven new sonnets. My reason for including the 1966 sonnets in *CP* is based less upon their final shaping of the story (which, as Berryman wrote to Robert Giroux, was his reason for writing them) and more upon the record of the point of view they offer. These new sonnets, as well as the prefatory Dream Song, represent Berryman's later response to his 1947 sonnets. Once we know that the last sonnets (107 and 112–17) were written in 1966 (by not capitalizing the initial letter of each new line in the 1967 edition, Berryman alerted readers that these poems are in some way set apart), we may read them as a coda to the narrative and a re-vision of his younger self.

Publication History of Sonnets: Berryman's decision to publish *Sonnets* might very well have originated as early as April and May of 1965, when he was awarded the Pulitzer Prize for 77 *Dream Songs* and a Guggenheim Fellowship to complete *The Dream Songs*. The two prestigious awards gave public notice of his national stature and seemed to double his expectations of himself. During the period of the Guggenheim, awarded for the 1966–67 academic year, Berryman's plan was to complete *The Dream Songs* in Dublin, Ireland, between September 1966 and spring 1967. The expenses for the year abroad with his wife and young daughter (and his wish to help with medical expenses for his mother) became matters of financial concern.

To supplement his income, Berryman taught a summer course on "Humanities and the Modern World" at the University of Minnesota from July 18 to August 20, 1966. His preparations and lectures demanded most of his time: the classes met daily, Monday through Friday, and he was grading finals the night before he and his family departed for Dublin. When one adds to his financial concerns and teaching duties the preparations for a year abroad as well as his organizing large files of MSS of Dream Songs and writing new ones, it is remarkable that he even considered taking on another project. But *Sonnets* was the most complete work at hand, and to publish the collection would bring in the income he needed. The double recognition of the Pulitzer and the Guggenheim assured that his next publication would be in demand.

Although Berryman told an interviewer in mid-June 1966 that *Sonnets* would "probably be published next Spring [1967]," he waited nearly two months before initiating publication. On August 11, he called William Meredith, a close friend whose opinion Berryman counted on, and asked him to read the MS of some "114 sonnets." If Meredith thought they merited publication, would he send the MS (actually the CTS-C) on to Berryman's publisher, Robert Giroux? Meredith sent the CTS-C to FSG and enthusiastically endorsed these "remarkable poems," as he wrote to Giroux on August 23. About the same time, Berryman and his family were sailing to Ireland; by the first week of September they were in Dublin.

The exhausting journey to Ireland seemed to intensify Berryman's capacity for alcohol and writing Dream Songs; *Sonnets* was far removed from his concerns. Meanwhile, Giroux had read *Sonnets*, and on September 28, he offered Berryman a contract. Both agreed that the collection should be published as quickly as possible, primarily because Berryman expected to complete *The Dream Songs* (that is, the last parts, published as *His Toy, His Dream, His Rest*) by the end of 1967. Neither Berryman nor Giroux wanted the publication of *Sonnets* to deflect attention from the completion of his epic work.

The advance Berryman had hoped for was part of the contract he accepted in a letter to Giroux on October 8, 1966. In early November, he sent four new sonnets—written in Minneapolis in August—to add to the 111 Giroux had in the CTS-C. (Berryman in fact sent Giroux two more sonnets in early February 1967 after the 115 were in galleys, but it was too late to add them.) Giroux sent the galleys to Berryman in early January 1967, and he promptly returned them on January 11 with a note written by Kate Berryman. She said that although John was ill, the galleys had been proofed. She asked Giroux to check the accuracy of six passages because they did not have a copy of a *Sonnets* MS. Giroux responded on 18 January: "I have checked the ms. against all the items you listed, and found a few other typographical errors too." No further changes or corrections were made, and *Berryman's Sonnets*—the title Giroux had suggested—was published on April 24, 1967.

Berryman's illness and preoccupation with writing Dream Songs during the process of publishing and proofing *Sonnets* ensured the probability of errors in the final copy. Both sets of galleys—one in JBP and the other at Columbia University—show only six HW corrections, which do not appear to be in Berryman's hand. It is certain, however, that he did not (could not, because he did not have the MS) proof the galleys carefully. I find seventeen errors of transcription

Appendices

in comparing the CTS-C with the FSG edition. Some of the FSG errors may be attributed to obscured or uncertain letters that were erased and changed in the TS-1 but only typed over in the CTS-C. For example, the first "g" in "springing" in 54.10 (*CP*) was erased on the TS-1 and retyped as a "t"; the carbon (CTS-C), however, was not erased, so that the word looks more like "springing" (which appeared in the FSG edition) than the corrected "sprinting."

But why did Berryman choose to publish the carbon copy rather than the original typescript with his 1947 changes? First, his circumstances did not allow him time to produce a clean TS for FSG. When Berryman called Meredith on August 11, 1966, he and his family were to depart for Dublin in two weeks. The hectic preparations—as well as the demands of the final days of the course he was teaching and his preparing to work on *The Dream Songs*—were foremost in his life. There simply was not time to retype and carry forward his HW corrections from the original 1947 TS. The only unmarked copy of *Sonnets* was the CTS; he need only change the names and places by hand.

That Berryman did not destroy his original TS suggests that he wished to preserve his final intentions of 1947. An experienced editor himself, he might very well have taken some delight in playing a sort of hide-and-seek and hoped to be found out. Whatever his reasons for saving the TS-1, it seems to me that it is nearer his "final" intentions than the CTS-C.

VARIANTS: Left of the] indicates the *CP* version that follows the original typescript (TS-1) with Berryman's HW changes; right of the] indicates the FSG edition. As I indicate in my Editor's Notes, Guidelines, and Procedures, I have regularized Berryman's arbitrary use of ellipsis points and quotation marks.

Title: Sonnets to Chris] *Berryman's Sonnets*
Epigraph poem ("He made, a thousand years ago")
  1.7 Let] let (*Editor's Note*: The CTS in file 2 shows a capital "L.")
  2.13: breasts . . My] breasts . . My
Sonnets
  3.7: crown] crowd (*Editor's Note*: In both TS-1 and CTS-C the word is clearly "crown.")
  4.5: Chris] Lise
  .5: where] when (*Editor's Note*: In both TS-1 and CTS-C the word is clearly "where.")
  .9: dánce] dance (*HW in TS-1*)
  5.12: Laught . . Well,] Laught . . Well,
  6.1: twist] grind (*HW in TS-1*)
  .11: whispers? . . Not] whispers? . . *Not*

7.7: *Editor's Note*: The TS-1 indicates "on . . . and"; I have deleted one point consistent with my editorial guidelines.

.9: **on! . . .'**] on! . .' (*Editor's Note*: I have added an extra point because the ellipsis appears in a quotation.)

8:1: **cocktails,**] flunkeys, and (*HW in TS-1*) *Editor's Note*: On TS-1, Berryman notes: "*cocktails* means also 'persons passing for gentlemen, but underbred' in *English* slang, as seems appropriate of an Anglophile college."

.5: **eternity? . . Your**] eternity? . . Your

9.2: **Chris**] Lise

10.4: **palm**] hand (*HW in TS-1*)

.9: **situation!**] situation, (*HW in TS-1*)

12.1: **in the half-light, & malignant,**] armed & suicidal (*HW in TS-1*)

14.2: **porchlight . . I**] porchlight . . I

.13: **Love**] love (*Editor's Note*: "Love" is capitalized in both TS-1 and CTS-C.)

15.1: **then? . . Cargoed**] then? . . Cargoed

.12: **signs**] sighs (*Editor's Note*: The TS-1 shows that the "n" in "signs" was first typed as an "h" and then erased and retyped as an "n"; the CTS-C was not similarly erased so that it reads erroneously as "sighs.")

.15: (***After Petrarch & Wyatt***)] (A F T E R   P E T R A R C H   &   W Y A T T)

16.4: **the wild fact**] local truth (*HW in TS-1*)

.13: **recovered . . Rack**] recovered. . . Rack (*Editor's Note*: The TS-1 indicates "recovered . . .   Rack"; I have deleted one point consistent with my editorial guidelines.)

.14: **Stockton street**] Rockwell Street

18.1: **Chris**] Lise

20.3: **Nassau street**] Knowlton Street

.4: **angel's**] angelic (*HW in TS-1*)

.9: **have here misabused**] here have been abused (*HW in TS-1*)

21.1: **upto**] into (*HW in TS-1*)

22.9: **ascotted groom,**] ascotted, still (*HW in TS-1*)

.10: **eyes . . No**] eyes . . No

.11: **tongue;**] tongue. (*HW in TS-1*)

.14: **for . . We**] for . . We

23.1: **may,**] may suppose, (*HW in TS-1*)

.3: **'love'; suppose**] 'love' and 'love', (*HW in TS-1*)

.6: **Wíth**] With (*Editor's Note*: The accent mark in the CTS-C is faint but the mark is clear in TS-1.)

.12: **false . . Blood**] false. . . Blood (*Editor's Note*: The TS-1 indicates "false

. . . Blood"; I have deleted one point consistent with my editorial guidelines.)

24.9: though! . . Who] though! . . Who

25: *Editor's Note*: Since the TS of Sonnet 25 is missing from TS-1, I have followed the CTS-C that FSG used. While Berryman made three HW changes in the CTS-C in 1966, I have admitted them because they are the same as those that appear in *Poetry* in 1952. The three changes are:

> **1.3: nearing]** near
> **1.4: Toward]** To
> **1.13: around]** about him

26.1: a ridge] a low ridge (*HW in TS-1*)

  .12: *Editor's Note*: In TS-1 and CTS-C "Negroes" is not capitalized; I have admitted the FSG capitalization.

27.8: synchrisis] syncrisis (*HW in TS-1*)

29.12: day . . Your] day. . . Your (*Editor's Note*: The TS-1 indicates "day . . . Your"; I have deleted one point consistent with my editorial guidelines.)

30.1: *Editor's Note*: In CTS-C "weeks-long" appears as "weeks'-long"; in the FSG edition the apostrophe is deleted. In the TS-1 Berryman indicated that the apostrophe should be deleted, which is the reason for accepting the FSG emendation.

31.2: unaware,] unawares (*HW in TS-1*)

  .12: not-come-up] *not come up* (*Editor's Note*: Berryman's HW marginal note "no ital." is in TS-1. The hyphens appear to be HW.)

32.1: shall] can (*HW in TS-1*)

33.3: Another . . Strange, so] Another . . Strange, (*HW in TS-1*)

  .10: moaned . . One] moaned . . One

34.2: Oúr] Our (*Editor's Note*: The accent mark in the CTS-C is faint but it is clear in TS-1.)

35.6: *adjustment*] adjustment (*HW in TS-1*)

36.13: in . . Open] in . . Open

37.1: ends . . I] ends . . . I (*Editor's Note*: The TS-1 indicates "ends . . . I"; I have deleted one point consistent with my editorial guidelines.)

39.14: Enter] Trying (*HW in TS-1*)

  .14: boiling] raving (*HW in TS-1*)

42.3: sleep . .] sleep . . . (*Editor's Note*: The TS-1 indicates "sleep . . ."; I have deleted one point consistent with my editorial guidelines.)

  .7: belov'd] beloved (*HW in TS-1*)

  .9: died . . Fill] died . . Fill

43.13: me, Than] me. Than (*Editor's Note*: In TS-1 and CTS-C, a comma follows "me" after which "Than" is capitalized. FSG emended the comma to a period, which I have not admitted. In the only extant HW copy of this sonnet, in a spiral notebook, "me, than" appears.)

45.3: twilight. . .] twilight . . (*Editor's Note*: I have added one point because the ellipsis appears in a quotation.)

46.1: night-] night (*HW in TS-1*)

  .2: bulge on the North Way] Attack on the dark road (*HW in TS-1*)

  .3: You] you (*HW in TS-1*)

  .4: Flushes] Joy bloods (*HW in TS-1*)

  .5: You writhed on Me] you writhed on me (*HW in TS-1*)

  .13: we (ah),] till we, (*HW in TS-1*)

47.9: Usk. . . .'] Usk . .' (*Editor's Note*: I have added two points because the ellipsis appears at the end of a quotation.)

48.2: cut] out (*Editor's Note*: The TS-1 is clearly "cut," which in the CTS-C could be mistaken for "out.")

  .5: Natasha] Katrina

  .6: wonderful! . . .] wonderful! . . (*Editor's Note*: I have added an extra point because the ellipsis appears in a quotation.)

49.3: *Editor's Note*: In TS-1, "Seconal" is spelled "secanol" and is not capitalized; I have admitted the FSG emendation.

50.2: Smother,] Batter, (*HW in TS-1*)

51.3: squibs,] squibs (*HW in TS-1*)

  .10: us . . —Ah] us . . Ah (*HW in TS-1*)

  .12: puisne] jackal (*HW in TS-1*)

53.9: an-crazy] antcrazy (*Editor's Note*: In both TS-1 and CTS-C the spelling appears as "an-crazy"; FSG changed it to "antcrazy" which I have not admitted.)

  .10: Pyne] Wyne

  .13: you . . No] you . . No

54.10: Sprinting] Springing (*Editor's Note*: The first "g" in "Springing" was originally typed as a "t" and erased and changed to a "g" on the TS-1; on the CTS-C, the "t" is typed over the "g," which was not erased, and could be mistaken for a "g.")

55.7: white and] white & (*HW in TS-1*)

57.1: tropic] heavy (*HW in TS-1*)

  .5: us-inured] us inured (*HW in TS-1*)

  .7: audacious,] audacious and (*HW in TS-1*)

  .9: incredible] unlikely (*Editor's Note*: On the CTS-C in 1966, Berryman changed in HW "incredible" to "unlikely." I have not admitted the change.)

59.2: Sucks out our best,] Sucks our best off, (*HW in TS-1*)

.8: we] wé (*Editor's Note*: The accent above "we" is erased in TS-1.)

.9: Left, before there we bloomed,] Left before there we bloomed (*HW in TS-1*)

60.4: creaked] got (*HW in TS-1*)

.11: in the platform's] and the platforms (*HW in TS-1*)

.13: So action and peace . .] Action and peace so . . (*HW in TS-1*)

.14: *come!*] *come* (*HW in TS-1*)

62.1: far] much (*HW in TS-1*)

.11: Chris] Lise

63.12: Win] Wid (*Editor's Note*: In TS-1 the word is clearly "Win," but in the CTS-C the "n" is an uncertain combination of two letters that could be mistaken for a "d.")

64.2: askew] not far (*HW in TS-1*)

.8: Chris] Lise

65.10: soon . . Deep] soon . . Deep

67.10 Chris] Lise

68.9: well . . I] well . . I

.13: will] well (*Editor's Note*: In TS-1 "well" was typed first but corrected to "will"; in the CTS-C the word looks more like "well" than "will.")

69.1: collared] collared O (*Editor's Note*: The "O" does not appear in either TS-1 or CTS-C.)

.2: redhaired] sandy-haired (*Editor's Note*: Berryman changed "red" to "sandy" in 1966 CTS; I have followed TS-1.)

.13: the great needle] and the needle (*HW in TS-1*)

.14: Chris] Lise

70.1: October's both,] Under Scorpion both, (*HW in TS-1*)

.2: thin winds worry] dry winds winnow (*HW in TS-1*)

.2: born;] born, (*HW in TS-1*)

.4: (frankly) has] has frankly (*HW in TS-1*)

.11: frightened,] frightened; (*HW in TS-1*)

72.4: ten-year old] ten-year-old (*Editor's Note*: In both TS-1 and CTS-C the hyphen appears only between "ten" and "year.")

.5: you forgot forgot forgot] forgot you, forgot you, (*HW in TS-1*)

73.8: LOVE' . . O] LOVE' . . O

74.6: Muster me into morning] Conducted me to-morning (*HW in TS-1*)

.7: In the South,] Two years, (*HW in TS-1*)

.8: fixed . . The] fixed . . The (*Editor's Note*: The TS-1 indicates "fixed. . . The"; I have deleted one point consistent with my editorial guidelines.)

75.15: Chris! be our surviving] Lise! be our bright surviving (*HW in TS-1*)

76.13: Chris] Lise

.15: **Koblegaard**] Kierkegaard (*Editor's Note*: In the CTS-C, in 1966, Berryman changed "Koblegaard" to "Kierkegaard"; I have followed TS-1.)

78.1: **wheat-sacks**] wheat-sacks, (*HW in TS-1*)

.2: **Sidney**] William

.13: **barn . . Princeton**] barn . . Kingston

79.12: **Chris**] Lise

80.14: **scrap us single, strap us**] split us painfully (*HW in TS-1*)

81.9: **brook-sheet**] water (*HW in TS-1*)

.12: **The complex patient,**] Brook near the postbox, (*HW in TS-1*)

.14: **four-square**] solid (*HW in TS-1*)

82.1: **Chris**] Lise

.10: **Fantasy! . . Forget.**] Fantasy! . . . Forget. (*Editor's Note*: The TS-1 indicates "Fantasy! . . . Forget."; I have deleted one point consistent with my editorial guidelines.)

.11: **—This pencil's**] —I write this (*HW in TS-1*)

.12: **I'm**] I am (*HW in TS-1*)

.13: **let—**] let (*HW in TS-1*)

83.10: **Eileen**] Esther

84.11: **ín**] in (*HW in both CTS-C and TS-1*)

85.7: *Editor's Note:* In TS-1, "protégé" appears incorrectly as "protegé"; I have admitted the FSG correction.

86.1: **hopelessly**] bitterly (*HW in TS-1*)

87.2: **Chris**] Lise

.11: *Editor's Note:* Neither the French nor the Anglicized spelling is "pavanne," as Berryman spells it in both the TS-1 and the FSG edition. I have emended the misspelling to "pavane."

88.9: '*. . . note . . . note . . .*'] '*. . note . . note . .*' (*Editor's Note:* I have added extra points because the ellipses appear in a quotation.)

89.10: *Editor's Note:* In TS-1, and CTS-C, Berryman misspelled "desiccation" as "dessication." I have accepted the FSG correction.

.14: **hopelets**] hope lets (*Editor's Note:* In 1966 on the CTS-C, Berryman changed "hopelets" to "hope lets." This is a questionable change because in both TS-1 and a HWMS (spiral notebook) "hope lets" appears as "hopelets." I have followed TS-1, which is confirmed by the HWMS version.)

90.4: **fled**] lost (*HW in TS-1*)

.8: **succor, as they can,**] succor as they can (*HW in TS-1*)

.11: **useful,**] useful (*HW in TS-1*)

92.2: **whistle you**] work you here

.3: **Become,**] Be

.5: **How far? Alive to**] Room still? Alive O to

.6: Or the] The

.7: in? . . Your] in? Your

.8: J.B., M´o, B´e, and F.S.] Bach, Mozart, Beethoven & Schubert

.11: . . deaf pride of art . .] . . they moved apart . .

.13: Across sometimes: neither admits he's] Sometimes, neither will say how he has (*Editor's Note:* Sonnet 92 apparently was retyped around 1947–48 with the above changes. The revised version is in TS-1, and the earlier version is in CTS-C and therefore in the FSG edition. A comparison of all extant versions suggests that the retyped version postdates the CTS-C version because the CTS-C closely follows his first HW draft.)

94.9: wére] were (*Editor's Note:* The accent mark is faint in CTS-C but clear in TS-1.)

.11: Spring] Fox

95.1: Smoky] Smokey

.1: Robin, Chris,] Peter, Lise,

96.8: coming . . Heavy] coming . . Heavy

97.8: shudder as I'd] scream as I would (*HW in TS-1*) (*Editor's Note:* Although the FSG edition does not reflect it, in the CTS-C Berryman crossed out, in 1947–48, "would" and wrote in "I'd" and wrote "shudder" above "scream" but did not cross out "scream." In the TS-1, he deleted "I would" and wrote in "I'd" and changed "scream" to "shudder.")

.9: l . . Only] l . . Only

98.3: below . . See] below . . See

99.11: German] Jersey (*Editor's Note:* In the CTS-C, Berryman changed in 1966 "German" to "Jersey." Although Stephen Crane was in fact buried in New Jersey, I have not admitted the emendation.)

101.7: '. . . was] '. . was (*Editor's Note:* I have added an extra point because the ellipsis appears in a quotation.)

.8 over . . .'] over . .' (*Editor's Note:* I have added an extra point because the ellipsis appears in a quotation.)

.14: *Editor's Note:* "triste" is spelled "trist" in TS-1 and CTS-C, but FSG emended it to the correct spelling, which I have admitted.

104.6: To'have] To have (*Editor's Note:* "To'have" appears in both TS-1 and CTS-C.)

.12: god] God (*Editor's Note:* FSG emended "god," which I have not admitted.)

105.8: Jerquer] Jerguer (*Editor's Note:* The "q" in "Jerquer" was typed as a "g" but typed over in TS-1; in CTS-C, the "q" could be mistaken for a "g.")

106.10: Nineteen Forty-seven] Nineteen XXXX

.11: McCosh] McIntosh (*Editor's Note:* In TS-1, sonnet 106 is 110; sonnets

106–9 are either missing from TS-1 or were not typed. In 1966, when Berryman made the changes in CTS-C, he crossed out "110" and wrote in "106.")

107.4: movement of] no of

   .14: a-conning] a-coming (*Editor's Note:* Berryman wrote this sonnet in 1966. In the HWMS of 107 in file 2 of the *Sonnets* box in JBP "no" is "mvt" in l.4 and "a-coming" is "a-conning" in l.14. In the TS, not a CTS, of Sonnet 107 at Columbia, the phrase "no of clocks" [FSG edition] appears as "n of clocks," but in the margin a HW change—not in Berryman's hand—indicates "movement," apparently for the "n." In the FSG edition, the "n" was changed to "no." In l.14 of the same typescript, "coming" is crossed out and in the margin "conning" is written, again not in Berryman's hand. I have emended the text to follow the HWMS in JBP.)

108.9: your] that (*HW in TS-1*)

   .10: nowhere] no where (*HW in TS-1*)

   .11: life like a mouse] times when your voice (*HW in TS-1*)

   .12: Cheeseless, but trapt.] Nearly I latched. (*HW in TS-1*) (*Editor's Note:* Sonnet 108 is 112 in TS-1. On the CTS-C in 1966 Berryman changed the number to 108.)

109.12: mais . . .'] mais . . .' (*Editor's Note:* I have added an extra point because the ellipsis appears in a quotation. Sonnet 109 is 113 in TS-1. On the CTS-C in 1966 Berryman changed the number to 109.)

110.1: us . . .'] us . .' (*Editor's Note:* I have added an extra point because the ellipsis appears in a quotation.)

   .5: Chris, whistling . . Knowing] Lise, whistling . . . Knowing, (*Editor's Note:* The TS-1 indicates "Chris, whistling . . . Knowing"; I have deleted one point consistent with my editorial guidelines. Sonnet 110 is 114 in TS-1; on the CTS-C, Berryman changed, in 1966, the number to 110.)

111.11: After, and] After, (*Editor's Note:* Sonnet 111 is numbered in HW on the CTS-C, but the original TS does not appear in TS-1. In file 3 of the *Sonnets* box in JBP, a TS appears to be the original of the CTS-C. On the TS, Berryman made the HW change in l.11 which seems to me characteristic of his handwriting during the 1947–48 period.) "Lies" in 113.1 is the Dutch spelling of "Lise."

113.8 and 117.3: *Editor's Note:* When Berryman wrote these lines in 1966, he used "Lise" rather than "Chris." In these two instances, I have not emended the name to conform to the 1947 sonnets.

113.11, 12: On the CTS, "clouds" is spelled "clound" and "freighter" is spelled "freighty." The HWMS and the FSG version show the correct spellings, which I have followed.

115 and 116: *Editor's Note:* Berryman sent these two sonnets—both written in August

1966—to Robert Giroux on February 4, 1967, with instructions to change Sonnet 115 to 117 and to number these new ones 115 and 116 respectively. Since I have included the published sonnets he wrote in 1966, it follows that his instruction to add these unpublished ones must likewise be observed.
Epilogue: *Editor's Note*: The epilogue "Judges xvi.22" appears only in TS-1.

HOMAGE TO MISTRESS BRADSTREET (1953)

The Copy-Text of Homage *for* CP: The author's galleys for the FSG edition of *Homage* (published October 1, 1956) are apparently lost. But since the FSG version is the same as that in *Partisan Review* (published in the September–October 1953 issue), the author's corrected galleys for *Partisan Review* extant are the primary copy-text for *CP*.

VARIANTS: There are no variants between the author's galleys of *Homage* for *Partisan Review* (1953) and the first printing by FSG (1956). I have added an extra ellipsis point in l.8, " 'Simon . . .'," because it appears in a quotation.

from HIS THOUGHT MADE POCKETS & THE PLANE BUCKT (1958)

The Copy-Text of Thought *for* CP: The copy-text for *CP* follows the author's corrected galleys. *Thought* was published by Claude Fredericks, Pawlett (Vermont) on December 15, 1958. Both the galleys and the printer's TS (actually a combination of a TS and a CTS) are now at the Washington University Libraries in St. Louis, Missouri. The final printed copy is faithful to Berryman's corrections in the galleys.

VARIANTS: No variants in the texts of the poems in the author's corrected galleys and the first edition.

Editor's Notes: Since "Sonnet XXV" in *Thought*, which follows "Scots Poem," is now Sonnet 25 of *Sonnets* in *CP*, it is not included here. "Sonnet XXV" is the only poem in *CP* deleted from those originally published in *Thought*.

The epigraph beginning "Henry sats in de plane & was gay" is not in the galleys but was added before final printing, presumably at Berryman's direction.

In the galleys of "Venice, 182-" (l. 25), "are" appears with a grave accent rather than the acute in the printer's TS. Since Berryman most frequently favored the acute accent, I have followed the printer's TS. I have also added an extra ellipsis point to " 'There . . .' " because it appears in a quotation.

Although neither the TS nor the galleys show opening quotation marks in l.23 and l.42 of "American Lights, Seen From Off Abroad," they do show closing marks. I have added opening quotation marks in both lines.

"Formal Elegy" (1964) (from SHORT POEMS, 1967)

Editor's Note: "Formal Elegy" was first published in *Of Poetry and Power: Poems Occasioned by the Presidency and Death of John F. Kennedy*, foreword by Arthur Schlesinger, Jr., edited with an introduction by Erwin A. Glikes and Paul Schwaber (Basic Books, Inc., New York, 1964) and collected in *Short Poems*. I have followed the text in *Short Poems*, but in keeping with my editorial guideline on single quotation marks, in l.67 I have emended "education" to 'education.'

LOVE & FAME (1971)

The Copy-Text of L&F *for* CP: The copy-text of *L&F* for *CP* is based on the page proofs, with Berryman's HW changes, which he sent to Faber and Faber in the spring of 1971. Although the FSG second edition, revised, of *L&F* was published a year after the FF edition, Berryman actually made his last revisions for FF. He revised the FSG edition in January 1971 and the FF edition in March and June 1971. The FF page proofs are at the Columbia University Libraries.

The printing errors in the FF edition, insofar as I have been able to determine them by comparing it with the FSG first and second editions, have been corrected for *CP*. I have followed the American rather than the British spelling of the FF edition except in those instances where Berryman, as was his habit, preferred British spelling, as in "Her & It," l.16: "cheques" rather than "checks."

Publication History of L&F: Similar to the intense period of composition of *Sonnets*, Berryman wrote the first drafts of most of *L&F* in two months. He wrote the first four or five poems on February 4, 1970; by April he completed the last. He made so many revisions in the first set of galleys in August that a second set of galleys, dated September 9, had to be done. The second galleys show a few HW corrections, not in Berryman's hand, but there are no substantive changes. The first edition was published on December 15, but before it was issued, he was at work on the second edition, revised.

Berryman's uncertainty, manifest in both his extensive revisions in the galleys and his requests for advice from a dozen friends, is partly explainable, he said, in that he had not written short poems in over twenty years. Less than two months after he wrote the first poems, he completed the first TS of *L&F* by March 23, 1970—forty-two poems (Parts I, II, and III), each numbered and untitled—which did not include "Eleven Addresses to the Lord." He sent photocopies to "a dozen of my friends," as he wrote in the cover letter with each copy, to read and "CRITICIZE." Most responded in April, among them Mark Van Doren, Richard Wilbur, Adrienne Rich, Edmund Wilson, Edward Hoagland, Franklin Reeve, Maris Thomes, and Deneen Peckinpah. By early August Berryman had proofed the galleys of *L&F*, which included "Eleven Addresses to the Lord."

The first unfavorable reviews of the first edition of *L&F* in November 1970 spurred Berryman to revise lines and delete whole poems in the collection. He wrote to Robert Giroux on January 25, 1971: "I hope to Christ the first edition sells out quickly and you can reprint." In the same letter, he enclosed a preface ("Scholia to Second Edition") and asked that six poems be deleted. "I'll send you—phone you if necessary," he added, "the very few corrections in the text." Of the 6,000 copies of the first edition FSG had printed, Giroux wrote on February 4, only 1,000 were left, but the second edition did not materialize until November 15, 1972. The revisions Berryman sent to Giroux in January 1971 were to stand as his final revisions for the FSG second edition, revised.

In the meantime Charles Monteith of Faber and Faber, Ltd. planned to publish *L&F* in England. He read the FSG galleys of the first edition in August 1970 and on the twentieth he wrote to Berryman that FF would offset from the FSG edition. Monteith had himself been corresponding with Berryman, and in December, when he learned of Berryman's revisions, he wrote to Giroux that FF would now offset from the second printing. But FSG's plans to publish the second edition in March 1971 changed to a later date, and FF proceeded with making up their own galleys. In mid-March, Berryman revised and deleted several poems—probably on an unbound copy, the extant manuscripts suggest, of the FSG first edition—and sent Monteith the revised copy. Monteith planned to publish *L&F*, as he wrote to Giroux, "in the early autumn [1971] in its revised form."

Monteith sent Berryman two sets of FF's galleys on June 2 with instructions to return one set, which Berryman did on June 21 with further comments and instructions: "Some of the typos are grave. All are listed on the front leaf. I've revised only a few details." He enclosed a TS of the "Afterword" which is, except for a sentence in the penultimate paragraph and the entire final paragraph, the same as "Scholia to Second Edition," which would appear in the FSG edition over a year later. The page proofs followed shortly thereafter, and Berryman made some twenty changes and corrections.

When FSG published the second edition, revised, of *L&F* on November 15, 1972—nearly two years after Berryman had made his changes—FSG assumed, apparently, that Berryman's revisions for the FF edition in March and June 1971 were the same as those he had made for FSG the preceding January. In any event, it is clear that Berryman's last revisions were in the FF edition.

VARIANTS: Left of the] is the FF author's corrected page proofs, except where noted; right of the] is the FSG second edition, revised.

"Cadenza on Garnette"

1.20: *Editor's Note:* The FSG two-point ellipsis of "Poets! . . Lovers" is accepted for *CP.*

"Shirley & Auden"

1.16: *Editor's Note:* The FSG spelling of "chauffeured," rather than the FF proofs spelling of "chauffered," is accepted for *CP.*

1.38: *Editor's Note:* The FSG two-point ellipsis of "Coquet . ." is accepted for *CP.*

1.65: *Editor's Note:* The italicizing of "first" in the FF proofs is a printing error, which I have emended.

"Drunks"

1.18: young] young new

"Olympus"

1.17: *Editor's Note:* I have followed the FSG version of "15 ¢" rather than the FF proofs of "*15c.*"

1.34: less] but never so

"Nowhere"

1.10: blues,] blues, at the Apollo & on records.

"In & Out"

1.8: *Editor's Note:* The FF page proofs show Corbière with an acute accent rather than a grave; the FSG version is correct and accepted for *CP.*

1.41: witty &] a little

1.43: beat] pounded

1.62: and slovenly, Zander] & slovenly, he (*Editor's Note:* "Zander" is printed as "Zauder" in the FF edition. Berryman's HW change in the proofs could be read as "Zauder," but his "n"s often look like "u"s. There actually was a Randolph Zander enrolled at Columbia at the time Berryman was there.)

"The Heroes"

1.9: *Editor's Note:* The FSG spelling of "maneuvered" and the circumflex on "rôles" are accepted.

"Crisis"

1.58: *Editor's Note:* The FSG spelling of "installment" is accepted for *CP.*

"Recovery"

1.10: *Editor's Note:* The comma after "wheel-chair" in the FSG edition is accepted for *CP*; I believe the missing comma in the FF edition is a printing error.

1.22: *Editor's Note:* I have emended "scholarship . . ." to "scholarship . ."

"Away"

Title: Editor's Note: The title of "Away" in the FSG edition appears as "Anyway" in the FF edition. Berryman did not correct the title in the FF proofs, but in the Table of Contents in the FF page proofs the title appears as "Away." I believe that he overlooked the FF printing error of "Anyway," and I have accepted the title "Away" as it appears in all other extant copies and proofs of *L&F*.

"First Night at Sea"

1.15: *Editor's Note:* Berryman misremembered the surname of the composer Walter Morse Rummel as "Memel." In letters to both his mother and Mark Van Doren in 1936, he spells the name as "Rumel." I have not, however, changed Berryman's spelling.

1.21: *Editor's Note:* The FSG comma after "ballads" is accepted; the period after "ballads" in the FF proofs is a printing error.

"London"

1.17: *Editor's Note:* The comma after "Hotel" in the FSG edition is missing in the FF edition; I have admitted the comma in the FSG edition.

"The Other Cambridge"

1.18: *Editor's Note:* The FF spelling of "sweart" is, I believe, a misprint; I have accepted the FSG "swear." But a more serious error occurs in Berryman's quoting what Essex actually said to Ralegh. It should be: "What booteth it to swear the fox?" rather than "What boots it swear The Fox." I have not emended the quotation.

1.41: *Editor's Note:* The FSG spelling of "Queens' " is accepted; the FF version of "Queen's" is a printing error.

1.21: Freans] Frean's

"Monkhood"

1.28: 'Satanic pride',] 'Satanic pride'

1.41: *Editor's Note:* The FSG capitalization of "One" is accepted; the FF lower case is a printing error.

"Views of Myself"

1.2 *Editor's Note:* FF proofs show a misspelling of *Advocate* which is corrected for *CP*.

1.27: *Editor's Note:* The FSG spelling of "bite" is accepted; the FF spelling of "bit" appears to be a printing error. The second part of the quotation—"am quiet"—suggests that the first part should be in the present tense as well, that is, "bite" rather than "bit."

"Meeting"

1.3: *Editor's Note:* The FSG spelling of "center" is accepted.

"Tea"

1.13: Lives] He lives

"Relations"

1.4: *Editor's Note:* In the FF galley proofs, Berryman changed "Peckinpah" to "Pekinpah." Since Deneen Peckinpah spells her name with a "c," and since the name is spelled correctly in the FSG edition, I have emended the FF version to the correct spelling.

1.8: resume] be

"Antitheses"

1.17: *Editor's Note:* I have emended "Leonardo . . ." to "Leonardo . ."

1.19: *Editor's Note:* The FSG spelling of "skeptical" is accepted.

1.23: *Editor's Note:* The FF version of "at" is, I believe, a misprint; I have followed the FSG version of "as."

"Have a Genuine American Horror-&-Mist on the Rocks"

1.3: *Editor's Note:* The FSG ellipsis in "Waal . ." is accepted.

"Damned"

1.7: *Editor's Note:* The FSG spelling of "mustache" is accepted.

"The Hell Poem"

1.4: except for when] except when

1.13: coming] she came

"Purgatory"

1.20: *Editor's Note:* The period after "67" in the FSG edition is accepted; the FF version is a printing error.

1.25: retired,] retired, frail,

"Heaven"

1.11: married before she died,] was killed in a car accident soon after she married,

1.15: whatever yen—] my lust for her

1.16: forgive] persuade me to forgive

"Eleven Addresses to the Lord: 1"

1.21: Peter and] Peter &

"Eleven Addresses to the Lord: 6"

1.3: blow-it-all] suicide

"Eleven Addresses to the Lord: 7"

1.7: never has] has never

"Eleven Addresses to the Lord": *A Prayer for the Self*

Editor's Note: In the FSG galleys (September 9, 1970) the number 8 was not deleted as it is in the first and subsequent editions. The only instruction in the September 9 galleys, not in Berryman's hand, was to move the number to a new position on the page. While it is possible that Berryman could have deleted the number after the galleys were corrected, and while one may reasonably argue that Berryman did not add the number to either the FSG second and FF editions, I have chosen to recover the number because it is more in keeping with the title of the series (i.e., *"Eleven* Addresses . . .") and because all the other prayers are numbered.

DELUSIONS *etc of John Berryman* (1972)

ABBREVIATIONS FOR *De:*

TS-4:   File 4 in Box 1 in JBP: *Delusions* and *Sonnets*, Third Inventory; see "The Copy-Text" section for a description of TS-4.

PMS: The printer's MS copy for FSG; the PMS is in the possession of Robert Giroux; see "The Copy-Text" section for a description of the PMS.

The Copy-Text of De *for* CP: The copy-text of *De* is based on a combination of the PMS and Berryman's working MS. Since Berryman did not live to proof the galleys, his last revisions, rather than his final intentions, must be carefully considered. Although any revision of a poem represents but one version of it, I have chosen, where I could determine them, Berryman's last revisions as the copy-text. The evidence in Berryman's papers, Robert Giroux's files, and the correspondence between them shows that *De* was in process of revision even while the galley proofs were being set. Because the poems were in process, as opposed to the revisions in *TD* eleven years after it was published, Berryman's last revisions must represent his final intentions.

In order to determine Berryman's last revisions, I compared all extant copies (TS, CTS, HWMS, photocopies, and photocopies with HW changes) of each poem in *De*. Most of the changes in the text of *De* for *CP* (i.e., different from the FSG 1972 edition) are based on the MSS that appear to postdate the PMS. All other changes taken from other MSS are noted in the "Variants" section below.

Toward determining Berryman's last revisions for *De*, I drew upon three major sources for the text of *CP*:

    1. Robert Giroux's personal file: letters to and from Berryman; several TSS and CTSS of Berryman's various tables of contents for *De*; photocopies of

twenty-nine poems, all of which Berryman either rejected or revised for the PMS (this file does not contain a complete MS of *De*)

2. The printer's MS (PMS): nine TSS; thirty photocopies of TSS; three poems photocopied from magazines and one cut out of the magazine in which it appeared

3. Berryman's MSS: HW fragments, HWMS, TSS, CTSS, and photocopies in JBP (ten files in the "Third Inventory, Published Poetry, Box 1: *Delusions* and *Sonnets*")

Of the ten *De* files of Berryman's notes and MSS in JBP, the four most valuable in determining an authoritative text of *De* are:

File 1: A photocopy of an October 1971 TS of *De*—probably the copy sent to Robert Fitzgerald, which he returned to Berryman with a letter (October 17, 1971); the penciled X's on the MS indicate Fitzgerald's recommendations for deletions

File 2: One HWMS, CTSS, and photocopies of most of the poems in *De*; the CTSS and the photocopies were typed in October and November 1971

File 4 (i.e., TS-4): TSS, CTSS, and photocopies—many with HW changes; the pages in this file are arranged numerically in an unbound black folder; some of the MSS in this file appear to have been written in October and as late as December 1971

Unnumbered file: Labeled, in Kate Donahue's writing, "Delusions, typed, corrected, rejected": primarily CTSS

In determining Berryman's last revisions, the nine original TS of poems in the PMS may be set apart from the photo- and magazine copies because the TSS appear to be Berryman's last revisions of them. The TSS include: "Nones," "Beethoven Triumphant," "In Memoriam (1914–1953)," "Gislebertus' Eve," "Scholars at the Orchid Pavilion," "The Handshake, The Entrance," "Navajo Setting the Record Straight," "Unknowable? perhaps not altogether," and "Facts & Issues." All the photo- and magazine copies in the PMS do not necessarily represent Berryman's last revisions; they have been compared with other MS copy.

Except for the original TSS in the PMS, the MS of *De* that contains most of Berryman's last revisions is file 4 (TS-4). That this MS is in a black folder, the only extant MS of *De* so filed, suggests that it was to be distinguished from his other *De* files of notes and MSS. The most compelling evidence that the TS-4 file was his working copy is that the photocopies in the PMS were made from it. TS-4 alone, however, has not determined all the changes in *De* for *CP*: several MSS in other files appear to postdate both the photocopies in PMS and the MSS in TS-4. Finally, where the magazine copy of certain poems in the PMS is different from Berryman's MSS, the MS copy prevails.

Publication & Composition History: Berryman's plan for the organization and contents of *De* began as less of a whole than his plan for *L&F*. In his first table of contents for *De* on August 4, 1970 (his first working title was *Last Poems*), he listed seventeen poems—about half of which appear in the final copy of *De*—and "the prayer in progr[ess]," presumably "Opus Dei." As his plans for the volume took shape, he periodically revised his table of contents (the extant "Tables" are dated September 14, September 25, December 28, 1970, and January 16, 1971). On January 25, 1971, he wrote to Robert Giroux that he had "50 poems at present" for *De*, which "may be ready by Easter *or* it may not be ready till Christmas."

Berryman wrote most of the poems for *De* between August 1970 and May 1971. He called Giroux in mid-May to tell him of his progress, and Giroux responded in a letter on May 19, 1971: "[De] as you described it on the telephone is really exciting. If it turns out to be ready for the fall of next year (and it sounds as if it will), I'd be delighted." But *De* was ready much sooner than Giroux anticipated. By late summer 1971, the first TS was completed, and in October Berryman sent a copy—some TSS, some photocopied—for the printer.

After the PMS was sent to Giroux, Berryman continued to revise several poems, and in a few instances he seemed to have lost track of whether or not the copy in the PMS included his latest revisions. Perhaps he was counting on making his further revisions in galleys as he had done in *L&F*; certainly he was following a similar pattern of revision in asking friends to criticize his MS. Berryman sent copies of the *De* TS in early October 1971 to Robert Fitzgerald and Richard Wilbur. In his letter to Wilbur (which Wilbur dates October 9, 1971), he wrote: "[I]n my prostrate opinion the book [De] is still raging w. trash. Questions: is it worth publishing? and if so, how much of it? Have no mercy." Both Wilbur and Fitzgerald responded favorably in general, but, as Wilbur wrote on October 20, "I don't find all of it best Berryman, and . . . my vote, for what it's worth, is for some deletions and additions. Had you not class and continuing oomph, I would not cavil."

Berryman made notes in the margins of Fitzgerald's and Wilbur's letters, and on a copy of his table of contents he tallied their favorable and unfavorable recommendations of poems to keep or delete. He revised his table of contents and wrote to Giroux on October 23: "Here's a better Table of Contents [of *De*]. I've kept several poems Dick Wilbur strongly supported (against Fitzgerald—without of course knowing it)." He enclosed a revised copy of "Nones" and added in the margin, "other revisions follow." On November 12 he sent the revisions, and three days later Giroux responded: "I've received the revised poems and the new table of contents. . . . Everything seems to be in order for the manuscript now."

Berryman's letters to Giroux in November 1971 concerning his revisions of

De do not give a precise record of all the poems he revised for the PMS. On November 12 he wrote to Giroux:

> Herewith, except: (1) I can't locate the carbons of several revised sections of Opus Dei—I may come on them over the weekend—or Bob Silvers has a revised master of the whole poem at The New York Review he could throw downtown; (2) Sonnet 116 has likewise disappeared and is to be replaced by 'The Handshake, The Entrance', enclosed. These others are substitutions and additions.

Although Berryman added a postscript indicating changes in "Damn You, Jim D., You Woke Me Up," " 'How Do You Do, Dr Berryman, Sir?'," and "Navajo Setting the Record Straight," the other "substitutions and additions" he mentions cannot be determined. (Some of the revisions were probably the TS of poems that were incorporated in the PMS.) Likewise, in Giroux's response two days after Berryman's November 12 letter, the specific revisions are not mentioned. Giroux does say that he is "expecting the final drafts of the 'Opus Dei' poems from Bob Silvers" and that he does not have a copy of "Gislebertus' Eve" (which Berryman sent to him two days later). Giroux's next letter was to be his last to Berryman (November 19, 1971); the only mention of revisions is Giroux's thanks for a copy of "Gislebertus' Eve."

Berryman did not proof the galleys of *De* because FSG posted them on January 4, 1972 three days before he died. The galleys were returned to Robert Giroux, who oversaw the collection through final printing. A second set of galleys was set on January 25, 1972. The FSG galleys of *De* were sent to Charles Monteith on February 3, 1972, and Giroux wrote to Monteith that FSG would have setting copy ready in a few weeks. Monteith received the finished copy on April 4 (FSG published *De* on April 28), and the FF edition was published on December 4, 1972, including several corrections that Giroux had written to Monteith about on April 7.

VARIANTS: Left of] is the *CP* text based on TS-4 unless indicated otherwise; right of] is the FSG 1972 first edition.

> *Editor's Note*: Although FF made several corrections in their edition of *De*, I have chosen the FSG edition as my comparative text because it is taken from Berryman's MS. I have taken into account the misprints in the FSG first printing.

Title: *Delusions etc of John Berryman*] *Delusions, Etc.*

> *Editor's Note*: Berryman's title in both TS-4 and the PMS is *Delusions etc of John Berryman*. On the title page of TS-4 and the PMS, "DELUSIONS

etc" is centered approximately ten line spaces from the top of the page; approximately twelve line spaces farther down the page on the same margin is "of John Berryman." In Robert Giroux's file copy of the title page (a photocopy of Berryman's title page), the "of" is crossed out, but Giroux's penciled note in the margin restores it: "Stet 'of' *not* 'by' per author." When the set copy was prepared for the printer, after Berryman's death, a second title page apparently was added to the MS with "Delusions, Etc." centered on a single page. In effect, two titles were published: the first with *Delusions, Etc.* on the first unnumbered page and the second with *Delusions, Etc. of John Berryman* on the third unnumbered page with FSG's colophon and credit. The longer title was easily overlooked by readers because the abbreviated title was most prominent and appeared as well on the jacket cover. Although Berryman referred to the volume in his correspondence as *Delusions etc*, there is no evidence in his MSS that he considered the abbreviated title for the final copy. I have restored the original long title based on the evidence in TS-4 and the PMS.

"Lauds"

    Editor's Note: See Stefanik, p. 134, on the misspelling of "parsecs" in l.4 of the FSG first printing.

1.9 raffish,] raffish. (*Editor's Note*: The photocopy in the PMS does not show a comma as clearly as the original TS in TS-4.)

"Matins"

    Editor's Note: Berryman misspelled "scotographer" in l.21 as "scoteographer"; I have accepted the FSG correction.

"Terce"

Title: "Terce"] "Tierce" (*Editor's Note*: In the photocopy of a TS in the PMS, a HW "i" is added to "Terce," but it is uncertain whether or not the change is in Berryman's hand. Since "Terce" is an acceptable spelling and since all other extant copies show "Terce," I have chosen to emend the spelling to that of the MS copies.)

Stanzas 7 and 8: *Editor's Note*: I have restored the two concluding stanzas (i.e., 7 and 8) of "Terce." Except for the PMS, all extant copies (CTSS, TS-4, and the copy in Giroux's file) show them. Neither Fitzgerald nor Wilbur recommended dropping the stanzas, and I do not find that Berryman made notes, as he often did, suggesting that he considered dropping them. Indeed, frequently his pattern of composition was to write the concluding lines or stanzas of a poem early (sometimes first) in composition and then work toward (or against) his ending. I find only one instance—from his earliest MSS to the end of his life—where he dropped the conclusion of a poem.

    And, too, one might wonder, in light of the concluding affirmations of all other "Opus Dei" poems, why "Terce" stands alone in its bitter ending: " 'In sex my husband is brutal, beating, dirty, and drunk.' / Has this become Thy will, Thou Reconciler?"

Berryman's writing habits and the restoration of the thematic movement consistent with the whole of "Opus Dei" seem to me reasonable arguments for recovering the stanzas, but a third circumstance suggests the most persuasive evidence. Since stanzas 7 and 8 appear on the second page of all extant typed copies of "Terce," it appears that somewhere in the process of routing the copy to Giroux and into the PMS it was mislaid. (The "master copy" of "Opus Dei" was sent by Bob Silvers of *The New York Review of Books* to Giroux; see above, in the "Publication & Composition History," the exchange of letters between Berryman and Giroux on November 12 and 14, 1971.) The printer apparently did not receive the second page, as the PMS shows.

1.30 *Editor's Note:* Berryman misspelled "Gethsemane" as "Gethsemani" which I have corrected.

"Sext"

Editor's Note: In TS-4, Berryman wrote in the margin of a TS of "Sext" the following stanza to be inserted between stanzas 3 and 4:

> I personally call it: outmoded biology
> of even mutation ignorant,
> and in that, that a bare one in 100 is benevolent.

Berryman noted, in his ledger comparing Fitzgerald's and Wilbur's recommendations, that Fitzgerald marked an X over the HW insertion. Nevertheless, since Berryman did not do likewise in TS-4 (he did not take several of Fitzgerald's suggestions), I have included the stanza.

1.17: In TS-4 and the PMS Berryman misspelled "millennia" as "millenia"; FSG corrected the error, which I have admitted.

"Nones"

Editor's Note: "Nones" is not in TS-4, but the original TS is in the PMS. The TS appears to be Berryman's final revision, the one he sent to Giroux on October 23, 1971.

"Vespers"

1.19: not] *not* (*Editor's Note*: On a photocopy of "Vespers" in file 2, Berryman noted: "Be very chary w. these italics leave *all* out when I re-type." The TS is TS-4 appears to be the retyped and revised version of "Vespers," but he changed only one italics, *"not"* to "not.")

1.20: only] only.

1.23: In TS-4 and the PMS Berryman misspelled "millennia" as "millenia"; FSG
corrected the error, which I have admitted.

"Compline"

1.20: thro'] Out (*HW in TS-4*)

1.23: engulphing] engulfing

1.31: snore & drowse.] hymn & sleep. (*HW in TS-4*)

"Washington in Love"

1.2: musketry (my first) is] musketry is

1.4: *Editor's Note*: I have emended the number of ellipsis points, that is, John
Adams of Massachusetts . . I] Adams of Massachusetts . . . I

1.6: 174'] 174´,

1.7: BRING THE WOUNDED, MEN.] *Bring the wounded, men.*

Editor's Note: The above emendations are taken from the TS in TS-4. Between
stanzas IV and V three asterisks appear, centered. On the photocopy of
"Washington in Love" in the PMS, Berryman queried the italics in l.7, "or
all caps?" On the CTS, in the unnumbered *De* folder, he wrote "*yes.*" The
original TS in TS-4 shows that he revised and retyped the poem after he
sent the PMS to FSG.

"Beethoven Triumphant"

Editor's Note: "Beethoven Triumphant" is based on the TS in the PMS.

1.38: often] Often (*Editor's Note*: The TS in PMS shows a lowercase "o.")

1.66: also,] also

1.127: class'] class (*Editor's Note*: The closing quotation mark is not in the original
TS in PMS, but in all extant versions before the TS, the quotation is closed.
Also, see Stefanik, p. 134, for a comment on "them] then" in stanza 27, l.128.

There are several variants between the TS in the PMS and the FSG
published version: in stanza 19, l.94 in the TS "á" is "à" in FSG; in stanza
22, l.107 in the TS "Winterreise" is "*Winterreise*" in FSG; and in stanza 24,
l.11 in the TS "Moliere" is "Molière" in FSG. I have admitted all the FSG
emendations except the italicizing of "Winterreise.")

"Your Birthday in Wisconsin You Are 140"

1.5: (the other reader)?] the other reader? (*HW in TS-4*)

"In Memoriam (1914–1953)"

Editor's Note: "In Memoriam (1914–1953)" is based on the TS in the PMS.

1.22: thát] that (*Editor's Note*: The printer missed the accent mark on "that" in
the TS in the PMS.)

"Gislebertus' Eve"

Editor's Note: "Gislebertus' Eve" is based on the TS in the PMS.

"Scholars at the Orchid Pavilion" (*Editor's Note*: Does not appear in the TS-4,
but the original TS is in the PMS.)

1.22: Halls,'] Halls'

"The Handshake, The Entrance"

> *Editor's Note*: "The Handshake, The Entrance" is based on the TS in the PMS.

1.3: 'Ain't] Ain't

1.4: yourself.'] yourself. (*Editor's Note*: At the beginning of 1.3 ['Ain't], in the TS in the PMS, the quotation mark is opened but not closed. FSG deleted the opening mark, but since ll.3 and 4 are a single quotation—as l.1 and l.2 are each quotations—I have assumed that Berryman forgot to close the quotation. I have restored the opening quotation mark and added the closing mark.)

"He Resigns"

1.10: ever] or ever (*Editor's Note*: The HW deletion of "or" is indicated in the PMS, but, perhaps because the PMS is a photocopy, the instruction is unclear; the HW deletion on the TS in TS-4 is clear.)

"The Form"

> *Editor's Note*: All the following changes are taken from Berryman's MSS in *De* files 2 and 3. The CTS in file 2 appears to be the carbon of the TS Berryman sent to *Esquire*, where it was published (LXXV, May 1971). Since the FSG and FF copy was taken from *Esquire* rather than from a MS, their version incorporates *Esquire*'s emendations and errors, which are not accepted.

1.1: &] and

1.4: kind] kind,

1.10: convulsing] confusing (*Editor's Note*: In the combination TS-HWMS of "The Form" in *De* file 2, "confusing" appears as "convulsing"; in the CTS in *De* file 3, "convulsing" is changed to "confusing." Although the CTS postdates the TS-HWMS, I believe the CTS spelling is a typing error.)

1.11: thro'] through

1.15: wide-eyed &] wide-eyed and

1.18: &] and

1.20: &] and

> *Editor's Note*: See Stefanik, p. 134, for a note on the roman / italics type of "The Form." In all of Berryman's extant MSS of "The Form," he does not indicate italics for stanzas 2 through 6 as in the FSG first printing. Giroux noted, in an April 3, 1972, letter to Charles Monteith of FF, that " ['The Form'] should be in roman throughout."

"Ecce Homo"

1.8: thro'] through (*Editor's Note*: No MS of "Ecce Homo" appears in the *De* files. In the PMS, the copy of "Ecce Homo" is cut out from *The New Yorker*

(XLVII, April 10, 1971, p. 38), and it is the same as the FSG version. I have followed the *New Yorker* version, with one exception. Since throughout Berryman's MSS of *De* he spells "through" as "thro'," I have assumed he spelled it the same in the copy he sent to *The New Yorker*.)

"A Prayer After All"

1.7 worshippéd] worshipped (*HW in TS-4*) (*Editor's Note*: The accent mark on "worshippéd" appears also in the PMS, which the printer evidently overlooked.)

1.21: *find none*] find none (*HW in TS-4*)

"Navajo Setting the Record Straight"

Editor's Note: This poem is based on the TS in the PMS.

"Henry By Night"

***Title*: By**] by (*Editor's Note*: In the CTS, file 3, the title appears as "HENRY BY NIGHT"; in the Table of Contents in TS-4, the title appears as "Henry By Night." "Henry By Night" is not in TS-4; the copy-text is based on a photocopy in the PMS from *The Harvard Advocate*, CII, Spring 1969, p. 13.)

"Henry's Understanding"

Editor's Note: The copy-text of "Henry's Understanding" is based on a photocopy in the PMS from *The Harvard Advocate*, CII, Spring 1969, p. 12.

"Defensio in Extremis"

Editor's Note: "Defensio in Extremis" is based on the TS in TS-4 that appears to postdate the photocopied version in the PMS.

1.2: depth] skill

1.5: however their] whatever their

1.6: in a study of stillness I read my single] in quietness I read my newly simple

1.7: my collapsed] so far

1.8: Oh even A, great E, & tender M] O even X, great Y, fine Z

1.9: my immusical procedures & crude loves.] my procedures and my ends.

1.10: some] their

1.11: half-ful] half-full (*Editor's Note*: Although "half-ful" would appear to be a misspelling, I have allowed it because I believe he intends the suffix "-ful," meaning not only "full" but also "characterized by" and "having the qualities of" [cf. Berryman's similar use of hyphenation in "Facts & Issues" in l.35, "far-away"].)

1.12: misunderstood orders.] insights.

"Damn You, Jim D., You Woke Me Up"

Editor's Note: The title in TS-4 is "Damn You, Jim Dickey, You Woke Me Up," but on the PMS "Jim Dickey" is changed to "Jim D." Between lines 3 and 4 in TS-4 is "(we're sounding just a bit like Frost here, aren't we?)." In Berryman's November 12, 1971, letter to Giroux, he said to "kill" the line; otherwise, the text of the poem in the FSG edition is the same as that in TS-4.

"Somber Prayer"

   Editor's Note: The CTS version in TS-4 appears to postdate the PMS version and is therefore the primary text for *CP*.

1.2: **spoken . .**] spoken . . .

1.12: **half-effective,**] half-famous & effective, (*HW change in TS-4*)

1.14: **worth.**] worthy. (*HW change in TS-4*) (*Editor's Note*: l.14 originally read "not worth much." On the CTS in TS-4, Berryman deleted "much" and placed a period after "worth." The change of "worth" to "worthy," which may or may not be in Berryman's hand, was done in ballpoint on the photocopy in the PMS.)

"Unknowable? perhaps not altogether"

   Editor's Note: The FSG version of this poem is different from the one in TS-4, but since the FSG text is based on a TS, I have accepted it as the correct version. Berryman misspelled "pizzazz" in l.9 as "pizazz," which FSG corrected and I have admitted.

"Minnesota Thanksgiving"

1.1: **great**] terrible (*HW on the TS in TS-4*)

1.14: *Editor's Note*: On the TS in TS-4, Berryman commented that *"conscience"* is the French word.

"Overseas Prayer"

1.7: **lest upon**] lest at (*HW in TS-4*)

1.14: **able tho' of integrity father**] able father (*HW in TS-4*)

1.20: **beg**] ask (*HW in TS-4*)

"Amos"

1.2: **vex will I**] will I vex

1.4: **horror; thus**] horror: so

1.6: **present', & the Urals**] presently, & the Urals,

1.7: **dachas,**] Omsk,

1.8: **home;**] home:

1.21: **them;**] them: (*Editor's Note*: This was l.13 in the FSG edition of *De* but is now l.21 in *CP*.)

   Editor's Note: The above changes of "Amos" are based on the TS in TS-4, which appears to postdate the PMS photocopy. The two new stanzas in *CP*—between stanzas 2 and 3 of the FSG edition—are in the same TS in TS-4.

"Certainty Before Lunch"

1.3: **forever—**] forever, (*HW in TS-4*)

"The Prayer of the Middle-Aged Man"

1.7: **medium**] mediam (*Editor's Note*: Berryman's HW instruction on the photocopy in the PMS is not clear as to whether "medio," as it appears in the MS, is to be changed to "mediam" or "medium"; the TS in TS-4, however, clearly indicates "medium.")

"How Do You Do Dr Berryman, Sir"

1.12 glory] glory)

    Editor's Note: None of the extant copies show that Berryman closed the parenthesis at the end of l.12.

"Facts & Issues"

    Editor's Note: "Facts & Issues" is based on the TS in the PMS.

1.35: far-away] faraway (*Editor's Note*: The TS in PMS indicates a hyphen in "far-away," which FSG either emended or overlooked.)

"King David Dances"

1.1: world] world,

1.3: sight] sight,

    Editor's Note: In l.4 of the photocopy in PMS, the phrase "slaughter devising" that appears in the FSG edition is "murder conspiring," but in TS-4 the phrase "murder conspiring" is crossed out and "slaughter devising" is written in. How the phrase in the FSG edition became the correct one, I am not certain (i.e., "murder conspiring" should be "slaughter devising" because the photocopy of the TS with a HW change in TS-4 postdates the PMS version). In any event, the FSG version is correct.

EARLY POEMS

from "TWENTY POEMS" *in* FIVE YOUNG AMERICAN POETS
(1940)

The Copy-Text of "Twenty Poems" *for* CP: Since the printer's MS and the galley and page proofs are lost, the copy-text for *CP* is based on the first edition. "Twenty Poems," Berryman's first book collection, was published in an anthology by New Directions (Norfolk, Connecticut) on November 19, 1940. Besides Berryman, the poets included are Mary Barnard, Randall Jarrell, W. R. Moses, and George Marion O'Donnell.

    Since eleven poems from *20P* appear in *TD*, with some minor revisions, they are not included in *CP*. The eleven poems are: "The Statue," "Desires of Men and Women," "On the London Train," "Letter to His Brother," "Parting as Descent," "The Disciple," "World-Telegram," "Conversation," "The Return" (the revised title in *TD* is "The Possessed"), "Winter Landscape," and "Caravan."

VARIANTS: None. The copy-text of the poems from "Twenty Poems" is based on the first printed edition.

from POEMS (1942)

The Copy-Text of Poems *for* CP: The copy-text for *CP* is based on the first edition. *Poems* was published September 28, 1942, by James Laughlin's New Directions (Norfolk, Connecticut) in "The Poet of the Month" series. The author's galleys and page proofs are lost, but the printer's MS is in the Houghton Library of Harvard University. The printer's MS consists of an unsigned, undated, twenty-two-page TS with HW instructions for the printer. The poem "1 September 1939" is missing.

I have compared the printer's MS with the published edition of *Poems* and have noted the variants below. Where the printer's MS is different from the published edition (in four instances), I assume that Berryman instructed the changes.

The six poems that appeared in *TD*, not included in *Poems* for *CP*, are: "The Statue," "At Chinese Checkers," "1 September 1939," "A Point of Age," "The Moon and the Night and the Men," and "A Poem for Bhain."

VARIANTS: Left of the] is the first edition of *Poems* accepted for *CP*; right of the] is the printer's MS.
Dedication: "To Bhain Campbell"
1911–1940] 1912–1940
"The Dangerous Year"
1.26: *The car is still upon the road,*] The car is still upon the road,
"River Rouge, 1932"
Title: 1932] 1933
1.17: dreamt a dream] had expected

Acknowledgments

To acknowledge, merely, the help of friends, colleagues, correspondents, and librarians hardly seems adequate recognition of their contributions to the editing of *Collected Poems*. An expression of my gratitude comes closer. At the beginning of this project, over three years ago, most of my friends were not fully aware (nor was I) of the complexity involved in editing John Berryman's collected poems. Simply type the texts (after all, the poems *have* been published), write an introduction of about five thousand words, and send the publisher the manuscript. So the scenario went. After about two years of indexing, comparing, typing, retyping, and annotating variants—and no clean manuscript in sight—I attempted to explain to them that editing, like a Byzantine icon, is deceptively simple. Whether or not they believed me is still open to question, but they were supportive when I needed them; as it turned out, their encouragement was as important to me as their advice on scholarly and critical matters.

Kate Donahue (Mrs. John Berryman) and Robert Giroux knew from the beginning what was involved in editing Berryman's poems. For their forbearance, encouragement, and confidence in me I am deeply grateful. They did all they could to make every document known to them available to me; even though they would have wished to accelerate the process, they seemed to have a sure sense of when to prompt me and when to leave me to Byzantium. John Berryman's brother, Jefferson, knew as well what the editing involved, and I appreciate very much his genuine enthusiasm for my work.

Several friends and colleagues kindly criticized my Notes on Texts and Introduction; some advised me on tracing obscure sources of quotes and spellings; others patiently listened to me rehearse almost weekly how I planned to solve the most recent crux. Each in his or her own way sharpened my thinking, polished my expression, and saved me from several blunders. To Eileen Simpson, Richard Kelly, E. M. Halliday, Kathe Davis, Philip and Ellen Siegelman, Patricia Brooks, and Mike Powers—some of whom gave detailed comments on my introduction—I am glad to have the opportunity to thank them publicly. Among my colleagues at St. John's and College of St. Benedict, I am particularly grateful to Florence Amamoto, Peter Carlton, S. Mara Faulkner, S. Nancy Hynes, and Ozzie Mayers for their close readings of my introduction. Lively conversations with them and other colleagues—Fr. J. P. Earls, Fr. Pat McDarby, Jane Opitz, Cyril O'Regan, Jon Hassler, Annette Atkins, and Bart Sutter—not only allowed me to follow the elbows and stops of my ideas but also gave me great pleasure. For administrative support that faculty at most universities would envy, I am indebted to Fr. Hilary

Thimmesh, S. Eva Hooker, Robert Spaeth, and Janet McNew. For financial assistance, I gladly acknowledge the support of the MacPherson Foundation.

I wish to extend my warm regards to William Meredith and Richard Harteis, who helped me determine some of the history of the publication of *Sonnets*; to Richard Wilbur for his help on *Delusions etc of John Berryman*; to James Laughlin for permission to photocopy Berryman's TS of *Poems*; and to Richard J. Finneran, Jerome J. McGann, and Carmela Vircillo Franklin for their criticism and counsel on editorial principles and procedures.

Alan M. Lathrop, Curator of Manuscripts Division, and his assistant, Vivian Newbold, did everything possible to facilitate my work on the large collection of manuscripts and proofs in the John Berryman Papers at the University of Minnesota Libraries. I appreciate their help all the more because they frequently put aside other pressing duties to assist me. I am also indebted to several library staffs for their promptness and efficiency in responding to my queries, particularly Madeleine G. Gosselin, Manuscript Department, The Houghton Library, Harvard University; Timothy D. Murray, Curator of Manuscripts, Washington University in St. Louis; and Bernard R. Crystal, Assistant Librarian for Manuscripts at Columbia University.

A special word of thanks to Ernest C. Stefanik, Jr., for *John Berryman: A Descriptive Bibliography* (1974). His meticulously researched work has been invaluable in comparing the embodiments of Berryman's published texts.

The editing of an author's collected works demands not only persistent attention to detail but also staying power. On both counts, I have indeed been fortunate to have Roger Ehresmann as my student assistant. His conscientiousness in proofing typescript and comparing texts and his perseverance through three dispiriting summers stake an important claim to the text of *Collected Poems*. Others helped in the early, fumbling stages of the editing; I am grateful for the careful work of Tim Herwig, Greg Machacek, and Maya Mannat. Pam Schrader typed and retyped most of the manuscript; her geniality made every stage of the project much more cheerful. Lynn Warshow of Farrar, Straus & Giroux has been a superb editor; her careful scrutiny of the typescript raised editorial questions I had not considered. Ann Marie Strukel assisted me in proofing the galleys; her dedication and alertness greatly improved the accuracy of the final text. I am, of course, responsible for any errors.

To Ozzie Mayers, Kathy Paden Thornbury, Herbert Thornbury, my mother (Mae Thornbury), George Connor, Hazel Paden, and Richard Kelly ("the lovely friends," as Henry says), I wish to say how grateful I am for your interest, kindness, and friendship. One of the pleasures of slowly accumulating the completed pages of the manuscript for *Collected Poems* has been my teenage daughters' amazement—"awesome" is the current word—at the *number* of pages it finally came to; it did not matter that John Berryman had written the poems; it did not matter that I was their temporary custodian. I would like to pay my own tribute to my daughters Kendra and Clare. Berryman's poems "terrify & comfort"; they cajole and make you laugh; they brood and they celebrate. His poems belong as much to your generation as they do to his and to my own.

Acknowledgments

Index of Titles and First Lines

[338

Index of Titles and First Lines

Index of Titles and First Lines

Index of Titles and First Lines

Index of Titles and First Lines

Index of Titles and First Lines